Kate

Also by Sean Smith

Robbie

Cheryl

Victoria

Kylie: The Biography

Justin: The Biography

Britney: The Biography

J. K. Rowling: A Biography

Jennifer: The Unauthorized Biography

Royal Racing

The Union Game

Sophie's Kiss (with Garth Gibbs)

Stone Me! (with Dale Lawrence)

Kate

Sean Smith

SIMON &
SCHUSTER

London · New York · Sydney · Toronto

A CBS COMPANY

First published in Great Britain by Simon & Schuster UK Ltd, 2011
A CBS COMPANY

1 3 5 7 9 10 8 6 4 2

Simon & Schuster UK Ltd
1st Floor
222 Gray's Inn Road
London
WC1X 8HB

www.simonandschuster.co.uk

Simon & Schuster Australia
Sydney

A CIP catalogue for this book is
available from the British Library.

ISBN: 978-1-84737-868-2 (Hardback)
ISBN: 978-1-84737-869-9 (Trade paperback)

Typeset by M Rules
Printed in the UK by CPI Mackays, Chatham ME5 8TD

For Garth – larger than life

Author's Note

Kate or Catherine?

It's difficult to know whether the star of this book is Catherine or Kate. Growing up, everyone called her Catherine. Her family and all her school friends still do. But when she left Marlborough College, she began to introduce herself as Kate. William met her as Kate and that's how she was known when the world first noticed her. To the cheering crowds who wished her happiness on her wedding day, she is Kate and always will be. That's good enough for me and for that reason I've decided to call her Kate throughout this story of her life.

Contents

Introduction

Something to Smile About

Chippy Pete Beedle got it right when he was talking about his distant cousin Kate marrying into the Royal Family: 'In these gloomy days it has put a smile on people's faces.'

Pete, who runs Beedle's fish and chip shop just off Cockton Hill Road in Bishop Auckland, Durham, comes from the same mining stock as the future Queen Catherine and is one of many working people up and down the country who have discovered they are related to the new royal. He loves football and for many years was the goalie for his local team, Cockfield United.

He has changed his menu to mark the Big Day when his second cousin once removed becomes a princess. Among the usual favourites will be Middleton's Mushy Peas, Buck House Burgers and Kate's Kod. The suggestion that he should name a saveloy 'Big Willie' after Kate's pet nickname for William has been abandoned on the grounds of taste. 'They'd be welcome to look in any time for a fish supper,' he says.

By coincidence Pete married his wife Karen on the same day in July 1986 as Prince Andrew and Fergie were married at Westminster Abbey – the last royal wedding to be held there.

Fortunately, his marriage has lasted a lot longer than that ill-fated match.

And then there's hairdresser Anna Partington, who runs The Barber Shop in West Cornforth, Durham. She's another who was thrilled to discover she is related to Kate: 'It's silly really but I got quite excited when I found out. I think if it was the other way round and I was marrying Prince William, Kate would want to know she was related to me.'

Kate Middleton brings all manner of places and professions to the royal melting pot. In addition to her mining roots in the north-east, her ancestors over the last two hundred years have included a nurse, a farm labourer, a joiner, a charwoman, a baker, a butcher, a road sweeper (who died of exhaustion in Hammersmith in 1893), a grocer, a solicitor, a cloth merchant, a steel worker, a plasterer, a bank clerk, a lorry driver and a pilot.

And at least two convicts. One, an old ancestor on her father's side of the family called Edward Glassborow, did time in Holloway Prison before it became exclusively for women. His offence is lost in the mists of time but his circumstances improved and he lived out his life in comfort. More colourful still was Samuel Hickmott, a ploughman from Kent who was arrested in 1840 and accused of stealing three lambs. He denied the offence but suspicious magistrates sent in the veterinary equivalent of CSI. They found the cuts of meat hanging in his shed and matched them to the discarded carcasses that had been carelessly abandoned near the scene of the crime.

Both Samuel and his brother Thomas were convicted and shipped from England to a penal colony in Tasmania. On arrival Samuel was assigned to a chain gang that broke up rocks to create the roads around the capital, Hobart. After bearing this awful punishment for ten years, he was eventually pardoned and freed to set up a new life in South Australia, where his son and daughter-in-law sailed to join him.

The daughter-in-law, Sophie Hickmott, is Kate's great-great-aunt. She was one of many female ancestors who struggled against adversity, living in poverty in a frontier town. She died an untimely death at the age of twenty-four after giving birth to her fourth child and first son, Henry Hickmott. He would become a respected farmer and long-standing member of parliament – another example of how fortunes can change between generations.

A royal source revealed, 'Kate does know about her sheep-stealing relation and thinks it's quite funny looking back at all the ancestors.'

She can't possibly know about *all* the branches of her complex family tree, which has strands reaching around the world. As well as in Australia, she can look forward to meeting more relations when she and William visit the USA and the state of Virginia in particular. Some of her ancestors emigrated to America in the eighteenth century and became one of the founding families of the now aptly named city of Williamsburg. Their descendants became wealthy landowners and can boast a city mayor among them.

In scrutinizing Kate's family history it becomes clear that, for the first time, a future queen will have a connection with the entire population – ordinary men and women who have lived real lives. Until Princess Diana came along, the Royal Family didn't have a clue how to relate to the general public. But Kate Middleton's family background has given her an unexpected head start in becoming popular.

In this media age the Royal Family are celebrities – they may not like it but they are. And the biggest celebrities in the country today are those anyone could aspire to be: Susan Boyle from a small village in Scotland, Cheryl Cole from the drug-ravaged mean streets of Newcastle or Robbie Williams from Tunstall, who grew up playing football in the local park with his mates.

Two current celebrities lurk in the branches of Kate's family tree. First, Helena Bonham Carter, who won a BAFTA in 2011 for playing the Queen Mother in the Oscar-winning film

The King's Speech, is a distant cousin. They share the same great-great-great-grandfather, a cloth finisher from Leeds called Joseph Asquith. Then there's Guy Ritchie, another distant cousin on her father's side.

Kate Middleton's most famous cousin is, by an extraordinary twist of fate, Prince William himself. They are twelfth cousins once removed, which is about as distant as you can get. Their common ancestor is Sir Thomas Leighton, an Elizabethan soldier, diplomat and, for forty years, the murderous dictator of the Channel Island of Guernsey. Today we would be sending in the troops to overthrow this tyrant. When he died there was literally dancing in the streets, so he is not the best role model for today's young royals.

I began this book with the realization that we all know very little about the woman who would be queen. She is quite an enigma. I'd seen photographs of her, of course, but like most everybody I didn't have a sense of her as a person until I heard her speak on a cold and frosty November morning when she sat next to Prince William, the man she had agreed to marry, for their TV engagement interview.

She is certainly very pretty, with a dazzling smile that can light up a room – a good start for a royal-to-be. She also sounded the part with a speaking voice every bit as upper crust as William's. She seemed very nervous but strangely composed during the inevitable superficial questioning. I didn't feel I knew much more about her by the end of it, though, which doubled my determination to find out more. For his part William seemed to have aged quite a bit. Responsibilities and a proper job have robbed him of the shy, boyish charm of his younger years.

The moment she started dating William, Kate Middleton became a celebrity – it usually takes a lot less than that these days. By the end of her first television interview, she had become the biggest celebrity in the country, which must be galling to every wannabe who has flogged their way through one or more of the reality television shows. Kate did it in one short interview and didn't even have to eat kangaroo testicles. Ironically, when she and Wills were 'on a break' in 2007, she was asked if she would be interested in going on *I'm a Celebrity Get Me Out of Here*. Fortunately she didn't have a brainstorm and agree or that would have been curtains for her royal ambitions.

By any standards Prince William is a dream catch. The world loves a fairy tale and nothing beats the one in which any little girl can dream of becoming a princess. But in these modern times there's more to a prince than a childhood fantasy. Prince William is a multimillionaire, a helicopter pilot and a friend of David Beckham – which covers most fantasies for the nation's women.

The *Daily Mail* columnist Melanie Philips was unimpressed that David and Victoria Beckham were going to the wedding. She observed that the wedding would be another glittering outing for the 'tacky and the tawdry who comprise our celebrity culture.' She argued, 'Anonymous Palace sources have insisted it will not be a "celebrity-filled wedding". But why have the Beckhams been invited if not on account of their celebrity? After all, what are they really famous for? For being stylish and fashionable – in other words, famous for being famous. This is particularly disappointing . . .'

I'm not too sure if inviting the most famous and arguably the most popular couple in the country to your wedding is a bad thing or even disappointing. Patrick Collins, the chief sports writer of the *Mail on Sunday* thought that David, in particular, could only 'raise the tone' of the whole affair. Hopefully, the Beckhams have been invited because they've struck up a friendship with the royal couple.

Much of the nation is still patriotic but, in my opinion, we want a Royal Family that's more approachable than in previous generations. Nobody wants a repeat of the Diana circus but even now, fourteen years after her death, she is more popular than the rest of the family put together – except for her two sons and now, possibly, Kate.

I was talking to an old friend of Kate's, who told me that her greatest fear was that nobody would like the new Royal bride: 'I am quite frightened that Catherine is going to be seen as quite snobby because she hasn't been seen talking to the public.'

Perhaps that fear has filtered through to the fixers in the royal household because Kate didn't wait until she was married to begin her public engagements. She looked a million dollars when she joined William to name a new boat in Anglesey and the following day dazzled in a red coat when she went back to St Andrews, where it all began for the royal couple. She really does have the most winning smile and perfect teeth and you can't coach that. The most noticeable thing, however, was that she needs to do something about her hair if she is going to attend many outdoors events in the future: it kept blowing in her face and she was forever having to disentangle it from her mouth. The Queen's hair hasn't moved in fifty years.

It was a good start though. I think we all want to know how she arrived at this point. That's what led me to 'leafy Berkshire' in the dead of winter, when it was freezing cold, covered in snow, foggy, dark and unwelcoming. Kate, by and large, had a happy time here, although I was unpleasantly surprised to learn the full extent of how she was bullied at school. She is fortunate to have a secure and supportive family unit and her parents have continued to be there for her as she has taken those first tentative steps into the limelight. I discovered that Kate comes from a line of strong women who have 'true grit'; it's a quality she shares. I also found out that Kate was more fun growing up than one might think from her carefully controlled public image.

As I retraced her steps to St Andrews University and beyond, I discovered her relationship with William had sparked into life before her now famous sashay down the fashion runway in her bra and knickers. What we think we know about Kate continually turns out to be not quite as it seems. The great break-up of

2007, when they split, proved to be a case in point. They were back together much sooner than everyone realized.

My task here is to present the story of her life so that we can get a better sense of who she is – the real Kate, who we so want to do well. I was explaining to another friend of Kate's that there is no point in everybody telling me how nice she is all the time. That won't make the public like her. Nor will it change the negative attitude towards her shown by certain members of the media. We like people more if we can relate to them – share their worries or fears, laugh at things they find funny or shed a tear when they're sad. The Royal Family didn't get that at all until Princess Diana and then the interest in her was so great it led to her untimely death. We can only hope they've had time to absorb that lesson before Kate joins their family.

PART ONE

CATHERINE

1

True Grit

Sadly for the romantics among us, Prince William did not slip a glass slipper on the dainty foot of Kate Middleton. Nor did he discover her a poor and downtrodden waif, washing the floors of her ramshackle cottage in the big forest. William did once visit her house travelling on the modern equivalent of a white charger – an RAF Chinook helicopter – but that's the closest he's ever come to being Prince Charming. And Kate has never been Cinderella, however hard the media might have tried to shoehorn her into that role. In any case, these days William would be far more likely to be searching for the girl whose foot would fit a Hunter wellie.

Kate's life might not be the fairy story observers long for but her family's path to the Palace would make a good movie, a captivating tale of working-class grit and determination more Catherine Cookson than Charles Perrault, the author of so many of the best-known fairy tales. It's a family saga in three parts: the heroine of the first instalment is her maternal grandmother, Dorothy Harrison; in part two, her mother, Carole, takes centre stage; and then, in part three, Kate herself is the focus of attention. The three women have overcome all manner of obstacles as they have striven to improve the quality of their own lives and the lives of their family.

The story begins in Durham in the north-east of England, where sons followed fathers and grandfathers down the unforgiving coal mines as soon as they had the strength to wield a pickaxe. Today, we can have little concept of the brutality of the miner's life – the long, dark hours, the minimal wages and the constant danger as greedy pit bosses cut corners on safety and had little concern for the health of their employees.

'They were slaves in all but name,' observes the writer Christopher Wilson, who first researched the life and times of Kate's ancestors. During the Victorian era the family moved from Byker, now a Newcastle suburb, and set up home in the villages east of Durham, in particular the grimly named Hetton-le-Hole. They lived in dreary two-up, two-down stone cottages with no running water, electricity or indoor toilet.

In such an impoverished environment, the grim reaper was a regular caller. Dorothy's grandfather, John Harrison, was fatherless at sixteen and already working in the pits in 1890. His son, Thomas Harrison, broke the mould, however, by training as a carpenter and using that trade as a springboard to escape the dark drudgery of the mines. He took the dramatic step of uprooting his young family and moving them south, where they settled in Southall, now a mainly Asian area but then a white, working-class suburb of London.

The old family home in Hetton has been bulldozed and nothing remains of the mine. Landscaped lakes and leisure facilities have replaced the looming presence of the old slag heaps. The older residents still remember the Harrisons but the closest they're likely to come to Kate Middleton is drinking in a local pub, the Prince of Wales.

The mining heritage of Kate Middleton has scarcely touched her own life. It was a long time ago, after all. But Thomas Harrison did bring one important characteristic of his life in the north-east down south with him: the Harrisons had a strong sense of community and family loyalty.

His youngest daughter, Dorothy, Kate's grandmother, who was born in 1935, shared her father's desire to improve the family's standing in the world. When she was eighteen and working as a shop assistant in Dorothy Perkins, she married a lorry driver called Ron Goldsmith at the Holy Trinity Church in Southall two months after the coronation of Prince William's grandmother, Queen Elizabeth II. They held their reception in a local pub and the new bride borrowed her going-away outfit from her sister-in-law. By all accounts Ron, who had left school at fourteen to earn his living, was a kindly man, devoted to his wife and the children they eventually brought up together.

The newlyweds had no money for a place of their own so they moved in with Ron's mother, the formidable Edith Goldsmith, who made up for her small stature by ruling her family with a rod of iron. If someone stepped out of line, she would swiftly take off her shoe and hurl it at the offender. The 'family home' was a condemned and spartan flat in Dudley Road, then one of the roughest streets in Southall. There was little privacy, especially with the one toilet next to the coal-fired boiler.

Dorothy had social ambitions for her family even if they had next to nothing. She took pride in her personal appearance and hated it when any of the family called her Dot, which she thought common; the family referred to her as 'Lady Dorothy' when she wasn't in the room. Her cousin Pat Charman told the author Claudia Joseph, who spent a year researching Kate's family tree, 'You couldn't imagine knocking on her door and finding her hair in curlers.'

Eventually Dorothy and Ron moved into a council flat nearby, before borrowing the deposit to buy their own small house in Arlington Road, Southall, where they were living when Carole was born in 1955. Ron, urged on by Dorothy, started to change the family's fortunes by setting up in business for himself as a jobbing builder. As a result, in 1966, the year England's footballers famously lifted the World Cup, they were in a position to upgrade. Carole was eleven and her younger brother Gary was one when the family moved into a semi-detached house in Kingsbridge Road, Norwood Green – a smarter area even though their home was surrounded by a council estate.

Buying an expensive house, which cost just shy of £5,000, was a very bold step for the family. Ron was doing well enough to keep his family afloat but they could easily have settled for a home they could have afforded more comfortably. It was further proof of the family's motivation: always try and make something better for yourself but you won't get anywhere without hard work and believing in your own abilities.

Dorothy Goldsmith may have had some airs and graces but she gave her young children all her time and attention. She gave up work to be a full-time mum when they were small but later also did her bit to bring in some much-needed cash by working for a local estate agent.

The Goldsmith family of Kingsbridge Road were united against the world and went forward as a unit – very much as Carole would do when she started her own family. And, gradually, as they pursued their ambitions, they began to leave behind members of the wider family. Perhaps unsurprisingly a family rift caused that to happen sooner rather than later. Ron and Dorothy fell out with his elder sister Alice over an apparent snub to her husband, Bill Tomlinson. He'd been barred from the house by Dorothy once when he'd gone to visit because they were 'too busy' for guests. He died two weeks later and the Goldsmiths weren't welcome at the funeral. In return the Tomlinsons wouldn't be invited to Carole's wedding in the summer of 1980.

Carole Elizabeth Goldsmith pictured a life for herself far beyond the grey horizons of Southall. While at school she worked in a boutique at weekends so she could afford the clothes and make-up to look her best. That paid off when she left school and secured a job as an air hostess with BOAC, which later became part of British Airways, in the days when it was considered a very glamorous way of seeing the world. Carole was a strikingly attractive young woman – slim, softly spoken and feminine but with the Goldsmith energy and resolve. She caught the eye of many of the male staff at Heathrow but soon found herself in a serious relationship with a dark and handsome young flight attendant called Michael Middleton. He was the son of a pilot and had ambitions to fly airplanes for a living too. He had impeccable manners and a social ease that would serve the couple well in their future ventures.

Michael's ancestors were wealthy, middle-class members of Leeds society, part of the Yorkshire city's elite. Their legacy would prove to be very important for Kate Middleton. Like Carole, Michael had his fair share of formidable women in his family tree.

One of them was one of the great thinkers of the Victorian Age, Harriet Martineau, a friend to the most famous people of the time, including Charles Darwin, Florence Nightingale and the writers George Eliot and Charlotte Brontë. Harriet, who might best be described as an early feminist, once wrote a novel called *The Peasant and the Prince* but she was better known for her strong words on social reform. She showed her resolve by travelling alone to the US – an unheard-of adventure for a young woman in the 1830s. Unlike her great-granddaughter Kate Middleton, Harriet was no beauty. On meeting her, Charles Darwin remarked, 'I was astonished to find how ugly she was.'

More importantly for Kate, a series of family trusts was set up more than a hundred years ago by her great-great-grandfather, Francis Lupton, a rich mill-owner and a shrewd businessman and entrepreneur who drew up plans to avoid death duties and keep his family's finances buoyant for generations to come. He had lived in a grand Victorian mansion in the Roundhay area of the city and, with his three brothers, had run the family textile and manufacturing business.

When he died in 1921 his personal estate was worth more than £70,000, which would be the equivalent of roughly £1.5 million today. His will reveals that he had already placed the bulk of his fortune, including his share of the business, in a family trust that to this day is still apparently paying an undisclosed sum to his descendants – including Michael Francis Middleton.

Lupton's daughter Olive continued his good financial habits, although she lived in a grand manner befitting an heiress. When she died in 1936 she left £52,031. As her father had done, she insisted in her will that her trustees invest the money wisely and, specifically, that they make provision to pay for her descendants' children's education.

The family business in Leeds no longer exists but subsequent generations have been well-off as a result of this prudence and forward planning. Michael's parents, Peter and Valerie Middleton, lived in a spacious country house in a village near Andover worth about £600,000. When Valerie died in 2006 she left Michael, among other legacies, £100,000 in cash. 'His family were upper middle class,' observed a family friend.

Michael was Carole's first serious boyfriend. Her mother, Dorothy, was said to be very happy when her daughter brought the well-mannered young man home. Carole appreciated his easygoing, gentle nature and he admired her energy and wickedly dry sense of humour – a characteristic she would pass on to her eldest daughter.

When the young couple decided to move in together, they found a small modern flat in Slough, which was handy for Heathrow. The town of Slough in the late seventies and early eighties was far from glamorous – more like a sprawling industrial estate than the modern town it is today. While the flat was a good starter property, it wasn't in an area where they wanted to bring up a family and it wasn't long before the couple were house-hunting in the country.

They eventually settled on a spacious semi-detached house in

Cock Lane, Bradfield Southend, a small Berkshire village about five miles from Pangbourne, where there was a railway station, and ten miles west of Reading. It would mean a longer journey to work at Heathrow but Carole couldn't wait to swap her air hostess outfit for the sloppy jumpers and jeans she much preferred.

West View, as their house was called, was the left-hand side of what was originally one big property that had been converted into two in Victorian times. When they moved in, it already had four bedrooms thanks to a loft conversion. A family friend observed, 'It was just an average house – not very big with no flashy furniture or gadgets. But Kate's parents were brilliant at giving it a homely feel.' The most memorable thing about the house as far as Kate's school friends were concerned was the address. One recalled, 'I will always remember that house as it was on Cock Lane!'

Everything was here for a flourishing local community – a doctor's surgery was just yards from the front door, the primary school was literally next door and the Queen's Head pub was a hundred yards away at the junction with the main road. There was also a war memorial, a rundown village hall and a post office in the village store.

Carole's most pressing task after they moved in just before Christmas 1979 was to plan their wedding for the following summer. This was an idyllic affair on 21 June 1980, a bright summer's day in the pretty Buckinghamshire village of Dorney, about thirty miles from their new home but, coincidentally, not far from Eton College where Prince William would go to school. They married in the picturesque church of St James the Less. Carole, wearing a traditional white wedding dress, travelled to the church with her father Ron in a horse and carriage. The day was very different from her parents' wedding in Southall and, instead of the pub, they held a lavish wedding reception in a nearby manor house. Her mother Dorothy's happiness was complete.

Dorothy died in 2006 – the year Kate would lose both grandmothers – sadly too soon to know that her granddaughter would marry the future king. She and her husband Ron lived out their final years near their grandchildren in a small cottage in Pangbourne. If she had lived, she would have been the future Queen of England's grandmother. From a condemned flat in Southall, via Cock Lane, to Westminster Abbey had taken the family just fifty years.

2

The Prophecy

Bradfield Southend was the perfect place for a young couple wanting to bring up a family in the country. That dream took shape when their first child, Catherine Elizabeth Middleton, was born on 9 January 1982 in the Royal Berkshire Hospital, Reading. New mum Carole was popular in the village, always stopping to chat as she wheeled her baby around. She made a big effort to immerse herself in village life, realizing perhaps that she might easily become lonely staying at home with a young child while her husband commuted. He was now a flight dispatcher, and had given up his flying ambitions for a job managing the planes on the ground. Catherine was christened the following June at St Andrew's, the local church situated on the banks of the River Pang. She wore a smart white christening gown for the occasion. A little more than a year later, in September 1983, Philippa Charlotte was born.

Pippa, as she is known, was just eight months old when the family went to live in Jordan in the Middle East. It was a dramatic move away from the peace and quiet of their English village to the modern city of Amman, where Michael had been offered a two-year posting as a manager for British Airways. Kate went to an English language nursery school in Amman when she turned three, while Carole, who was on extended maternity leave, looked after Pippa at home. Kate was able to sing 'Happy Birthday' in Arabic before she learned it in English, which amused everyone back in England.

Carole was expecting her third child when the Middletons returned to Bradfield Southend in September 1986 so Kate could start school in England. The village primary school was next door but, thanks to Michael's family legacy and the money they had saved in Jordan, they were able to enrol her in St Andrew's School in Pangbourne, ten minutes away in the car and, even in those days, more than £4,000 a term.

The family soon settled back into village life. For the two little girls, it was just another adventure. They were fortunate that being close in age they were able to do things together as children; for instance, joining the local Brownie pack at the same time. The Brownies are a throwback to more innocent times, especially in a village where there were farms to visit, woods to explore and hearty stews to help cook.

Carole was determined not to go back to her full-time job at BA. Pippa went to the village preschool playgroup, where Carole could chat to other mothers in similar situations and plan the children's outfits for the Christmas nativity play. Every week one of them seemed to be trying to find the time to organize a birthday party for one of the children. There just weren't enough hours in the day to sort out balloons, games and a local conjuror. Carole always remembered one of her childhood birthdays in Southall when someone had forgotten to buy the balloons and none could be found at the last minute: nothing, it seemed, had changed.

She explained, 'I was looking for party stuff for my own children's parties. It was impossible to find anything easily in the shops and trying to find value for money party bag presents was a complete nightmare. So I came up with the idea for Party Pieces.'

Thousands of mums up and down the country dream of having that great idea that will enable them to bring up their children, work from home and make lots of money. Carole couldn't have known it then but her simple plan for a one-stop party mail order store for harassed mothers would change her family's lives.

She cleared a space in the garden shed, installed a desk and a phone and fixed up electric lighting. When Kate and Pippa were tucked up in bed for the evening, she would assemble the made-up party bags that were the initial product. To begin with, she would take these along to the local preschool group to try and interest the other mothers. Their positive reaction gave her the confidence to press on. Carole was fortunate in that her husband Michael also saw the possibilities and was very supportive from the beginning. A neighbour observed, 'They are a very entrepreneurial family.' The Middletons' third child, James William, was born in May 1987, which meant she had to be even cleverer juggling her time, but Carole was determined to make Party Pieces a success.

St Andrew's preparatory school is impressive, especially when you are four years old and slightly bewildered that you are not joining all the high-spirited boys and girls over the garden fence at the village school. The sign for St Andrew's is on the main road approaching Pangbourne from junction 12 on the M4, but it's nearly a mile down a long winding drive through the school's fifty-four acres of woodland and grounds. The main building, a Gothic-looking old Victorian manor house, is hidden from the road but suddenly springs into view, coming out of nowhere like Hogwarts. Unlike Harry Potter's famous school, St Andrew's is neither scary nor full of magical powers but, according to one classmate of young Kate, 'simply a fantastic school with a brilliant atmosphere.'

When the old house was turned into a school in 1934 there were just eight boy pupils. When Kate started, that number had grown to a couple of hundred boys and girls. One of its great advantages was that there were no more than fifteen children in a class. St Andrew's is a very English and privileged place to begin school life. The school was determined to turn out young ladies and gentlemen. For starters, Carole had to buy her eldest daughter two school uniforms – an ordinary day one and a Sunday best – from the outfitters Jackson's in Reading. The store on Jackson's Corner would prove a regular stop for the Middleton family over the years, providing Brownie uniforms and all manner of sporting kit.

The ordinary uniform consisted of a grey shirt, a grey jumper and black trousers. The Sunday best was a vision in green: a green jumper, a green blazer and a white shirt with a green tie emblazoned with the letters SA. The ensemble was topped off with a shiny black briefcase, which was compulsory. When school ended for the day at 5.30p.m., lots of little commuters would run out to greet their parents struggling to find somewhere to park their 4 × 4s or, as in the case of the Middletons, the family Volvo estate in the circular drive outside the school entrance. Fortunately it was one way so there were no three-point turns to cause further traffic chaos.

'It was all very posh,' recalls actor Kingsley Glover, who was in Kate's class when she started. 'Over the years, I've tried to say to people that the school wasn't posh, and that it was rough like any school. But, no, it was posh. There were a lot of moneyed people who went to the school. There were also a lot of aspiring middle-class families who wanted to turn their children into "gentlemen". They would pack them off to this boarding school in the country where they would be taught to be nice.

'I don't recall there being too much of an emphasis on the academic side of things. The main enduring thing they always used to say was that if you haven't got anything nice to say, don't say anything at all. You were taught to be polite more than anything else.'

As part of the polite strategy the children were encouraged to speak well. Kingsley remembers that the teachers would always pick students up on their speech if they weren't speaking correctly. 'We all arrived with regional accents but they kind of trained it out of us. I mean, if you dropped an "h" you were picked up on it. If you said "f" instead of "th" you were picked up on it. They taught us how to speak "proper" and we were all "terribly terribly". There was an awful lot of that going on.'

Away from the classroom the children would try and sound as 'London' or 'estuary' as possible – the Guy Ritchie school of speech. 'And then the teachers would all turn up and you would have to sound "terribly, terribly" again.'

Kate has clearly never forgotten the elocution standards encouraged at St Andrew's and now speaks posher than a royal prince. She also learned good manners and the importance of etiquette. All the children had to queue up to enter the big dining hall. When everyone was seated, the headmaster, Dr Acheson, a popular figure in his schoolmaster robes, would say grace. A teacher sat at the head of every table and one of the kitchen staff, Mr Peters, brought out the food. Even if it was revolting, you weren't allowed to leave your place at the table until you'd finished everything. And Mr Peters would be on hand throughout, with a large bowl in his hands, encouraging you to have some more.

Two things enabled Kate to stand out as a youngster: she was brilliant at sport and she was a leading light of the choir. She was much taller than her contemporaries, and in her early school pictures she seems to have drifted into the frame by mistake, standing head and shoulders above the rest. As a result, she was a girl that people noticed. Kevin Alford, who taught French and German as well as sports, observes, 'She was a 100 miles an hour kind of girl and put full concentration into everything she did. She did well academically but it was on the sports field that she excelled.'

Kate was captain of the netball team and broke many school swimming records. She was also very good at hockey, cross-country running and, in particular, tennis. Every year the school would organize a skiing trip and Kate was always one of the first to sign up. Not surprisingly she showed a huge aptitude for whizzing down the slopes – a skill that would serve her well years later when she was invited on the royal skiing trip to Klosters.

In her final year at St Andrew's, Kate, then thirteen, was named best all-round sportswoman. She loved 'games' and would always be the first to help clear away the equipment. Denise Alford, wife of Kevin and also a teacher at the school, recalls that at the end of the games lesson she would never have to worry about the thirty or so netballs strewn all over the pitch: she knew that Kate would collect them.

One of the most popular teachers was called David Gee, who a classmate recalls 'was a great guy – young, fun and the sort of teacher who made you want to perform well. He always had a joke or two up his sleeve but got great results. He also taught Kate mathematics, another thing she was really good at.'

Kate had a lovely singing voice as a girl and was quickly snapped up for the school choir, run by Mr Miles. St Andrew's was a Church of England school and religion played a big part in daily life. Every morning a short church service would follow assembly and the headmaster would always say grace before and after school dinner.

Sunday, understandably, was the big day for the choir. Even though she was a day girl, which meant she went home every day, Kate was expected to sing at the Sunday service in the school chapel. She and later Pippa were renowned for always being the first of the choir to arrive. 'The Middletons are here' would be the first remark from the others when they entered the church. Kate progressed well in the choir, eventually earning a Dark Blue, presented by the Royal School of Church Music as part of their 'Voice For Life' project. When she joined she wore a black cassock, then, as a fully fledged member of the choir, she wore a white cassock, progressing to a light blue ribbon and then a dark blue. In choral terms, it's about halfway to the top award, a green ribbon awarded to a King's Chorister.

The Sunday service was an opportunity to practice for their more public singing at various services at the local St James's church in Pangbourne, especially at Christmas time when the highlight was the annual candlelit Christingle service in aid of the Children's Society. Kate and her fellow choristers would also sing outside pubs and restaurants to raise money for charity.

In 1994 St Andrew's choir were among the thousands who entered the BBC's 'Song for Christmas' competition. Two of Kate's best friends, Emily Bevan and the wonderfully named Chelsie Finlay-Notman, wrote an original song that they had to submit to a panel of judges at BBC Pebble Mill. Kate and another girl, Zoe de Turberville, did most of the singing and there was great excitement in the school when they were one of the fifty runners-up and received a special commendation.

Kate was very musical as a girl and both she and Pippa played flute in the school chamber orchestra. The highlight of her time as a performer was at the summer concert in 1995 when the orchestra performed 'Jupiter' from Holst's *The Planets* suite and the theme tune from *The Muppets*. The piano was not her strongest instrument and she took extra lessons for three years, as did Pippa, James and Carole, from the local teacher, Daniel Nichols. He recalls, 'I don't think anybody expected her to be a concert pianist but she did what was asked and she enjoyed it, which is the main thing.'

At this stage of her life Kate was universally known as Catherine. In class the teachers would address her as Middleton C to distinguish her from Pippa, who was Middleton P when she joined two years after Kate. For young Kate, life revolved around St Andrew's and she wanted to do well. She may not have appreciated it at the time but she was enjoying an education far better than her mother's. Kevin Alford remembers her as a very hard worker who would often stay behind in an empty classroom to keep ahead of her studies while her school friends were outside playing.

Kate was by no means brilliant at everything. One classmate recalls that she was terrible at Craft Design Technology, or CDT as it is known: 'She was good at the design side but not the practical part of a project. I remember her being pretty inept with the tools and machines she had.' Mrs Sharman's classes were huge fun but Kate's efforts at making tie-dye T-shirts and fashionable accessories weren't destined to impress.

While much of Kate's daily routine involved the school, life at home was very stable and secure. West View, though a semi-detached house, was made more spacious when her parents added a ground floor extension, which made the kitchen bigger and created a playroom that was much needed when the youngest of the three children, James, was born. In comparison with Prince William's turbulent childhood, Kate grew up in a calm environment.

A few of her friends would often come back after school for a play in the garden or they would come over at the weekend. As a girl she loved 'cooking parties' involving fairy cakes and cookies and all the treats her mother wouldn't allow. Her favourites were simply 'anything that Mummy would normally never allow me to have. They were always such a treat.' Her favourite party memory was 'an amazing white rabbit marshmallow cake that Mummy made when I was seven.' Even though she could be a little shy, Kate loved dressing up and recalled one outfit she loved was a 'wonderful' pair of clown dungarees that her grandmother had made her. They were white with big red spots and a small hula-hoop for the waistband.

When she was growing up it seems Kate was a mixture of this girly-girl who liked dressing up and making cakes and a tomboy who loved sport and adventure. On one family holiday to the Lake District she discovered a love of hillwalking. She particularly enjoyed the school trip to Snowdonia when she was twelve. On the first day they climbed Glyder Fawr and could see for miles when they reached the top. On another day they went gorge-walking and wore hard hats and life jackets so they could bomb into the water and whizz down a water slide.

Carole continued to be as supportive as possible to her children despite the growing pressure on her time from Party Pieces. She was one of the star players in the mothers and daughters' rounders matches. On sports day, when not cheering Kate on, she and Michael would set up a large picnic for their children and all their friends.

Not everything Carole did went like clockwork, however. On one memorable occasion she took Kate, then nine, off to St Andrew's in her best school uniform for the first day of the winter term. The only problem was it was the second day. A classmate recalls, 'It was very unusual for her as they were normally so well organized. We were in the middle of a maths lesson when Kate and her mum walked in. They were so embarrassed.'

Kate thrived at St Andrew's and, before she left, was made a prefect with several of her best friends, including Emily and Chelsie, who became head girl. Chelsie's family home was a spacious detached house in Bucklebury, a village a few miles from Bradfield Southend where the Middletons aspired to live.

One evening Kate and Emily had an eye-opening confrontation with Kingsley Glover. By this time Kate had become an occasional boarder to prepare her for life away from home when she went to senior school. One of her duties as a prefect was to patrol the corridors with Emily to make sure everyone was tucked up in bed and all the doors were secure and locked where necessary.

Kingsley, who was staying at the school temporarily while his parents were away, didn't realize you were supposed to stay in the dormitory at night and had run down the main staircase to retrieve his toothbrush from his locker, grabbing just his dressing gown to put on. 'I came to the big double doors at the bottom and opened them when a big gust of wind blows my dressing gown wide open. I'm stark naked underneath and the two pre-fects, Catherine and Emily, are standing straight in front of me. As you can imagine, it was highly embarrassing for all concerned. I went bright red and there was a lot of giggling involved. They were very nice about it but they must have told somebody. I was hoping it wouldn't get round but, of course, these things do. The whole school took the mick out of me for that.'

Towards the end of Kate's time at St Andrew's, boys and girls started noticing each other. Up until the last year the girls seemed to travel in packs and the boys too were in theirs. Then some of them started to pair off in class. Kate, who was tall and skinny, was not in demand. One of her classmates unkindly described her as a 'beanpole'.

Kingsley, a little more gallantly, observes, 'She was a bit lanky, which sounds a bit derogatory. She was tall and skinny and didn't have much of a fantastic figure. She wasn't the girl all the boys chased after at school.

'Looking back, it's all a bit hilarious, the boy/girl thing at twelve or thirteen. But I don't remember Catherine seeming to be interested. She was always very content with sport. You usually think someone so sporty would be attracting quite a lot of attention from the boys but she wasn't.'

Denise Alford confirms that Kate wasn't a looker: 'She wasn't particularly pretty as a young girl and she wore braces on her teeth from the age of twelve. She was thin and much taller than the other girls – quite gangly really. Her sister Pippa was the more beautiful of the two at that age.'

One of the reasons for Kate's lack of interest may have been her lack of success. When she was ten she was chosen to play Eliza Doolittle in a school production of *My Fair Lady*. Kate won the part because of her singing voice. Professor Higgins was played by Andrew de Perlaky who, using the stage name Andrew Alexander, would later become a member of Teatro, a singing group in the style of Il Divo. Andrew is very complimentary about the passion and conviction Kate brought to the role.

Kate saw plenty of Andrew because they both played flute in the school chamber orchestra. She obviously liked him and, though only ten, decided to ask him out. He turned her down. He would later tell the *Daily Mail*, 'I was only ten and Kate seemed so mature at the time. I remember being flushed all of a sudden and getting tongue-tied. I think I caused myself more embarrassment than I caused her.'

Kate also took part in school productions of the Tchaikovsky ballet *The Nutcracker* and *Rats!*, a modern musical for schools by Nigel Hess, a well-known composer of TV theme tunes and a ballet based on Prince Charles's story *The Old Man of Lochnagar*. *Rats!* was adapted from the famous Robert Browning poem *The Pied Piper of Hamelin*. Kate played one of the children kidnapped by the pied piper.

The most interesting of Kate's acting forays at St Andrew's was the sixth form review, which all school leavers had to take part in during their final year. Part of the hour-long perform-ance has become a YouTube classic, with fourteen-year-old Kate taking the leading role of Maria Marten in *Murder in the Red Barn*, a Victorian melodrama that had been a feature film in the 1930s. It gave the master, Mr Boyd, the chance to put together some very funny sketches within the framework of the play – more like a melodramatic pantomime than anything else. Kate recited some moving war poetry and joined in a sketch in which the students sang famous war songs like 'Pack Up Your Troubles'. Her performance at the review has lived on because of a now famous 'prophecy' about her leading man, called William.

This most extraordinary piece of dialogue takes place between Kate, wearing a white dress with black lace piping and a big black belt, and a fortune-teller, who says she will marry 'a handsome man, a rich gentleman.'

Kate asks, 'It is all I have ever hoped for. Will he fall in love with me?'

'Indeed he will,' replies the fortune-teller.

'And marry me?' asks Kate.

'And marry you.'

'Will he take me away from here?'

'Yes. To London.'

'Oh, how my heart flutters,' says Kate, theatrically.

As the cliché goes, 'you really couldn't make it up'. When William, who was played by Byron Rodgers, the son of the popular television actor Anton Rodgers, later drops on one knee and asks her to marry him, she replies, 'Yes, oh yes, dear William . . . Ah, to think I am loved by such a splendid gentleman.'

The only grey cloud to this amusing prophecy is that in *Murder in the Red Barn*, Kate's character, who by then has a child, is abandoned by Squire William. The play itself is based on a real murder that took place in Suffolk when Squire William strangled Maria and buried her in the red barn. Unsurprisingly the media failed to report this grisly outcome, preferring to dwell on the romance of a fictional prophecy coming true in real life.

For a girl entering her teenage years, being thought lanky didn't do wonders for her confidence. Even worse, she developed bad eczema but, being tall, she couldn't hide away. A fellow pupil recalls, 'She was really self-conscious about it.' The eczema may or may not have been caused by the nerves Kate suffered from, especially when performing in front of an audience or getting up in class. She developed a coping mechanism that betrayed her when she was nervous: she would push her palms down towards the floor as if trying to calm herself. She has never lost the mannerism. It is evident during her first public interview following the announcement of her engagement to Prince William.

One of the products of being highly strung and constantly on the go was that she never seemed to put on any weight, which was a particular worry for her mother – she just had too much nervous energy. There was always the concern that if Kate was upset and forgot to eat she would become even thinner. Denise Alford recalls, 'Catherine had a very high metabolic rate and that was always a concern for her mother, particularly when she started boarding. She had a tremendous appetite but because she put so much effort into everything she needed a constant supply of calories.'

Catherine Middleton left St Andrew's with a beautiful speaking voice, impeccable manners and a very strong will. She was like the product of an expensive finishing school except that this was just the start of her education. She certainly wasn't prepared for what came next.

3

Billy the Kid

Prince William's ancestral history is rather dull compared to Kate's. There is little variety, consisting as it does of kings and queens, princes and princesses, dukes and duchesses and all manner of aristocrats. There are no road sweepers, sheep stealers or coal miners. But he can boast of having two of the most famous women in the world in his immediate family: his maternal grandmother, the Queen, and his mother, Diana, Princess of Wales, who was the biggest celebrity of the latter half of the twentieth century.

William Wales is five months younger than Kate Middleton. Inevitably, he was born under a microscope with a greedy public wanting to know everything about Diana's little boy. The whole world, it seemed, wanted his life to be one long fairy tale, not realizing for one second that his mother, whom everyone adored, was chronically unhappy, suffered from bulimia and threw herself down the stairs while she was pregnant.

With unintentional irony, Diana, the daughter of an earl, declared, 'I want my children to have as normal a life as possible.' Neither Diana nor her husband, Prince Charles, had enjoyed the luxury of a normal childhood themselves. Diana had been crushed at the age of six when her mother, Frances, left the matrimonial home. She had been brought up by a succession of nannies whose clothes she used to throw out the window. She described it simply as a very unhappy childhood.

Charles was a lonely little boy who only saw his mother twice a day for thirty minutes at a time. He would be left with his nanny for weeks – sometimes months – on end while his parents carried out official engagements abroad. On their return they would greet their son with a formal handshake.

Both Charles and Diana did their best to give William something more. Diana would get into her little boy's bed at night to give him hugs and cuddles. She declared, 'A child's stability arises mainly from the affection received from his parents and there is no substitute for affection.' Even his father was known to clamber into the night-time bath to help his son play with his favourite toy, a plastic rubber whale that spouted water all over the place. It would soon become clear that they felt far happier with their son than they did in each other's company.

The early pictures of baby William and his very proud parents are unavoidably sweet, and none more so than those taken during a photo session in Kensington Palace, his first home, when a laughing Diana holds her son up in the air and he gurgles with delight. In another photograph, his father holds him as Diana entertains him with a multicoloured rattle. They resemble the happiest snaps of a million families up and down the country – except they are posed.

Even William's christening in the Music Room at Buckingham Palace was not the happy day it seemed. William, wearing the same gown his father had worn thirty-three years earlier, bawled incessantly when it came time to take the family pictures with the Queen and the Queen Mother. Diana later revealed that she had felt totally excluded, wasn't very well and just 'blubbed her eyes out'. Diana had just turned twenty-one and was suffering from post-natal depression.

William's 'normal' childhood continued with his first royal

tour to Australia and New Zealand when he was still in nappies. Diana had already prepared herself to leave him behind when, out of the blue, the Australian Prime Minister, Malcolm Fraser, suggested that the baby should come too. Diana was thrilled, even though, in practical terms, William would see far more of his chief nanny, Barbara Baines, than he would of his own parents. Baba, as he called her, was a constant presence for the first years of his life.

From beginning to end the royal party were treated as celebrities, bigger than any Hollywood stars. It was as if they had won the World Cup and were doing a tour for the fans parading the trophy, which in this case was their son. William was just nine months old when they touched down in Alice Springs and one of the assembled media famously shouted out, 'Here's Billy the Kid.'

William, Nanny Barnes and assorted protection squad officers were whisked off by private plane to a remote sheep station called Woomargama in New South Wales while his parents encountered mass hysteria everywhere they went. Charles and Diana saw William whenever their schedule allowed and were thrilled to discover their son, whom they called Willie Wombat, had started crawling and was already developing a highly destructive streak.

Diana told listeners to a radio phone-in that William had once pressed the panic button at Balmoral and had an entire police squad speeding to the scene. He had also flushed a pair of his father's very expensive shoes down the toilet. William was proving to be Diana's means of connecting with the public.

The absurdity of the world's obsession with a tiny tot was never better illustrated than when the whole jamboree moved on to New Zealand and William, now ten months old, granted his first news conference on the lawn of Government House in Auckland. He hadn't started speaking but he could at least entertain the media with a fifteen-minute demonstration of his ability to crawl.

William, wearing an apricot and peach romper suit, was placed on a rug between his doting parents and, helped by Diana, didn't disappoint his public as he crawled around for the cameras like an adorable puppy. Someone even thought they heard him say his first word – 'Dad-a' – although it was probably wind. The late Victor Chapman, the press officer on the trip, couldn't conceal his exasperation when asked yet another inane question about William. 'He's one year old, for chrissake,' he barked.

The trip was a public relations triumph and cemented Diana's position as the most photographed woman in the world. The crowds loved her. More than one million well-wishers and gawpers came to wave flags at the royal couple. Ostensibly it was a resounding success, but it drove a permanent wedge between Charles and Diana. Christopher Wilson, author of *The Windsor Knot*, observes, 'He became hugely jealous of her popularity. He could hear the groans of the crowds when he got out of the car and they realized they had been standing for hours on the wrong side. Diana loved the attention. He hated the lack of it.'

There was really only one person they wanted to see and that was the statuesque young blonde, over six feet tall in her heels, and not the diffident, balding heir to the throne more than thirteen years her senior. Diana, for her part, soon became addicted to her own publicity and her day would be ruined if she didn't see her picture in the newspapers. She hated it and loved it at the same time – the classic dilemma of a superstar.

William's baby brother, Harry, was born on 15 September 1984, a little over two years after his elder brother, who seemed delighted that he would have someone to play with who wasn't a nanny or a member of the nursery staff. Charles, who was hoping for a girl, memorably said at the birth, 'Oh God, it's a boy, and he's even got red hair.' Diana, in the tape recordings she made for the author Andrew Morton, confessed, 'Something inside me closed off.'

William's parents' marriage was effectively over after the birth of his brother. Diana would later admit that she knew that Charles had never stopped loving Camilla Parker Bowles. 'There were three of us in this marriage so it was a bit crowded,' she said.

William, with his baby brother in tow, became, for a while, a very boisterous if not objectionable little boy. He could hardly be blamed, for he lived in an utterly absurd world. He was the centre of his own little court in Kensington Palace, or KP as his mother called it. William's universe, known as 'the nursery', was like a little house within a big house. It included assorted play-rooms and bedrooms as well as a kitchen and a dining room. He had three full-time nannies and several part-time ones, various bodyguards and a driver. On Fridays, the boys would be driven to Prince Charles's country home, Highgrove, where they had exactly the same comforts and familiar staff. William knew from a tender age that he was a Very Important Person and was not afraid to let others less fortunate know it.

Nothing conveys the ridiculous world the little boys lived in better than a description by Patrick Jephson, Diana's private secretary, of an incident at KP: a distinguished cavalry colonel bowed deeply to Harry, then just three, and bellowed 'Sir', almost causing an astonished little prince to fall off his tricycle.

At his local preschool, Mrs Mynors' Nursery in Chepstow Villas, William would lord it over the other children, declaring, 'If you don't do what I want, then I'll have you arrested.' Things did not improve when he attended his first school, Wetherby Pre-preparatory School, close to KP in Notting Hill. One of the few constants in his life, Nanny Barnes, left on the day he started there after clashing with Diana, who was jealous of her son's affection for her. William burst into tears when he was told she was going.

At the school, William was given the nickname Basher Wills, which sounds a far too jolly description of a young royal bully. On one occasion, a birthday party for another child, William was told to behave himself when he had a food-throwing screaming tantrum. William responded by shouting, 'When I'm king, I'm going to send all my knights around to kill you.'

His long-suffering protection officer had to break up many a playground fight, usually started by William. He always enjoyed rough and tumble with his protection squad and once remarked, 'I don't want to be king. I want to be a policeman.'

William didn't get it all his own way, though. He barrelled up to Sir Bob Geldof, the mastermind of Band Aid, who got on well with Diana, and rudely shouted, 'He's all dirty. He's got scruffy hair and wet shoes.' Sir Bob, unperturbed, replied, 'Shut up, you horrible little boy.'

Amateur psychiatrists would have a field day asking how much of William's high spiritedness was a cry for attention in a fractured home. He was too young to understand his parents' infidelities and infighting but he was old enough to sense the atmosphere. Patrick Jephson memorably described the marital discord as 'like watching a slowly spreading pool of blood seeping from under a locked door.'

William's personal bodyguard, Ken Wharfe, observed that the deep, loving bond between Diana and her two sons was 'truly wonderful to witness'. He recalled how her face would light up whenever she saw them, even if they had been away from her for only a short time. None of the staff, however, could possibly know how much William was affected by his mother's growing emotional fragility.

Andrew Morton in the now famous book *Diana: Her True Story* describes the suicide attempts, which included slashing her wrists with a razor-blade, cutting herself with a penknife and the serrated edge of a lemon slicer, as well as hurling herself at a display cabinet full of glass. For most of her married life Diana was an emotional wreck and her eldest son found himself unprepared for his role as comforter, forever beseeching his mother not to cry.

The tantrum-filled little pest of the early years did not last long. By the time he left Wetherby in 1990, William's exuberance was more likely to be channelled into sports and games than mayhem. Like St Andrew's, Wetherby was intent on turning out youngsters with impeccable manners and a strong sense of responsibility. William changed from being a self-centred little boy into an extremely polite and thoughtful one. His tendency towards seriousness even prompted his mother to start referring to him as 'my little old man'.

He continued to be watched over by a circling pack of media buzzards. When he was seven, he was caught short during a school sports trip to the Richmond Athletic ground and had a pee in a bush. Sure enough, the future king was photographed in the act and the pictures made the next day's tabloid press with the headline 'The Royal Wee Wee'.

During his three years at Wetherby, William mirrored Kate's sporting prowess, becoming the school's champion swimmer. He also had a strong singing voice and starred in several Christmas concerts. Riding was one interest William and Kate did not have in common. She had never been a girl who yearned for a pony, mainly because she was allergic to horses. William, however, was brought up watching his father play polo as often as time would allow. The young princes' horsemanship improved when Diana started taking riding lessons from the handsome James Hewitt. The dashing army officer would roll up to Highgrove when Charles was away and help the boys with their trotting and cantering. They probably had no idea that Diana was having a passionate affair with their riding instructor.

William left the security of home in September 1990, at the age of eight, when he began life as a boarder at the splendid Ludgrove prep school, set in more than one hundred acres of wooded countryside near the Berkshire town of Wokingham and just twenty-one miles from where Kate was going to school at St Andrew's. Unlike Kate's mixed school, Ludgrove was all boys. After an initial bout of homesickness, William settled in well. It was easier to protect him there – and keep him away from the more unseemly publicity surrounding his parents.

He couldn't fail to be affected by the rows and quarrels he observed during the school holidays. After one spat at Highgrove, Diana locked herself in a bathroom in floods of tears. William, concerned for his mother, thrust some tissues under the door with a note saying, 'I hate to see you sad Mummy.'

One of the most striking differences between Kate and William's childhoods was that she was part of a united family linking arms together against the world while the divisions in William's family seriously undermined his confidence.

The most dramatic event of William's school life occurred in the summer of 1991, when he was accidentally smashed in the head by a golf club. He had been larking around in the school grounds with some friends when he was unfortunately caught by a swinging club. Diana was lunching with friends at one of her favourite restaurants, San Lorenzo in Chelsea, when she heard the news. She sped off to the Royal Berkshire Hospital in Reading; Charles, equally alarmed, was driven from Highgrove.

After a CT scan, it was decided that William should be transferred to the Great Ormond Street Hospital for an immediate operation. He had a depressed fracture of the skull and would require surgery under general anaesthetic. Diana travelled in the ambulance along the M4 with Charles following behind in the Aston Martin. While Diana fretted outside during the 75-minute operation, Charles, satisfied that the boy was in safe hands, left for his next official engagement, a performance of *Tosca* at the Royal Opera House in Covent Garden, where he was hosting an evening for European Union officials, including the Environment Commissioner.

Although the operation and aftercare carried some risks, and there was a possibility there might have been some brain damage from the initial blow, William proved to be absolutely fine. As Diana held William's hand for hours after his ordeal, his father hopped on the royal train to travel to Yorkshire for an environmental conference.

Charles had been raised in a stern environment where duty took precedence over family. He was forever being seen as cold-hearted by the media, especially when compared to his wife. It was unfair because both parents loved their sons to bits. After the accident, the *Sun* carried the supremely hurtful headline 'What Kind of Dad Are You?' The old battleaxe columnist of the *Daily Express*, Jean Rook, wrote: 'What sort of father of an eight-year-old boy, nearly brained by a golf club, leaves the hospital before knowing the outcome for a night at the opera?' By the following evening, when Charles returned to spend an hour at his son's bedside, it was too late to alter public opinion.

The dilemma of royal duty versus loving family is one that William and Kate will have to face up to themselves in the years ahead. Christopher Wilson observes, 'I think William is a bit like his father. When Prince Charles was young he was a very dutiful boy. He was warned early of the responsibilities he has had to face up to as a future king. William is made of exactly the same stuff.'

William was able to resume life at Ludgrove within a few days of the incident, although he was advised not to be too daring on the sports field for a while. He still bears the scar from his operation, referring to it jokingly as his 'Harry Potter scar'.

His parents had been briefly reunited in their anguish but there was no way to patch up their dreadful marriage. At least within the beautiful haven of the school, William could be spared the very public death of a nation's hopes as everyone became grimly fascinated by the marriage meltdown. He was out of the limelight when several key events took place: the publication of *Diana: Her True Story* in June 1992 and the serialization of the book in the *Sunday Times*; and, in August 1992, the publication of intimate conversations between Diana and James Gilbey, called Squidgygate by a press that likes to add the word 'gate' to anything scandalous. (It would be another two years before the publication of the authorized biography of the Prince of Wales by Jonathan Dimbleby, in which he admitted adultery, whereas Diana admitted her marital transgression in the notorious *Panorama* interview with Martin Bashir in November 1995.)

All of these controversial events helped to change the public perception of the Royal Family. For many people they were now an upmarket version of *EastEnders*. When Charles and Diana officially separated in December 1992 it was more of a constitutional surprise than anything else. The Royal Family's golden couple were just like the rest of us after all. The news was formally announced by Prime Minister John Major, who, without a trace of irony, said that the decision had been reached 'amicably'. His statement added that the Queen and the Duke of Edinburgh hoped that intrusions into the privacy of the Prince and Princess would now cease – a ludicrous request considering the amount of information Diana and Charles had put into the public domain themselves.

Behind the scenes, the most difficult part of the marriage breakdown had been played out a week earlier in a private room at Ludgrove. Diana had driven down to make sure her boys heard the news from her and not from a roving reporter or classroom gossip. What do you say to children to sweeten the truth in these circumstances? William was deeply affected by the news, even though he put on a brave face at the time. 'I hope you will both be happier now,' he said. William was having to grow up much faster than the average ten year old, offering his younger brother support while privately grieving for his parents' marriage.

Reports coming out of Ludgrove said he would wander around the grounds, head down, as if his whole world had fallen in. William had become a thoughtful, sensitive boy. His uncle, Diana's brother Charles Spencer, described him as 'a very self-possessed, intelligent, and mature boy and quite shy.' William could be forgiven for deciding on those solitary walks that marriage might never be for him. In the future, he would want to be absolutely sure before he made that commitment.

As a schoolboy he continued to thrive at Ludgrove and his success mirrored the progress of Kate Middleton at St Andrew's. He loved acting and was secretary of the school dramatic society. He was still a fish in the swimming pool but now he was an accomplished tennis player as well as captain of the school's rugby and hockey teams.

On several occasions he made the twenty-one mile trip to Pangbourne to represent his school against St Andrew's. Catherine Middleton was one of the hoards of schoolchildren lining the pitch when William took to the hockey field. The crowd for a first eleven hockey fixture was never so big as when William was in the opposition. A classmate recalls, 'It tickles me to think she watched her future husband from the touchline all that time ago.' It was the closest she would get to him for six years.

4

Snogging and Marmite

Sometimes your life can take a most unpleasant and unexpected twist. Kate had been happy and secure at St Andrew's, confident in her sporting ability and popular with the other girls. And she had a stable, secure home life that so many, perhaps William included, could only envy. That was about to change in a horrid fashion.

Kate's parents, Michael and Carole, had chosen the prestigious girls' boarding school, Downe House, as the best senior school in the area for Kate. Situated in lovely grounds in Cold Ash on the outskirts of the small Berkshire town of Thatcham, it took just fifteen minutes to drive there from the house in Bradfield Southend so it would be ideal for Kate to pop back at weekends for some home comforts.

The school boasted an impeccable reputation with outstanding academic results as well as a strong emphasis on sport and drama. Some famous former pupils included the racing expert and broadcaster Clare Balding, the model Sophie Dahl and the current Queen of Comedy, Miranda Hart. It wasn't cheap, at more than £22,000 a year, but it seemed a perfect place for Kate to develop as a teenager. Unfortunately, she ran into a pack of bullies who made her life an absolute misery and reduced her to an emotional wreck.

Kate just didn't fit in, as her contemporaries formed cliques that she was not invited to join. Kate had so far been educated at a mixed school and had no experience of how bitchy girls could be. She was the outsider who was probably too nice for her own good. It didn't help that she was so tall and self-conscious about her eczema. Many of the girls came from private schools in London and Kate, brought up in a semi-detached house in Bradfield Southend, seemed an unworldly young teenager by comparison. Emma Sayle, who was four years above Kate but became her friend when they were both in their twenties, believes that Kate simply wasn't pushy enough. Another, more unkindly, told the diarist Richard Kay, 'In our peer group she was regarded as a nonentity. All the social-climbing girls – and there were lots of them at Downe – thought she was not worth bothering with.'

The bullying was far worse than just knocking her school-books out of her hands or pushing her to the back of the lunch queue: the bullies actually put faeces in her bed. Poor Kate was lonely, homesick and frequently in tears.

Fortunately, when her parents realized how horribly she was being treated and how unhappy she was, they yanked her out of school in the middle of the academic year and set about finding a more welcoming environment. This was not a case of sticking it out so it will be the making of you – Michael and Carole had very strong concerns about their daughter's emotional state.

About half an hour further west of Downe House lay the famous public school Marlborough College, which, in keeping with its go-ahead attitude, had become fully co-educational in 1989. The school is centrally situated in Marlborough, which boasts the longest main street of any market town in the country, assorted antique shops and tearooms, as well as a Waitrose supermarket right in the middle. Anyone driving through might see the gates of the main school but the buildings are hidden from view around an impressive inner court. The central Queen Anne-style house is surrounded by beech trees and streams, while immaculate lawns lead onto the downs.

To send three children there today would require an annual income of not less than £200,000. The fees of £29,000 per year are even higher than those of Eton College. In terms of prestige, Marlborough is probably ranked in the group just below Eton and Harrow, although it enjoys a far less stuffy reputation and attracts parents seeking a more relaxed and cosmopolitan education for their children. The sporting facilities are outstanding, with six grass hockey pitches, ten netball courts and twenty-four tennis courts. Marlborough had its share of aristocrats but it also enjoyed a reputation for diversity. The most famous old girl pre-Kate is probably Samantha Cameron, wife of Prime Minister David Cameron who, by coincidence, was at Eton before Prince William.

One Old Marlburian, the illustrator Emily Faccini observed, 'Marlborough gave you the freedom to discover who you were and to stop caring what other people think. You couldn't take yourself too seriously.' Perhaps this would be the place for Kate.

Michael and Carole went to see the headmaster, Mr Ed Gould, to explain the situation and asked him if Catherine could join the school in the middle of the summer term. Mr Gould, a former international rower and Oxford rugby blue, had a blossoming reputation in the world of education. He had arrived at Marlborough in 1993, when it had received unwelcome publicity following a series of sex and drug scandals and the expulsion of pupils found half naked together. A big, bald man of great physical presence, he had won the confidence of the pupils and restored the school's prestige. His educational goal was to produce 'someone who is capable of making a sound individual judgement by the time they are in their early twenties.'

Mr Gould listened sympathetically to Kate's parents and was happy to help. He decided that she should be placed in the all-girl house Elmhurst, which enjoyed a reputation for sporting excellence under the encouragement of its houseparents, Anne and Mitch Patching.

Before Kate arrived, the house matron, Miss Gould – no relation to the headmaster – rounded up all the girls in the common room and told them that a new girl, Catherine Middleton, would be joining them. Jessica Hay, who would end up in the next bed to Kate in the dorm, recalls, 'Miss Gould was an absolutely lovely woman and she told us to be aware that Catherine didn't get treated very well at her previous school and we all had to try and make her comfortable. So, as we were all fairly down-to-earth people, there was no problem with her fitting in at all.'

Kate undoubtedly needed that support. One of her new schoolmates, Gemma Williamson, remembers her arrival: 'She looked very thin and pale. She had very little confidence.'

It's impossible to say for sure why Kate was the victim of bullying. Jessica believes it was because Kate had the 'whole package'. She explains, 'She's intelligent, she's sporty, she has no airs and she is a very nice, soft person. She was not the kind of person who could necessarily stick up for herself in an argument, although she probably could now she is older!

'She was always well turned out and perfect in that respect. No, at that age not the type of person to stick up for herself and so I think they saw something that they could pick on. Gangs of girls can be quite ravenous and very quickly spoil somebody's education.'

Kate, although rather subdued and lacking in confidence to begin with, was able to settle into her new surroundings more quickly than might have been expected. The girls at Elmhurst had a lot to do with that, readily accepting the nervous young teenager into their midst. Gradually Kate was able to tell Jessica and her new dorm friends the full extent of her misery at her previous school. She told them how much she 'absolutely hated it' and the awful story of how the bullies had put faeces in her bed. One friend observes, 'She was very, very badly bullied. It was not a good school for her at all.'

The headmaster came to Elmhurst during Kate's first week when many of the girls were in the common room watching television. Jessica recalls, 'He was so involved with the pupils – with everybody, not just one or two. I think he played a massive part in improving Catherine's confidence. He came in and he said hello to all of us but I knew that he really just came to see if she was all right. And I heard her say to him, "I am so happy."'

Not long afterwards came further proof of that happiness. The girls decided to play their version of the television game show *Blind Date* in the common room. It was one of the party evenings they had from time to time when everyone got together to play games and have fun after supper. Kate was nominated as the host, Cilla Black, and entered into the spirit of it all with great gusto.

Kate, who as a teenager wasn't into fashion at all, had to borrow her outfit from Jessica, which made everyone laugh because the two girls were such different heights: 'I lent her this really short black skirt, black fishnet tights and this kind of lime-coloured blouse. And then she put a wig on. It was so funny because she was so much taller than me.' Kate has never minded dressing up and was giggling along with everyone else. In her best Scouse accent, she introduced each of the 'contestants': 'Now then, luv, what's yer name and where d'you come from?' 'Our Kate', as Cilla might say, had been accepted.

Kate was also fortunate that, as well as her new friends, she had the benefit of a school counsellor, Mrs Bryant, who taught drama and art and was married to the school's drama director. She would come into Elmhurst twice a week to see how Kate and other girls were coping and if they had any problems they wanted to discuss. One of the other girls said, 'She is a fantastic woman, an absolute saint.' Her mentoring helped to bring Kate out of herself.

Once a week at 5p.m. Kate would knock on the door of one of

the study rooms and go in to spend half an hour telling Mrs Bryant about her week and talking through any problems. One week the problem was pretty self-evident when she appeared with grey hair. She and Jessica had spent the afternoon dying their hair: 'Kate was absolutely mortified. It was meant to be blonde.' Mrs Bryant was able to suggest quietly that Kate spend the evening in the bathroom washing the dye out. She was also prepared for her next pupil – Jessica, sporting bright ginger hair.

Elmhurst was a very sporty house, thanks largely to the efforts of Mr and Mrs Patching. Anne Patching was an excellent tennis player and her husband Mitch was outstanding as a hockey coach. The matron, Miss Gould, was also a formidable hockey player. Kate built her day around sport. Tennis and hockey were the two main sports for girls at the school but Kate also played in the netball team.

Jessica, who had won a sports scholarship to the school, shared Kate's enthusiasm. They were teammates throughout their school career, ending up in first team hockey together and playing doubles as the first tennis pair. Jessica describes Kate as being an 'amazing' tennis player.

The schoolday would begin with the bell waking them up at 7a.m., but nobody moved, of course, until matron banged on the door demanding they get up. After grabbing some breakfast in the house kitchen, they would be ready for classes between 8.30 and 9a.m. Lunch would be at 12.30p.m. so they could make hockey practice at 1.30 before afternoon lessons. At 4.30p.m. there would be another half hour's hockey practice before they returned to Elmhurst for a two-hour study period and supper. And then at 7p.m. there was an hour's homework to do before any thoughts of *EastEnders*. It was a very long day.

They could go to the main hall, known as 'the big hall', for supper but more often than not they chose to fix themselves something in the house kitchen, which was usually well-stocked with Kate's favourite things – peanut butter, Dairylea cheese tri-angles, very hot Peperami and Marmite.

Kate's speciality was a sort of Marmite double-decker sandwich that Carole used to make her at home. Jessica tried it when they were perched together on the kitchen counter while chatting about their day. She was very hungry so Kate told her to 'try this' and proceeded to grab some rye bread, smother it with butter and Marmite, fold it over twice and then shove it in the microwave. 'It came out after about twenty seconds all soft and gooey. I absolutely loved it. The next weekend she came back to my house in Hampshire and made it for my mum, who went "Oh my gosh . . .".'

After the first year, Jessica and Kate shared a dorm by themselves. The previous occupant had left a picture of the young Prince William above Jessica's bed. He was fishing – not exactly a pin-up shot. Contrary to popular belief, Kate did not put the poster up and she didn't gaze at it every night. Instead, while the two girls didn't take the picture down at first, Kate was more concerned with putting up her favourite, the male model from the Levi Jeans ad minus his shirt. Next to it she hung a poster of Kate Moss, then the most famous Kate in the country and the woman whose looks and style she most admired.

One thing that is true, however, is the girls would exchange light-hearted banter about the William poster. Kate would look at it and declare, 'I'll be his wife one day.' Jessica would respond, 'No you won't because I will be going out with him.' It was just a laugh, although, as Jessica says, 'It's funny when you think of it – like fate, I suppose.'

In her early teens Kate had filled out a bit from the lanky girl at St Andrew's. The braces had come off her teeth. Although still the tallest girl in class, she was chunkier thanks to her sports regime – more like a size ten than the catwalk-like size six of today. She showed little interest in clothes, make-up or boys. Her hair was very frizzy and not yet styled. She only turned heads because of her height.

Next door to Elmhurst was the all-boys house, Barton Hill, where the boys would compile a 'flavours of the month' list of all the girls they currently fancied in the school. Kate never made it on to the list, nor did Jessica, but their dorm-mate, Hannah Gillingham, seemed to be a regular 'flavour'. Jessica recalls, 'They used to pin it up on their dining-room wall. It was awful. Catherine used to say to me, "How sad. I'm going to grow up and be a princess, so I don't care."'

Teenage hormones were kicking in among her friends and there was a fair bit of 'preening' for the benefit of the boys. Kate seemed less interested than the rest, although that was more to do with confidence at this point. She did, however, join in when they used to tease the Barton Hill gang. After lights out, at about 9.30p.m., a group of girls would gather in Kate and Jessica's dorm, put on their make-up and parade up and down in front of the windows for the benefit of the pining boys in the adjacent house. They saw themselves as sophisticated models. On an agreed signal they would all stop – Kate included – and moon the hapless bunch. The boys across the way would shine flashlights through the windows to try and get a better view.

Jessica laughs, 'We used to have a little fun and tease them a bit. The next morning we would all trot over to have breakfast in the Barton Hill dining room. I can still hear Catherine protesting, "Keep me out of it, you guys. It's nothing to do with me." We used to have a lot of fun as girls.'

About a dozen of the boys and girls from Elmhurst and Barton Hill would get together to go on picnics to the picturesque village of Great Bedwyn, which is about six miles and a short train journey from Marlborough. One girl's parents lived in the village, which gave everyone the excuse to head off for a weekend visit. The boys would supply the booze, usually wine and vodka – Kate's favourites – while the girls would bring some snacks. Kate usually took Peperami. They would make their way to the same field each time and drink and chat and sunbathe under their favourite tree.

After sitting their GCSEs, the friends decided this would be the perfect place to celebrate. 'We just got absolutely pissed,' recalls Jessica. 'Even Catherine, though she wasn't as pissed as the rest of us. She usually kept a little bit of composure. She sort of has a stop button, which every group needs. She would be the person who would be nominated as the driver if we all went to a party.

'She had the last laugh the next morning when the rest of us were dying with our hangovers. She was like, "Look at me, I'm fine." And I was like, "You bitch!" It was great fun.'

Kate had one too many drinks only once during her school-days. She and her host of friends were invited to a country house party at the home of the international horseman William Fox-Pitt, whose younger sister Alicia was at Marlborough. One of the girls at the party explained, 'You do tend to have these kind of random parties in the country where the young gentry get invited, drink a whole lot and kind of puke up on the sofa.' Kate didn't puke up on the sofa, preferring instead to be sick outside on the lawn.

Kate was very lucky that in Jessica, Hannah Gillingham and her two other dorm-mates, Camille Koppen and Rebecca Johnston, she found kindred spirits. They were neither the coolest girls on the block nor the uncoolest. Jessica observes, 'Elmhurst was a great house for bringing people together who were in the middle.'

As was the case at prep school, everyone called her Catherine. Nobody used Kate and certainly she was never referred to as Middlebum, one of many inventions about the young woman's life. Kate and her friends were all boarders but they were able to go home to celebrate birthdays or special events.

Kate's home was now considerably more upmarket than it used to be. The success of Party Pieces had far exceeded Carole Middleton's initial ambition – so much so that Michael made the bold decision to give up his job at British Airways and con-centrate on the 'family business'. They joined the online revolution in 1992 when they registered the Party Pieces domain name and set up the website that would transform their fortunes. Within three years they were on the move.

They found Oak Acre in Chapel Row, a hamlet on the outskirts of the larger village of Bucklebury, which boasted several celebrity residents, including Chris Tarrant, Kate Bush and the television presenter Melinda Messenger. The five-bedroom red brick house, worth £1 million, was covered in vines and wisteria, and was hidden from the road by some impressive oak trees. Estate agent Dudley Singleton observed, 'Hardly anyone knows that the house is even there. We have more than our fair share of multimillionaires living here but you'd never guess because they are discreet.' Michael and Carole didn't want to transfer their business to the garden shed so they bought some ramshackle old farm buildings at nearby Ashburton Common, which would give them the opportunity to expand and take on some staff.

Carole set about turning Oak Acre into the sort of stylish home she had always dreamed of. She liked the modern open-plan style of house so they set about knocking down walls to create large reception rooms that they filled with antiques from weekend trips 'antiquing' in the Berkshire and Wiltshire countryside. One visitor to the house described it as 'modern mixed with old'. Carole placed photos of Kate and Pippa's sporting achievements on many of the surfaces – school pictures of them in the hockey and netball teams. Kate found space in her room for her collection of Cabbage Patch dolls and chose a tasteful, understated colour scheme – a cream satin duvet with blue and cream pillows; Pippa's room down the hall was eye-catching red.

In the garden was a large garage, which the Middletons used as a games and party room. Kate would celebrate her birthdays there and invite about a dozen of her closest school friends along. They could play music as loud as they liked while their parents enjoyed drinks in the house with Michael and Carole. Kate loved rap music, a pleasure she shared with Prince

William, although he wouldn't have been so impressed at the worrying stage she went through when she was obsessed with Whitney Houston and would waltz into Elmhurst singing 'I Will Always Love You' at the top of her voice.

Kate has always been a mixture of introvert and extrovert. Like her father, she can melt into a room so you barely realize she is there. Or, more like her mother, she can suddenly burst into life and start singing or dancing. She just needed a little encouragement to be the star of her school musical, join in *Blind Date* or, later, parade down the catwalk in a fashion show. But her friends will testify that she can be unexpected fun. On one of Jessica's birthdays, for instance, they organized a trip to Madame Tussaud's in London where Kate had everyone in stitches by standing next to the waxwork of Winston Churchill and doing an impersonation of the great man, pretending to smoke a huge cigar. One school friend recalls, 'Kate may have been a little shy sometimes but she likes the theatrical stuff.' She loved the film *Dirty Dancing* with Patrick Swayze and the *Rocky Horror Show* and always hoped to go to one of the cult productions where all the fans dress up in costume.

One of the Marlborough traditions was called the 'House Shout', when all the houses would compete against one another in a sort of *Glee* competition. One year Kate, Jessica and Camille sang 'I'll Be There For You', the famous theme tune from *Friends,* backed up by a huge chorus. In another life you could imagine Kate auditioning for Andrew Lloyd Webber's television talent shows *How Do You Solve A Problem Like Maria?* or *Over the Rainbow.*

Kate was beginning to mature and grow into herself. The summer after GCSEs was when she transformed from an awkward teenager into a beautiful young woman. The catalyst was the month she spent travelling around Brazil and Argentina on a school hockey trip. Kate played centre forward and was the star of a team that lost only two matches on the whole trip. More than that, away from the restrictions of school and home, she was able to blossom and enjoy the company of the handsome South American boys she met. Jessica, who was on the trip, observes, 'It was her first taste of having a social life and going out. The boys' team came as well and we were all on a bus together and then placed with various families whose daughters we were playing against.'

Kate, perhaps to her surprise, found that the local boys really fancied her. She was keen to reciprocate, although not everything went smoothly. One evening she managed to get off with a particularly handsome Argentinian boy and was happily snogging him on the steps of the veranda of the house where she was staying when the phone rang. 'Hello, darling. It's Mum.' The awkward situation was made funnier when Jessica, who was kissing another boy a few feet away, was called by her parents at the same time.

Her South American adventure took Kate out of her comfort zone. While she always enjoyed the summer fair in Bucklebury, with its familiar country stalls, falconry displays, dog races and hog roast, this was much more exhilarating – a wild and beautiful country. She loved, for instance, her trip to the Iguazu Falls, the spectacular series of waterfalls that marks the border between Argentina and Brazil and can rightly claim to be one of the wonders of the modern world.

Kate returned home a changed girl. She was tanned and healthy, and had a confident spring in her step. All her friends noticed. One of her school contemporaries, Gemma Williamson, observed, 'It happened quite suddenly. She came back an absolute beauty.' And Jessica confirms, 'I think there is a major transition that girls go through at this time and this was Kate's. Her hair was still the same but she looked completely different. She had grown into her body. She was more mature and had a different outlook on things.'

Kate was now a sixth former. She had passed all eleven of her GCSEs and for her A levels decided to study art, chemistry and biology. At last, now sixteen and a half, Kate started to attract the attention of boys at Marlborough, particularly the ones a little older, probably because she was still that bit taller than most girls of her age, but also because of her new maturity. She never went out of her way to encourage it, however. She never wore tight jeans or other flattering clothes, preferring always her 'trackie bums' and a baggy top. Sometimes she would slob out all day in her hockey shorts and shirts.

Once in a while she took part in a Marlborough ritual – the arranged snog. The girls would spend their Friday afternoon lessons passing each other notes about which boy each of them would like to snog at the weekend. When the snoggable target had been chosen, it was all arranged with the utmost decorum. A friend was enlisted to act as a go-between to see if the desired boy was up for it. If so, a suitable time and place was arranged.

Around the school pond you might get a dozen young couples pairing off as pre-arranged. Kate usually favoured round the back of Barton Hill because it was nearer and more discreet. The snog itself was more businesslike than a passion marathon and the clinch would last only a few minutes before the couple would separate and return to their houses. There the girls would get down to the more important business of the evening – comparing notes.

Kate's favourite snogger was a very handsome blond boy with a chiselled jaw called Willem Marx, although she never had a proper relationship with him. Other boys have been suggested, like Oliver Bowen and Charlie von Moll, but these are wide of the mark. The former was a year below Kate and the latter was older and had already left the school. Willem and Kate have an ongoing friendship, probably because he has never spoken of their teenage lip-locking, which is even more praiseworthy considering his future employment as a journalist.

Kate was definitely not a serial snogger. 'She has always been quite picky,' observes Jessica. 'She would never go for a man because he was "fit" or "rich". Even back then she would rather concentrate on making sure her life was okay. If a guy comes along – well, it's a bonus.'

Her new-found maturity did not signal a period of going off the rails. Kate never smoked, referring to cigarettes as 'cancer sticks' whenever Jessica was having a crafty fag out the window of the dorm. She never wanted to try drugs, and was concerned with the effect they could have on her contemporaries. Jessica explains, 'She didn't agree with drugs and thought it was degrading.' Instead, every Wednesday when there was no hockey practice, Kate and her friends would walk purposefully into Marlborough to have tea at The Polly Tea Rooms, where they would all pretend to be 'ladies' and Kate would order her favourite blueberry muffin.

Kate was brilliant at sport as a girl, winning a cup for outstanding sporting achievement at St Andrew's School in Pangbourne. She was a star of the swimming team (second row, third from left).

She played centre forward at hockey, here celebrating scoring a goal, aged thirteen.

In the netball team she played goal defence, although she changed to goal attack at Marlborough College.

On her final day at St Andrew's she posed with friends behind the house parent, Kevin Alford, who said she was 'a 100-miles-an-hour kind of girl'.

Kate fitted in easily at Marlborough, where she formed close friendships with the girls, relaxing at a sleepover aged sixteen, and below, grinning next to pal Gemma Williamson.

On the catwalk: the famous outfit that Prince William saw from the front row of a charity fashion show.

It wasn't all about William at St Andrews University. Kate revelled in student life, including the annual foam fight which was the culmination of the 'Raisin Weekend' celebrations.

Smiling on graduation day when she received her degree in art history.

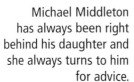

Michael Middleton has always been right behind his daughter and she always turns to him for advice.

Her mother Carole loves to join Kate shopping and is credited with helping to shape her daughter's sense of style.

Kate and William only rarely show signs of affection in public but they were caught embracing after he took part in the Eton Field Game in March 2006.

Kate shows off her well-toned figure on board a yacht in Ibiza in September 2006.

When Kate moved to London she was a constant target for the paparazzi.

Who wouldn't look miserable on a number 19 bus?

The paparazzi were waiting for Kate when she left for work on her twenty-fifth birthday. It was not a happy start to the day.

Every time they went skiing, there would always be a photographer to capture a tender moment. At Zermatt in March 2007, Kate was used to ignoring them.

Younger brother James keeps a low profile and is rarely photographed with his big sister.

The 'sizzle sisters', Kate and Pippa Middleton, out on the town.

In 2007 Kate showed the world what William was missing while he was away on military training. She showed her knees at the Badminton Horse Trials.

For a night at Mahiki, she showed her knees and her slender thighs.

It was her toned middle on display after the Rampant Rabbit party at Kitts Club in June.

5

William's Pain

William was asleep in his bedroom at Balmoral when his father woke him with the news that his mother was dead. It was 31 August 1997 and Diana had died four hours earlier. William was fifteen years and two months old and, at first, too shocked to cry. He had spoken to his mother only the day before, after she'd touched down in Paris for the last night of her holiday with the international playboy Dodi Fayed.

William had a moan to Diana about yet another media photo call at Eton, where he was due to start a new school year the following week. She said she would see if she could change it when she returned the next day. The conversation was light and Diana was looking forward to seeing both her sons after their annual royal holiday to Scotland with their father and grandparents, the Queen and Prince Philip.

William insisted he wanted to be with his father when he went to wake Harry, who was only twelve. All three could be heard sobbing down the silent corridors of the Scottish castle. It would be wrong to assume Charles, a sensitive man, didn't share the moment of desolation. He was grieving for the mother of his sons and for the boys themselves. Life for them, he realized, would never be the same. They cried until dawn.

The world missed a heartbeat when Princess Diana died. She was thirty-six. Her premature death would guarantee her immortality in much the same way it had Marilyn Monroe, James Dean and John Lennon. They never grow old; their youthful images remain forever frozen in the collective mind.

William and Harry have never got over the loss of their mother. To say they were devastated is inadequate. The emotional difficulty for the two young boys was made worse by the absurd if understandable level of public fascination with their private grief. They were never left alone to mourn.

Harry explained to NBC's Matt Lauer: 'When she passed away there was never that time, there was never that sort of lull. There was never that peace and quiet for any of us due to the fact that her face was always splattered in the paper the whole time.'

William agreed that they were always thinking about it and added poignantly, 'Not a day goes by when I don't think about it once in the day.'

The events of that fateful summer night in Paris are well known. Diana, Dodi and her personal bodyguard, Trevor Rees-Jones, were in a black Mercedes that was driven at furious speed through a tunnel by a chauffeur, Henri Paul. They were being pursued by a posse of paparazzi when Monsieur Paul, whose blood contained more than the permitted level of alcohol, crashed into a pillar. Only the bodyguard survived.

Conspiracy theories about the crash began almost at once and have never stopped. The young princes have had to cope with their grief while wondering what really happened in the tunnel that night. Harry admitted that he will never stop wondering. William hates the constant questioning and regurgitation of events: 'There are always rumours and stuff brought up the whole time. There are a lot of people feeding it – the conspiracy side of things – unnecessarily I think.'

Diana's life and shocking death had changed the country's expectations of the Royal Family. The nation's mood, caught by the Prime Minister, Tony Blair, demanded a public display of grief. The Royal Family's way of dealing with tragedy, however, is to cry behind closed doors while maintaining a public face of fortitude. They went to church the morning her death was announced and then retreated behind the royal gates.

Anyone who has seen the film *The Queen*, starring Helen Mirren, will appreciate the conflict behind those gates as Tony Blair sought to persuade the Queen that the public needed to see the human side of her family. He described the Royal Family's reluctance to speak publicly about her death as 'bizarre'. The day after her death he captured the 'tidal wave of grief and loss' when he memorably described her on television as the 'People's Princess' – an idea he had scribbled on the back of an envelope. The Queen was not so speedy to address the nation. Eventually, nearly a week later, she told the world of her family's grief and acknowledged the public despair. Harry and William went on a short walkabout outside Kensington Palace to inspect the hundreds of floral tributes that had been piled high outside the gates. A mourner among the watching crowd offered William a bouquet, which he took with a simple 'Thank you'. The princes had a cruel duty to show their faces.

Each day brought a fresh ordeal but none more so than the funeral on 6 September. Strangely, no image of Diana's life can match the iconic one after her death when her two young sons, heads bowed, walked solemnly behind the coffin. William was stooped as if wishing the ground to swallow him up. Prince Charles walked on one side, their grandfather, Prince Philip, on the other and their uncle, Earl Spencer, in the centre, but nobody could take their eyes off William and Harry. That included Kate Middleton in the common room at Elmhurst. She was just one of millions around the world who watched the funeral on television. It was, as Tony Blair said, a global event.

William hated the thought of the long walk in public. At first he absolutely refused to do it. Tony Blair's press secretary, Alastair Campbell, recalls that the young prince was 'consumed by a total hatred of the media' after the accident, especially since many blamed the paparazzi chasing the car for causing it. He wanted nothing to do with a stunt to appease the media and was adamant that he would take no active role in the funeral.

Campbell also says that royal courtiers were hugely troubled at the prospect of the crowds turning against Prince Charles, which would have made the day a disaster. William was apparently persuaded by the suggestion from Palace staff that it was what his mother would have wanted. Ironically, Diana was a master of the photo opportunity. William was more likely still to have been swayed by his grandfather, who advised him he would always regret it if he didn't walk. Prince Philip said that he too would walk behind the coffin if William would join him – and he stayed next to William for the whole of the procession. Perhaps, however, what ultimately persuaded William to change his mind was his own highly developed and precocious sense of duty.

Both the Queen and the Queen Mother, William's great-grandmother, understood that he required special attention because he would be king one day. He needed to be groomed for the role. Growing up, he would take the short walk between Eton and Windsor Castle to have tea with the Queen each week and tell her what he'd been doing. She would give him advice on how to behave. At family lunches the Queen Mum would invariably sit next to William and tell him stories of the Second World War, bringing the nation's hardships to life. The young boy looked up to her and admired her strength of character: 'Whenever I was ill, I always used to remember that in the same circumstances she would battle on, no matter how she felt.'

William had to battle on through the funeral service at Westminster Abbey. The funeral was a curious mix of regal solemnity and celebrity – a reflection of Diana's life and how she had changed the Royal Family. In a throng of 1,900 mourners that included the Queen, Mrs Thatcher and Hillary Clinton were Tom Cruise, Tom Hanks, Cliff Richard, George Michael and Chris de Burgh. Elton John sang 'Goodbye England's rose' in his reworking of the classic 'Candle in the Wind', which became the biggest selling record of all time in the UK. William and Harry were clearly moved and upset but, for once, were spared the gaze of the cameras as the BBC had agreed not to focus on grieving members of the family during the service.

Diana's brother, Earl Spencer, gave the funeral address. In the years that have passed, his speech has been judged less favourably for its apparent criticisms of the Royal Family. At the time, his halting, tearful words captured a mood that drew a round of applause from those at the service inside and among the crowd outside. He told the boys, 'How great your suffering is, we cannot even imagine.' He also declared that he and Diana's family would do everything in their power to make sure that her sons' souls would not be crushed by duty and tradition. The sentiment that chimed most with William's own feelings was his uncle's barb at the media: 'of all the ironies about Diana, perhaps the greatest was this: a girl given the name of the ancient goddess of hunting was, in the end, the most hunted person of the modern age.'

A long day, which had begun at 11a.m. with the sounding of the death knell at Westminster Abbey, ended at 6p.m. on a small island in the grounds of Diana's family home at Althorp in Northamptonshire. William and Harry joined a few family members, including their father, for a private burial – at last free from public scrutiny. Diana's final resting place was chosen so it would remain a private place, inaccessible to the public, that her sons could visit without the threat of a long-range lens capturing the moment.

The outpouring of global grief now, nearly fourteen years later, seems completely excessive. The Elton John song was the soundtrack to the general woe but it is neither performed nor played any more. Even Tony Blair admits that the phrase the 'People's Princess' seems 'like something from another age, corny and over the top.' But at the time it did reflect the mood of the country.

Her death is still talked about all the time. *Loose Women,* for instance, were discussing it in February 2011: Lisa Maxwell pointed out the legacy of the funeral was that it gave people the opportunity to cry openly – not just for Diana but also for themselves, for those whom they too had lost.

Most importantly the funeral gave William an unshakeable popularity and affection that the years haven't diminished – a place in the hearts and minds of the nation that will help protect Kate in the future. To many, however, his father will always be the pantomime villain of the piece.

Just four days after their longest day, Charles drove William back to Eton, where there were six hundred letters waiting for him in his room, many of them from his schoolmates. It was the start of his third year and from uncertain beginnings he had flourished at the famous public school.

Both Diana and Charles had been keen to avoid Gordonstoun in Scotland, where the Prince of Wales had been famously miserable. Eton is also a tough school where the only privilege a young prince could enjoy was bullet-proof glass in his bedroom window and having a personal protection officer sleeping in the next room. William had to have a panic button with him at all times to alert security, which didn't impress his schoolmates when he showed them: they grabbed it from him and chucked it in the Thames.

The cameras had been there to record William's first day when he nervously signed the school register in the wrong place. It was one of the few occasions when his mother and father were together following the split that would eventually lead to divorce.

William had to face the embarrassment of his mother's private life being paraded on the front pages of the newspapers.

When he started at Eton, for instance, there was intense speculation surrounding her friendship with the swarthy England
rugby captain Will Carling. Whenever William and his brother
joined his mother for outings, the inevitable front pages followed: days out to Thorpe Park and Alton Towers seemed more
like photo opportunities than happy family excursions. Behind
the scenes courtiers were working out when Charles would have
access to his children and when it would be Diana's turn – the
nuts and bolts of any divorce settlement.

Perhaps the worst media intrusion for William came with
Diana's notorious *Panorama* interview in which she spoke frankly
to Martin Bashir about her life and her love life. It was toe-
curling stuff as the Princess admitted adultery and talked about
her husband's infidelity. While tales of unfaithfulness, bulimia
and marriage breakdown had all been well aired in print, this
was an admission on television, the medium of the age. William
was said to be furious with his mother and refused to speak to
her on his next visit home. She had to promise him that the 'de-
bacle', as it was called by her private secretary, Patrick Jephson,
would be her first and last 'celebrity' television interview.

William was protected as much as possible by his renowned
housemaster, Dr Andrew Gailey, an easygoing Irishman who
had a strong rapport with the boys in his care. His protection
was even more vital during the lonely days after the funeral. At
Eton William also had an unofficial 'protector'. This would be
an older boy who would help and guide the younger pupil
through early school life, a mentor who was there to discuss and
offer counsel on any problems. William's protector was Nick
Knatchbull, the son of Lord and Lady Romsey and the great-
grandson of Lord Mountbatten, who had been an important
presence in the life of Prince Charles until he was killed by an
IRA bomb in 1979. His grand family home, Broadlands in
Hampshire, was the venue for the first part of Charles and
Diana's honeymoon.

By a twist of fate, Nick, who was a year older than William, would prove to be Kate's first proper link with the Royal Family. Jessica Hay, her dorm-mate at Marlborough, met Nick at the wedding of her friend Isabella Norman, who married into the Mountbatten family. Nicholas was a page boy and Jessica caught his eye. Two weeks later he asked her out, beginning a three-year teenage relationship. Through Nick, Jessica often met Wills, as he was generally known, when she went over to Eton to visit. She also saw him at Broadlands for shooting parties and hunts. There, she met the Queen and other members of the Royal Family. Back in the comfort of the dorm, Kate wanted to hear all about it but Jessica had to disappoint her because, as Kate would discover herself, it would be considered bad form to be too chatty about her royal connections. Jessica had a unique insight into a world that, at school, Kate could only watch from afar.

Jessica met the Queen for the first time at a dinner at Broadlands. She had nothing to wear but fortunately Nick's mother, Penny, came to the rescue and lent her a suitable dress because Jessica didn't have anything 'that posh'. She recalls, 'I was freaking out and Penny came up and she actually taught me how to curtsy properly and, you know, how to behave. But when I went down to dinner, it was so funny because they were all standing in a line. There was Prince Philip, the Queen, Nick's father, Norton. And I curtsied and Prince Philip was like, "You don't need to do that", making me feel like a "silly woman" . . . and then I had to sit next to him.

'But he was a complete hoot. He is so funny and I know that Catherine gets along so well with him. The table is set boy, girl, boy, girl and the protocol is you talk to the person on your left. Everything is concentrated around the Queen, who doesn't need to say anything at all. You could be talking to the person on your left or talking across the table but she wouldn't speak. But then she says one word and the whole place goes silent. It's amazing. She has great presence but she is such a lovely person.

'Funnily enough she and Catherine are very alike in terms of humour. They are both very dry and very sarcastic. The only difference is that Catherine doesn't really know anything about horses and the Queen does tend to go on about horses quite a bit. It's all she goes on about. Basically, though, they are a lovely family and the Queen and Prince Philip are a normal, old-fashioned couple.

'One thing about the Queen is that she can integrate with anyone. There was always a wonderful butler at Broadlands and the Queen would ask him to come and sit down and say, "Would you like a brandy?" She was very, very friendly.'

Whenever the Queen visited Broadlands, there would be a presentation line for dinner and, if he was there as well, William had to stand in it. Jessica recalls he would roll his eyes as if to say, 'Don't worry about it.' Harry would also have to stand in line and shake hands with the women as they came down for dinner.

After the meal the men and the ladies would split up and go to separate rooms for port and brandies and a natter. For many, the television hit *Downton Abbey* is the closest they will get to such grandeur but Jessica, a teenager from Marlborough College, was living it. The younger guests, however, were pretty bored by it all. William, Harry, Nick and Jessica used to go and sit on the lawn outside. There was a dip in the grass so that you couldn't be seen from the house if you wanted to have a crafty cigarette, which William often did.

If there was a shooting party the next day, then the ladies, including the Queen, would be 'beaters' for the day, a curious occupation where women, usually in headscarves, would plough through thickets and scrub beating the ground and making as much noise as possible to drive the birds out into the open and up into the skies, so that the men, armed with shot-guns, could shoot them down.

Princess Diana wasn't the least bit interested in such country pursuits but Jessica did meet her on occasion and found her to be 'quick witted with a warm sense of humour'. Jessica had the day off school to attend the funeral. When she returned to

Marlborough, she talked to Kate about it: 'Kate said she'd watched it in the common room and that she did get quite upset. I think everybody did. I remember that three days later we both went to the school's own memorial service for her in the chapel. The headmaster wanted to commemorate her life.'

William, meanwhile, had to carry on as usual. Jessica bumped into him at Eton not long afterwards: 'He seemed like he didn't have anything to worry about but you could tell in his face he was mourning because he was so very close to his mother. But he just got on with things. He had grown up with the belief that you had to get on with it and I think his mother would have been really insulted if he kind of let everything go.

William has never had a normal life but at Eton he could at least forget his public duty safe in the knowledge that nobody would be making a video of his efforts in a school karaoke competition to put on YouTube at a later date. Every building and area of the school grounds was dotted with security cameras fitted since his arrival, but the filming was strictly for the eyes of his protection staff.

Among a family not renowned for its brain power William stood out as being thoughtful and intelligent, comfortably passing twelve GCSEs with A grades in English, languages and history – Dr Gailey's subject. Prince Charles, a keen painter and student of art, was particularly pleased when William chose to study history of art at A level, along with geography and biology. He didn't know it at the time, of course, but choosing history of art would help to shape his future life.

Mirroring Kate's school career somewhat, William was better than average academically but well above average in sports. He was useful at football and rugby but excelled at swimming and water polo, eventually captaining the school in both disciplines. Like Kate, he became a prefect. William was elected to the Eton Society, commonly known as Pop, which is considered a great achievement. In effect, he became a senior prefect with privileges, the most notable one was that he could wear any elaborately designed waistcoat of his choosing. This was a good thing where William was concerned as he needed smartening up. He had a reputation for being a bit scruffy at school, forever borrowing friends' jumpers that didn't fit him properly and wearing his hair with his fringe unfashionably long.

More importantly for his future career, William won the Sword of Honour, awarded to the school's top military cadet. The Combined Cadet Force, or CCF as it was known, is a feature of most public schools and promotes discipline and leadership among pupils. William had signed up for the army section and his success at school was a good omen for any future military career.

6

Mind the Gap

Catherine Middleton arrived at Marlborough College an uncertain, bullied, nervous girl. She was embarrassed by her eczema and worried about fitting in. She left five years later, in 2000, a well-groomed, poised young woman ready to leave her teens behind. She was still tall but now she was more elegant than lanky. Her education had given her all the social skills she could want, although her experience of the opposite sex was confined to the occasional snog. She was well on the way to being 'Kate' and finding her feet in the real world.

She had yet to decide which university to attend. Her A levels were good but nothing that was going to guarantee a place at Oxford or Cambridge. She was keen to study history of art and her first choice at this stage was Oxford Brookes, a new university that had formerly been the well-known Oxford Polytechnic and was founded in Victorian times as the Oxford School of Art. The *Sunday Times* ranked it as the best new university and, from Kate's point of view, it had the advantage of having a strong reputation for history of art. A second positive was its proximity both to London, where the leading art houses had their bases, and Bucklebury, just thirty miles away. The University of St

Andrews was no more than a possible at this stage. She had plenty of time to decide. In the meantime, her parents were keen for her to see something of the world during her gap year – that time between school and university when many privileged teenagers have the chance to travel before the next stage of their education.

After a summer spent topping up her tan in the garden at Bucklebury, Kate flew to the beautiful Italian city of Florence to do a twelve-week course in Italian and history of art at the British Institute in Palazzo Strozzino. Established in 1917, the Institute has the grand aim of fostering cultural understanding between Britain and Italy. The course would give Kate an important edge when she started university. While the trip was an adventure for any teenager, Kate was under orders from her parents to take it seriously: this was not an excuse for three months of partying.

Instead, it was an idyllic interlude in Kate's life and probably the first and last time she was able to escape completely by herself. It was as if she were starring in her own James Ivory film. Her distant cousin, Helena Bonham Carter, had starred in one of the great director's finest films, *A Room with a View*, based on E. M. Forster's classic novel, in which the heroine, Lucy Honeychurch, came of age on a holiday to Tuscany.

Miss Honeychurch is also from a small English hamlet and her passions are ignited by a kiss in a cornfield from a dashing Englishman abroad, George Emerson. While the stirrings in Kate weren't quite so strong, she did see a lot of a young man called Harry. Though not a prince, Harry had also been to Marlborough and so had something in common with Kate.

While Kate was happy to socialize with the other students, she took the course a little more seriously than the majority. She did, however, join everyone for happy hour cocktails in the fashionable L'Art Bar in Via del Moro, a few steps from the River Arno. One of her fellow students remembers the evening he tried to chat her up: 'I failed miserably but she didn't make me feel bad about it. I liked that about her. When she left someone explained to me that she was hung up on this bloke Harry.' The *Mail on Sunday* later speculated that Harry had been a bit of a heartbreaker as far as Kate was concerned. It was certainly true that Kate, while socially adept, wasn't experienced in handling confident young men.

Even though Kate wasn't the finished article yet – her hair was naturally curly and her clothes uninspiring – she stood out among her new friends on the course. Another student recalls that Kate was very popular among the girls because all the barmen fancied her and would keep the free drinks coming: 'Italian men can be quite persuasive but Kate would never overreact to compliments. She definitely was not a giggly sort of girl, batting her eyelashes.' Kate's apparent coolness was, of course, extremely attractive to young men.

Clearly Kate was a girl who didn't like to lose control or was worried what she might do if she did. One of her fellow students observed, 'She couldn't really handle her drink and would get a bit silly after a few glasses, so then she would stop. She didn't want to be the centre of attention. She didn't want to try drugs although she was quite interested in what effect they had.'

One of the big social events of her course was a fashion show organized by an American university in Florence and held at a small club where the students all sat on cushions and downed shots and cocktails in what would become a very drunken night. One student there recalls, 'Kate made a glass of wine last the whole evening. She was sociable though and did plenty of dancing.'

While those around her most certainly were interested in getting drunk away from the gaze of parents and teachers, Kate was keen to develop her growing passion for photography during her stay. She had always taken holiday snaps but now she was in her element amid the breathtaking Renaissance architecture. She shared a top floor apartment with four other girls on the course and could walk straight out onto cobbled streets and scenic squares all begging to be photographed – and that was before the more famous buildings came into view.

Curiously, there was speculation during Kate's time in Florence that William might be coming to Italy for a pre-university course. The rumour mill had sprung into action after Prince Charles had lunch with the mayor of Florence. William, it was said, would be taking a course in Florence, Venice and Rome along with seven of his fellow Old Etonians. Nothing came of it. That didn't stop the gossip from reaching the British Institute, where Kate and her friends wondered if they would get to hang out with him. Kate, however, was more interested in her current romantic problems than speculating half-heartedly on the prince.

Kate *not* meeting William is almost like a movie in itself. She could have met him when he played hockey at St Andrew's prep school. She might have bumped into him if she had popped over to Eton with her friend Jessica Hay. They might have had a drink together if he had come to Florence to study art – but he didn't.

Halfway through the course, Kate's parents flew over to see her and the sights. Kate was able to show them round and introduce them to her fellow students. They stayed at the Grand Hotel and were happy to entertain Kate and her friends to drinks. One recalled that Kate seemed to take after her quiet father much more than her gregarious mother.

At this point Kate was still bound for Oxford Brookes and not St Andrews. She certainly didn't tell any of her fellow students that she had chosen the Scottish university. At some stage she changed her mind about going to Oxford Brookes and opted for St Andrews instead. Conspiracy theorists love the thought that Kate went to the Scottish university specifically to ensnare the future king – but that would also be pure Hollywood. Jessica Hay recalls that Kate's parents definitely knew that William was going to St Andrews. It was common gossip over dinner tables among their friends, the parents of other Marlborough pupils. His presence would enhance the university's prestige and that fact is more likely to have influenced her parents: they would have been thinking of her future career and not her marriage prospects.

While Kate enjoyed the cultural delights of Florence, Prince William was on his hands and knees helping to clean lavatories in a Chilean shanty town alongside half a dozen young hairdressers and former drug addicts all taking part in a Raleigh International Youth Development Programme (YDP). The initiative gave disadvantaged children the chance to experience life and work in places they could never have imagined visiting. William's small band was part of a larger group of about a hundred young people on the expedition.

It was a steep learning curve for the young prince, who had originally intended to use his gap year to improve his polo and go backpacking in South America with friends. His father quickly vetoed that plan. Prince Charles was worried it would be perceived as one long jamboree by a public having to foot the bill for his travel and security costs.

Polo and backpacking were out and in their place were a series of worthwhile projects, which began before Kate had even started to pack for Florence. In September William was already in the mosquito-infested jungle of Belize in Central America for a week's survival training with the Welsh Guards. The heat and humidity were a rude awakening. Only a couple of weeks before he went to Belize, William had been in the fashionable Cornish resort of Rock, where he got into shape for his ordeal by sunbathing, surfing, drinking and chatting up an endless supply of teenage girls. The only small comfort was that when he eventually embarked on training for a full-time career in the military, it was unlikely to be as hard as learning to survive in the harsh environment of Belize. William may have been top cadet at Eton but now he was trekking through the jungle watching out for poisonous snakes, scorpions and wild boar. Accommodation was a hammock with a blanket of mosquito netting, because the threat of malaria was a constant one. TV survival experts would have been heading for the nearest Holiday Inn. William later described his Belize adventure as 'exhilarating'.

Civilisation was only an email away, however, and his father was in touch with his respectable A level results: an A in geography, a B in history of art and a C in biology. William had by this time decided to study history of art at St Andrews but it's worth noting that geography was actually his best subject.

After Belize, William was able to discard the combats when he flew to Rodrigues, a beautiful island off the coast of Mauritius in the Indian Ocean, where he spent time studying coral reefs as part of a Royal Geographical Society conservation project. He had a proper chance to relax and enjoy himself snorkelling and scuba-diving. He could stroll along the white sands or ride an old motorbike around the nine-mile-long island confident in the knowledge that no picture would appear of him in shorts and flip-flops.

For some reason he checked into a tin-roofed hut on the island using the pseudonym Brian Woods and was delighted when it worked. His room had no television or telephone and no privacy – a thin curtain hung where the door should have been. But after the hammock in the jungle, it was paradise. William was even able to teach some of the local children the finer points of rugby without the accompanying click of intrusive camera shutters. The resort housekeeper, Michelette Eduard, who served him breakfast every morning, was one of many who failed to recognize him: 'We had no idea it was Prince William. We only realized after he had left the island and people started talking about his stay.'

William probably would have liked to stay longer but duty called him back to England. He had to give his first solo press conference as part of a deal to be left alone during his Raleigh International adventure.

William's good intentions to be one of the gang when he

travelled to South America were slightly tarnished at the beginning when he flew first class. But once established in the village of Tortel, he mixed easily with young people of widely differing backgrounds. He managed to put everyone at their ease with a surprisingly good impersonation of Ali G demanding respect for the 'Chilean Massive'.

He was met by a greeting party that included Sasha Hashim, a very attractive trainee beauty therapist, who had been living in a Merseyside hostel when she won a place on the expedition. She recalled, 'He was brilliant. He was much less stuck up than some of the other people, who I think looked down on us a bit.'

Tortel is a remote logging camp in the depths of Patagonia surrounded by a rugged Andean landscape. Most visitors arrive, as William did, by river raft. William had an easy rapport with his own group. One of them, Tom Kelly from Liverpool, recalled, 'Becoming friends with him has really boosted my confidence. He even gave me his personal email so that we could keep in touch. At the end of the day he's been through bad times as well, so even though we're from different backgrounds it made me realize that everyone is human.'

Certainly, William had to get used to some plain speaking. A trainee hairdresser, who lived in a hostel in Birkenhead, asked over a campfire drink if he was a virgin, which so surprised the prince that he went bright red. Another told him that her mum wanted her to get off with him.

The biggest dose of reality came when William joined them for some drinking and dancing at the local nightclub, a clapboard-covered building where everyone let their hair down at weekends. William apparently made a play for Sasha, not fully appreciating that this wouldn't go down well with her new boyfriend, whom she'd met on the trip. For once William should have kept his chat-up lines to himself. The boyfriend explained, 'It was nothing nasty because he and I get on very well. But I don't care if you are the future king – you don't start messing with other people's girlfriends. I had to lay down some ground rules.' Fortunately this did not involve a punch-up and William was able to calm the situation.

He spent another night salsa dancing with the local girls, all of whom asked him to dance. He showed off some fancy foot-work with the girl who operated the local switchboard, one who worked in a shop selling soap powder, the wife of the local harbour master and the teacher at the local primary school. It made quite a change from the double-barrelled set he was used to.

One of the things their gap year experiences reveal is that Kate and William have very different personalities. To celebrate her last night in Florence, Kate nursed one glass of wine and kept her cool. William got pissed on rough red wine and didn't care what anyone thought. He was determined to have fun.

In keeping with the strange parallel lives they were leading, William returned to England, while Kate made plans to join the next Raleigh expedition to Chile. One of many rumours about the couple was that they met briefly when William gave the new recruits a pre-expedition pep talk about his experiences. It was described as a 'Hi, Bye' encounter, although neither of them has ever confirmed it.

In January 2001 it was Kate's turn to catch the seventeen-hour flight to Santiago and join a group of young people from different backgrounds. It was her turn to visit Tortel and work on building an adventure playground for schoolchildren, enjoy the company of the locals and, of course, clean the toilets. Rachel Humphreys, who was on the expedition with her, recalls, 'Kate had a certain presence. She was a popular girl, particularly with the boys, and she was a great member of the expedition. But she was always in control of herself and impeccably behaved.' Rachel's observations confirm the view of those who met Kate in Florence: she was always careful to be in control whether drinking a glass of wine in an Italian bar or scrubbing the toilets in a Chilean school.

Rachel had received some unfortunate headlines just before

William's trip to Chile: she was thrown off the expedition at the last minute when it was discovered she was a BBC journalist – a sign of William's enduring paranoia about the press. She was already in Patagonia when she was given a day's notice to pack her bags. It was feared William would withdraw from the expedition if she were allowed to stay, even though she offered to sign a confidentiality agreement. Rachel was offered a place on Kate's trip instead.

William's whirlwind gap year continued in more sedate fashion when he worked on an organic dairy farm owned by Simon Tomlinson, a close family friend who runs the Beaufort Polo Club. Despite his work in Chile and Belize, William would later reveal that this was the toughest part of his gap year: 'It was very hard. I was exhausted after only a week as a dairy farmhand, and the guy I was working with did it every day of his life. They didn't care who I was and made me do the jobs I should be doing, like mucking out and driving tractors in the fields.'

At least after the farm work, William would be on his way to Kenya, which was fast becoming his favourite place in the world to visit. He had been to the country for the first time the previous summer when he was still at Eton and had instantly loved it.

Kate needed something to do for the summer because she still had quite a long time before university started and she didn't want to spend all of the summer at home. By now she was leaning towards St Andrews, accepting her parents' advice that this course of action would serve her better in the long run. In the meantime, she applied to be a 'corporate crew member' on the BT Global Challenge yachting programme in the Solent. She was accepted for interview and was one of twelve school leavers taken on to look after guests sailing on corporate regattas during the summer season.

Simon Walker, managing director of the Challenge, observes, 'The most important thing was to have good social skills. We were looking for smart, good-looking people who would make the guests – typically middle-aged, successful business men and women – feel at ease.'

Ironically, Kate's job was remarkably similar to being an air hostess. All the yachts taking part in the Global Challenge race had a skipper, a mate and a crew member responsible for hospitality during the sails with sponsors and press. Kate's boat was skippered by Duggie Gillespie, a round-the-world yachtsman and popular figure in sailing circles.

Kate's day began bright and early, when she put her marigolds on to scrub the yacht to make sure it was gleaming in time for the guests' arrival. She then helped to load the food and drinks and serve coffee and breakfast to the guests as they arrived. After breakfast she would run through safety regulations, and make sure each guest had the right clothing and had been issued with a life jacket. At last the important business of the day began and Kate could help hoist the 85-foot sails and get the boat away from its berth and into the water. She made sure the guests were involved with the sailing even if they were next to useless and kept them topped up with drinks the whole time – and that was before she had to serve lunch! At the end of a long day she had to help lower the sails, pack them away and bring the yacht back into berth in Southampton. There was just time for another spot of cleaning before all the crew members would make a beeline for the Los Marinos tapas bar, a gangplank away from the yachts. Simon Walker observes, 'They loved the job. It was hard work but they were out on the water most days and had a great social life.'

Kate hit it off with a fellow deckhand called Ian Henry, who was from Taunton and was due to go to Oxford in September. Ian recalls a side to Kate that not many see: 'She is a fun girl. I would call her bubbly, outgoing and down to earth. She is also very reserved.'

Kate loved the camaraderie of the sailing scene and enjoyed sleeping on the boat in her own cabin. Some days there would be races but if not there was always more cleaning to be done.

Kate

Kate's gap year ended with a summer holiday to Barbados with her family. They stayed in the Sandpiper Hotel in Holetown, on the west coast of the island, a favourite spot they had visited before. Ian came along for some sun and relaxation but, to his credit, he has only ever said that he and Kate were 'very good friends'. He was off to Oxford, while she was heading to Scotland. William's gap year was remarkably rich and varied but, by any normal standards, Kate's was brilliant too.

7

Bring on the Girls

Kate was much slower out of the blocks where the opposite sex was concerned than Prince William. He could boast one of the best chat-up lines known to man: 'I'm going to be king one day. Are you dancing?' William was well protected at Eton, especially after his mother died, so the press were in the dark about his schoolboy successes. A royal source, however, observed, 'I think William did rather well with girls while he was at Eton.' William wasn't at all shy about approaching girls at parties and was renowned for having a bit of a roving eye. If there was a circle of excited young girls at a do, then usually it was William who would be at the centre of the group, swigging nonchalantly from a bottle of beer.

His first love was rumoured to be a girl in Kate's class at Marlborough but this was idle speculation. His teen romances were often with girls from the Highgrove horsey set, who had one precious attribute as far as the nation's most eligible bachelor was concerned: they never told.

William was a handsome young man with a winning smile and lots of blond hair. The irony is that he did not have to be good looking at all to be the most sought-after teenager in town. He was Princess Diana's son and that was all that mattered to teenage girls around the world. He had a taste of that blind adoration in March 1998 when, still fifteen, he travelled to Canada with his father and witnessed what one royal watcher described as the modern equivalent of Beatlemania. Wherever he went he was greeted by literally thousands of swooning, screaming girls who saw him as the Justin Bieber of the day. He absolutely hated it, although in public the smile never left his face.

The lack of any concrete evidence of a teenage girlfriend meant that the media could have a great deal of fun at William's expense. The saga of the prince and Britney Spears is priceless and whoever dreamed it up deserves a medal for sheer advertising balls. The thought that the Queen's grandson, who was seventeen at the time and studying hard for his A levels, and the most famous teenage pop star of the time were smitten with one another occupied page upon page of press coverage. It didn't seem to matter that she was in a serious relationship with Justin Timberlake at that time.

The story first surfaced towards the end of 1999, when it was revealed that William had a crush on Britney. He was a schoolboy and she was a teenage hottie fancied by millions, so no one could blame him for being one of that particular crowd. She apparently sent him a selection of photographs and a signed copy of her first album – a classic marketing ploy.

Nobody seriously believed a romance would ever be on the cards but it was trotted out whenever a suitable opportunity arose. Sure enough, when it was announced that Britney was buying a million-pound mansion twenty minutes from Highgrove, feverish speculation followed about her popping round to take tea. Then sources close to Britney allegedly reported that she broke down in tears when she heard he was dating someone else.

In their shared memoir, *Heart to Heart*, Britney's mother Lynne reveals William is a 'big fan of Brit's' and they were supposed to go to Buckingham Palace but William called it off because he was foxhunting that day. Britney was also quoted in the press as saying, 'Marry Prince William? I'd love that. Who wouldn't want to be a princess?'

This would all be great fun if there wasn't a serious point about the business of celebrity and the way William was perceived as public property. He doesn't like it. His only reported comment on the one-sided romance was contained in a press statement on his eighteenth birthday: 'I don't like being exploited in this way but as I get older it's increasingly hard to prevent.' It just made William determined to keep his private life out of the headlines.

William had been an entirely normal teenage boy, apparently lusting after the odd lads' mag favourites, such as the busty Barbi Twins, as well as the blonde supermodel Claudia Schiffer, whose picture he used to have on his wall at Eton. There's a wonderful photograph of William in the summer of 2002 fulfilling a boyhood dream and kissing Miss Schiffer after she presented him with a prize for winning a charity polo match. It was his first public kiss and he had the look of a young man whose birthdays had all come at once. He was positively purring. The match at Ashe Park, near Basingstoke, was another indication that, like it or not, William was part of the celebrity circuit. At the event he was joined by Cilla Black, Carol Vorderman and two of the cast of *Coronation Street*, Tracy Shaw and Shobna Gulati.

Another blonde he was supposed to have taken a fancy to was Baby Spice, Emma Bunton, the cute smiley one in The Spice Girls. He is also said to have had her poster on his very crowded wall. They did meet after a Spice Girls concert when he was thirteen and kept in touch. He was even reported to have voted for her when she competed in *Strictly Come Dancing*.

The first member of the Highgrove horsey set to be named as a romantic attachment was a strikingly pretty blonde called Rose Farquhar (pronounced Farcar). She is the daughter of the popular master of the Beaufort Hunt, Captain Ian Farquhar, and had known Wills since childhood. She was one of the 'Beaufort Belles', as the press called them. They were the girls often seen at the Beaufort Polo Club, where both William and Harry used to join their father for matches. It proved a happy hunting ground for the brothers as far as the opposite sex was concerned.

Rose and William got together after his A levels and enjoyed what was a summer holiday romance. Some sources suggest she was William's first love but she is more likely to have been his first that summer. Their dalliance did give rise to one of the great William stories when they were reportedly caught by a local farmer in one of his fields. It's a good tale but may or may not be true.

Like many of the girls in William's life, Rose remained a good friend after their paths went in different directions. Rose has ambitions in the music business and just missed out on a place in Andrew Lloyd Webber's television talent show *How Do You Solve a Problem Like Maria?* She studied in New York before joining a band called Rocket #9, which never really took off. She has now launched a solo career and her songs can be heard online as she records them. On her Facebook page she urges that we bring back fox hunting, which slightly undermines her street cred.

Rose was unusual among the girls linked to William in the early days because she didn't have a double-barrelled name. The well-connected Davina, Duckworth-Chad was swiftly followed by Natalie Hicks-Löbbecke, but there was really nothing serious going on. Davina, who was William's second cousin, was just the sort of girl whom the more old-fashioned royal watchers might have expected him to choose.

Davina, whose brother James was an equerry to the Queen – an officer who helps the Queen on her daily engagements – was one of a number of girls invited on a royal holiday cruise around the Aegean Sea in the summer of 1999. This cruise was a curious affair in that William appeared to have asked a whole harem of the best-looking young ladies around to join him. Besides Davina, Emilia d'Erlanger was one of those on board. Coincidentally, she was at Marlborough with Kate and on her return to school that autumn she was able to tell her friends all about the cruise.

Prince William drew much of the media attention on that summer cruise – far more than his father or Camilla Parker Bowles, who were also on board, taking their first holiday together in the public eye. That was, of course, the plan: to get everyone used to having the heir to the throne's ex-mistress around as part of the furniture. William went along with it but behind the scenes was not too pleased at being 'used' by his father to win back public esteem. Christopher Wilson, biographer of Charles and Camilla, observes, 'Charles was ruthless in his determination to use his children to legitimize his relationship with Camilla. There was a moment when her children and his were all shoved into a photograph to give the appearance of one nuclear family. And William and Harry were old enough to resent this.'

The 'love boat' was nothing more than a smokescreen – a group of young friends enjoying sun and sea at dad's expense. William was far more likely to pursue romance behind the doors of Highgrove, where he and his brother had the run of the cellar, which had been converted into their private entertaining area called Club H. This was their own personal pub, although Charles insisted there was to be no alcohol while they were under age.

The single most important aspect of any new romance for William was that it was conducted discreetly. He would much rather people found out about something when it was all over than ruin it while the relationship was developing. It was a policy that would later serve him well with Kate just as it had when he met another girl he liked – the willowy, dark blonde Jecca Craig.

William met Jecca, short for Jessica, when he visited Kenya during his last year at Eton. He was keen to go back to the country he had so enjoyed visiting, and eventually returned twelve months later when he was finishing his gap year. He wanted to see Jecca again. She was a girl who shared his passion for the outdoor life. She favoured safari clothes and hats and seemed to William like a rugged frontier girl.

Jecca's parents, the conservationist Ian Craig and his wife Jane, owned a 45,000-acre estate called Lewa Downs. There, the Craigs set up a rhino sanctuary in 1983, which later became the Lewa Wildlife Conservancy. William could join Jecca for her daily horseback ride around the amazing countryside, home to white and black rhino, rare zebra, elephants, lions and giraffe. He would spend his days learning about conservation, mending fences, checking for poachers and watching for the beautiful rhinos. One of his tasks was to build a metal bird hide that promptly sank when he tried to put it up in a swamp. Fortunately, it was rescued and is still there to this day. William thrived on the isolation and the feeling he was at one with nature when he stayed at Lewa. He was free temporarily from the millstone of responsibility. In the evenings he and Jecca would watch the sunset together. Jecca's father said, 'William just loves Africa, that's clear. He's a great boy.'

A school friend of Jecca's observed, 'She's a lovely down-to-earth girl.' William, it seemed, liked down-to-earth girls. Rumours would continue for years about William and Jecca. It would be something Kate would have to put up with. They may have had a teenage fling but that soon passed into an enduring friendship. His love of Africa, however, became a lifelong passion. In the future Lewa would also have great significance for Kate too.

While at Lewa William and Jecca were reported to have held a mock engagement when he got down on one knee in the African wilderness and asked her to marry him. He was so annoyed when this story later leaked out that Clarence House issued a rare denial that it had happened or that there was anything romantic between Jecca and William. The Royal Family rarely bother to react but this was an indication that it offended William's sense of fair play: he was upset that a good friend he was genuinely fond of should have to suffer this kind of publicity because of who he was.

On his return to Highgrove, William struck up a romance with yet another 'first love'. Arabella Musgrave was again a member of the horsey set, the daughter of Major Nicholas Musgrave, who runs Cirencester Park Polo Club in Gloucestershire. Over the years he had seen her around at polo when she was just another gawky teenager. She had grown into a lovely young woman when he saw her again at a party held at the house of family friend Hugh van Cutsem. Bella stood out from the usual country set. She had long, glossy brunette hair, a healthy tan and a figure she showed off to great effect in the latest designer fashions. She may have been brought up in the country but she had an air of the girl about town in much the same way as the Middleton sisters have.

William was reportedly mad about her during their summer fling which, according to a friend, was 'very passionate'. They were often spotted laughing and being affectionate in local pubs like the Tunnel House Inn near Highgrove, where they would linger over a discreet meal. William could feel relaxed away from media scrutiny and happy that people knew who he was with when they went out. It was only later, when he was involved in a serious relationship with Kate Middleton, that he became paranoid about them being seen together in public and the paparazzi attention that would result. William and Bella's fling didn't survive the classic breaking-point encountered by thousands of boyfriends and girlfriends that September: being separated when one of them went to university many miles away.

PART TWO

WILLIAM AND KATE

8

The Smouldering Temptress

The first time William really noticed Kate she was wrapped up warm in a fleece jacket and jeans, watching a rugby match on the touchline at St Andrews University. She wasn't looking glamorous nor was she flashing her underwear on a catwalk – that would come later. Instead, she was one of the few girls braving the elements on a cold winter day because she liked rugby. She had been introduced to William because they were on the same course together and were on different floors of the same hall of residence, but they hadn't had a conversation. Instead she later admitted, 'I went bright red and sort of scuttled off feeling very shy.'

Kate's mother, naturally, was dying to know if she had spoken to him but there was nothing to report until they started chatting about rugby and William realized that Kate knew what she was talking about. He was impressed that she seemed such a sporty girl – not necessarily what one might expect from someone studying art history. She was able to tell William that she had seen him play hockey when she had been at the other St Andrew's, her preparatory school in Pangbourne. And they shared a laugh or two together about their gap year experiences with Raleigh International in Chile, quite forgetting about the match they were supposed to be watching. There was a spark between them. As William would later reveal during their engagement interview: 'She's got a really naughty sense of humour, which kind of helps me because I've got a dry sense of humour.'

William had already formed a little clique of half a dozen Old Etonians and other public school boys he could trust in St Salvator's Hall, more commonly referred to as Sallies. They were known as the Sallies 'Yahs' among the more down-to-earth students. Her touchline conversation was Kate's passport to that world. She was allowed to sit with William and his friends at the table they always occupied in the dining room. Helen McArdle, who had the room next to Kate's, recalls, 'She was the only girl allowed into their gang and you would see her with them, laughing and joking every breakfast, lunch and dinner. It sealed their friendship.'

Helen recalls her first impression, 'She introduced herself as Kate. I thought she was very posh! She seemed extremely well-to-do and upper class to me. But she also seemed quite quiet and kept herself to herself.'

When Kate arrived at Sallies as a 'fresher', or first-termer, there was a lot of speculation about which hall William would be assigned. He wasn't due at the university for another week. Hall warden Paul Boyle called Kate and the other residents to a special meeting in the dining room at Sallies. 'We were all sworn to secrecy,' recalls Helen. 'We were told to treat him like any other resident and on no account to speak to the press about him while he was there.'

Kate couldn't have known in advance that she would be in the same hall as William. Admittedly Sallies seemed to get most of the Old Etonians but it was sheer chance that she was assigned that particular hall after filling out her student forms. She had to state whether she preferred a shared or single room, and what kind of person she wanted to share with – an outgoing type or a quieter girl who liked to stay in. She ended up sharing with a quiet girl, similar to herself, called Sarah Bates, who enjoyed country pursuits.

Kate and Sarah's room was on the second or 'A' floor. Twenty girls' rooms were on one side of the stairwell and about twenty for boys on the other. Each side had a communal kitchen as well as showers and a bathroom. The room itself was quite basic: it had two single beds, a study desk and a sink with a mirror above it. It was like being back at school. The best thing about the room was the view from the window out to sea. Downstairs, on the ground floor, there was a dining room, a common room that housed the television and the daily newspapers, and the reading room that was used for studying and was pretty empty except when everyone was panicking over their exams.

St Andrews is an easy town to get to know, consisting in the main of just three streets – North Street, Market Street and South Street – all packed with pubs, bars, cafés and restaurants catering for an ever changing population. Besides the university, St Andrews is most famous worldwide as the 'Home of Golf', where the town's historic links is the most frequent venue for the Open Championship held each July. Tiger Woods has won there two times, including 2005, the year Kate would graduate.

Kate made a good impression during Freshers' Week, determined to join in as much as possible. The other students in Sallies nicknamed her 'Beautiful Kate' because of her immaculate elegance. Most everybody had a nickname at Sallies and Kate's was a lot better than some – William's old school friend Oliver Baker was known as 'Hairy Oli'. She cemented her position as 'Beautiful Kate' when she turned heads at the traditional Freshers' Ball.

One of them belonged to a final year law graduate, Rupert Finch. He was an all-round sportsman and, in particular, an excellent cricketer. He was also the son of wealthy Norfolk landowner and, being tall, dark and handsome, would be considered an excellent catch by most standards. His involvement with Kate, an undergraduate four years younger than him, was a sign of her now eye-catching good looks and maturity. Fellow students don't recall seeing them out and about in the town as a couple. Helen McArdle, for one, doesn't remember ever seeing him in Sallies so it would appear to be a relationship Kate kept pretty quiet.

Kate's university life started a great deal more promisingly than William's. He was far from happy to be greeted by more than 3,000 gawping onlookers as he rolled up for his first day in the scenic seaside town. His father drove him and his bodyguard in a dark green Vauxhall, no doubt believing it inappropriate to roll up in the Aston Martin. William, in a navy blue jumper and jeans, did his best to flash a toothy grin for the crowds even if it was the last thing he wanted to do. He got out of the car and strolled over to the side of the pavement to share small talk and shake a few hands. He was like the smoothest of politicians on the election trail. In his pre-university interview, William tried to shrug off public interest: 'I'm only going to university. It's not like I'm getting married.'

St Andrews at first seemed a surprising choice for a royal heir, breaking the traditional stranglehold of Oxford and Cambridge. It is, however, almost as old. Founded in 1410, it dominates the centre of the town, where cobbled streets and narrow alleys, ancient buildings and pristine quadrangles give the place a sense of history in much the same way as its illustrious southern neighbours. William explained his decision: 'I do love Scotland. There is plenty of space. I love the hills and the mountains and I thought St Andrews had a real community feel to it. I just hope I can meet people I get on with.' Coincidentally, during William's first year a study revealed that St Andrews had the worst record in the UK for recruiting students from state schools. Only fifty-nine per cent of students came from that sector, eighteen per cent below target.

William moved into a single room on the third floor of Sallies, two above Kate. He had the luxury of an en-suite shower and a toilet. He also had bullet-proof glass in the window and a heavy-duty door. He had two security officers in rooms on either side along the blue carpeted corridor. One of them the students nicknamed 'Johnny Vaughan Man' because he resembled the TV presenter and DJ. William didn't escape the vogue for nick-names – he was known as 'P Willy', a play on P Diddy and inspired by his love of R & B music.

William at first preferred the company of the few people he knew, such as former classmates Fergus Boyd, Oliver Baker and Ally Coutts-Wood, who would all become good friends to Kate. William might have integrated with more students if he had turned up to Freshers' Week, the introduction to university life that gives undergraduates the chance to mix, make friends and discover what activities and bars were good for the future. William, it had been decided, would give it a miss so as not to disrupt it for everyone else. He admitted, 'It would not have been fair on the other students. Plus, I thought I would proba-bly end up in the gutter completely wrecked.'

For the first week or so he was very wary of any media that might be lurking, even though the university's Lord Rector Andrew Neil, the former editor of the *Sunday Times*, had helped broker a deal that he would be left alone to enjoy university life. This agreement was not just for William's benefit but also for the other students around him, both on his course and in Sallies. Kate, in particular, would benefit from not having a member of the press nonchalantly trying to buy her a drink in one of the town's bars.

Hilariously, this agreement was broken, not by one of the tabloid newspapers but by William's own uncle, Prince Edward. William was much aggrieved to discover that a television crew was trying to film him and his fellow undergraduates after all the other media had, as agreed, left the town. When his security intervened, it was discovered that they worked for Ardent, the production company owned by Prince Edward. Apparently they were shooting a television show for America called *The A–Z of*

Royalty that was going to provide a much-needed cash injection for the company. Edward was forced to apologize after Prince Charles phoned him and, according to one report, shouted at the top of his voice that he was a 'fucking idiot'.

Mark Bolland, who was responsible for William's press, observed with masterly understatement that 'nobody expected it to be a family member who would breach the embargo.' Andrew Neil added, 'You just couldn't make it up. It set a terrible example for the rest of the media.'

After the crew had left town, William could at least relax a little and joined one university club, the water polo team – not exactly the most glamorous choice. He had, however, always been a star player and was keen to continue playing. He also quickly found a girlfriend to take the place of Arabella. Kate hadn't come into the picture just yet, so he took up with another tall, stunning brunette called Carley Massy-Birch, who was in her second year studying English and creative writing. She was also renowned for having the shapeliest booty in town. One of her friends reportedly joked, 'Carley's bottom has been sculpted by the gods.' Carley's parents ran a farm and camping park near the pretty village of Axminster in Devon and she described herself as a 'bit of a bumpkin'. Her relationship with William was a brief fling that her mother Mimi Massy-Birch confirmed: 'She went out with William for six or seven weeks when they first arrived at St Andrews. They are now the best of friends.'

The press embargo was evidently working because no media carried the story of William and Carley, which would have made her life intolerable considering how brief their relationship was. Carley obeyed the golden rule that Kate would also have to observe: she never blabbed. Her romance with William, though brief, was a chance for him to forge a relationship with someone outside his normal circle of polo and shooting enthusiasts.

William wasn't finding life at St Andrews anything like as much fun as Kate. Shortly after his split from Carley, his absence was noticed at one of the great events of the first year at St

Andrews – the 'Raisin Weekend', an annual tradition or excuse for students to get extremely drunk. The freshers are entertained by their academic parents, older students who are their designated mentors when they arrive. The student mother invites them to an alcoholic tea party before the student father takes them on a pub crawl. One student described it as 'pretty much forty-eight hours' solid drinking'. Those still standing on Monday take part in a fancy dress party in the quad outside Sallies, where they have a shaving foam fight. Kate wore shorts, a white T-shirt and a baby's bib with teddy bears on it. And, harking back to her favourite childhood clown costume, she painted bright red rouge circles on her cheeks. In a picture of the event that would later surface she is clearly having a whale of a time.

William had disappeared for the weekend, perhaps disappointed at his break with Carley or disenchanted with university life. One rumour suggested he went home to Highgrove and sought consolation with Arabella. Another was that he had a brief fling with a slim, blonde first year Edinburgh student called Olivia Hunt whom he had met at The Hirsel, the Scottish seat of the Earl of Home, a friend of the Queen. If there was anything between her and William, it was a case of blink and you missed it. They stayed good friends, however, and he did sometimes pop down to the Scottish capital to take her to her local pub, the Cumberland. He would later claim that he wasn't homesick but was simply 'daunted' at what university life entailed.

And then he went to watch one of his mates play in a uni rugby match and met Kate. William once admitted, 'If I fancy a girl and I really like her and she fancies me back, which is rare, I ask her out.' William was lucky in that he didn't really need to ask Kate at all. After their touchline encounter, he saw her every day. Some mornings he would join her for a run before breakfast – usually a bowl of healthy muesli because Kate didn't want to return home in the holidays fatter than her sister Pippa – and then they would have lectures together. When William had the odd responsibility away from campus or if he went home to Highgrove, it would be Kate who would lend him her notes to catch up.

Some days they would go swimming together at the Old Course Hotel and most evenings Kate would be the last person he saw before heading up to his room. They would literally chat for ages outside her room – revealing right from the start how relaxed they are in each other's company and how their conversations never dry up. Kate was fast becoming his favourite person to talk to. Sometimes they would stay up late and sit talking in the dining room. They would be the last to leave, happily chatting while the cleaners cleared up around them.

They couldn't really talk in Kate's room because Sarah would be there and it wouldn't be fair if she was trying to study or sleep. And going to William's room would have caused all sorts of gossip mayhem. Both his father and his security staff wanted him to enjoy university life but they had warned him of the potential booby-traps he might face with unscrupulous people looking to make fast money by selling stories to the press. Kate never gave William a moment's doubt concerning her ability to be discreet and keep a secret.

When they went home for Christmas at the end of the first term, William and Kate agreed to meet up in the holidays for a drink. It would be low key, away from student gossips, but it would officially be their first date. William drove over to Bucklebury from Highgrove and they went out to the pub. Kate would later tell friends that she wanted her parents to meet him – presumably just in case they didn't get another opportunity. Then the two of them slipped out to enjoy a glass of wine at the Middleton family's favourite pub, the Old Boot Inn at Stanford Dingley. The atmospheric listed building had been their local when they lived at Bradfield Southend and was still only two miles away. The family were well liked there and so could ask the landlord, John Haley, not to say anything about William's visit.

Both he and Kate's parents passed an important test with flying colours because William and Kate's date never appeared in the newspapers. Over the years, Kate and William always felt they could slip into this pub for a quiet drink, unbothered and unreported. John admitted, 'The first time we saw him everyone was slightly nervous but they often came in so we're used to it now.' John would have his reward for his discretion in the future when he was invited to the royal wedding. Kate and William have never forgotten that this was where they enjoyed their first proper date.

They had much to talk about because William was having serious doubts about returning to St Andrews for another term. Despite the attraction of seeing Kate's smile over breakfast every day, William did not find life at St Andrews nearly as enjoyable as she did. He discovered that he was not well suited to his chosen course and felt unable to relax, feeling that everyone was staring at him whenever he went out to buy a pint of milk. He felt trapped. Kate had got stuck into the late Baroque art studies of the first term but William, it was said, seemed more absorbed in playing noughts and crosses during lectures. During his gap year, William's interest in art had waned and, inspired most of all by his trip to Africa, he was increasingly attracted to environmental issues.

Kate suggested that he could try a different course, mindful perhaps that they would be seeing far too much of each other if they continued to study the same thing if and when they became more seriously involved. They would also be in competition – not always a healthy thing for a relationship. William agreed that he would think about it over Christmas, much to Kate's relief.

Prince Charles was equally concerned when he heard of William's misgivings. It would be a PR disaster if William left St Andrews after just a term because he would be marked as a 'quitter' for years to come. Prince Edward never lived down dropping out of his marines training after just four months.

The university's reputation would have sunk and the relationship between the monarchy and Scotland soured. Charles was sympathetic but also advised his son that it would look bad and that he needed to consider his royal duty.

Fortunately, for everyone concerned, William got over what he described as a 'wobble' and agreed to continue, provided he could change his degree course to geography, a subject he felt more comfortable studying. His good friend Fergus Boyd was also studying that subject and would be on hand to help William catch up.

The timing of Kate's split with Rupert Finch and becoming an item with William is a grey area but it's not one that ever seemed to worry her ex. When questioned about it later by journalists, Rupert made it quite clear that he would never talk about Kate or how it ended. The reality was that he would soon be leaving the university, while Kate was still an undergraduate – not a formula for success in a relationship, as he would be starting his working life many miles away at a London law firm.

Life became rosier for William when he returned to St Andrews in the second term and Kate had much to do with that. William immediately found that the geography degree course was more to his taste. He definitely had a spring in his step, even if it was only February, when the small coastal town could be very grey and unappealing.

Kate told him that she had put her name forward to take part in the annual Don't Walk student charity fashion show sponsored by Yves St Laurent at the swanky five-star Fairmont Hotel. Kate had no idea then that an outfit chosen for her to wear on the catwalk would become one of the most famous pictures of the decade.

A former fashion student called Charlotte Todd had designed a sheer silk skirt for her fashion degree a couple of years before and the show organizers phoned her up out of the blue and asked her if they could use it. She had knitted together gold and black fabric and then added a blue ribbon trim to the top and bottom. She recalled, 'I only made it as a skirt but they pulled it up on Kate and she wore it as a dress. She had the perfect figure for it.'

The dress was completely see-through so on the night all the guests at the show could judge that she had the perfect figure for it. William had a front row seat along with his friends from Sallies. Fergus Boyd joined Kate to do some modelling but William couldn't be persuaded to take part. Instead, he had the best view of the new girl in his life sashaying down the catwalk in a transparent dress revealing black underwear – a bandeau bra and black bikini bottoms. William was impressed and turned to his friends and whispered, 'She's hot!' It wasn't, as some thought, a sign that he was noticing her for the first time; it was more pride that this knockout girl was going out with him. Fellow student Jules Knight was astonished that 'reserved' Kate had turned into such a 'smouldering temptress'.

Kate looked fantastic. Fashion expert Alison Jane Reid observed, 'The dress was great fun but she had to have some confidence to pull it off. A lot of young women wouldn't have that confidence, especially with Prince William watching. Kate must have a degree of self-possession.'

Kate and William had already made a conscious decision that it was in their best interests not to make it too obvious that they were an item. William temporarily forgot that arrangement at the aftershow party at a student house in Hope Street, swept along by how 'hot' Kate had been, even though she had now changed into her own clothes. According to eyewitnesses, he had leaned forward to kiss her and been rebuffed. It was really a case of 'Don't make it too obvious, Wills.'

The ruse to keep things low key proved to be a success, however, with Kate being linked to Fergus Boyd, who had been photographed chatting to her backstage without his shirt. But it was William she was with at the Sallies Hall Ball later that month. With Kate by his side, William was at last able to settle into student life. His happier state of mind was particularly noticeable to the other students in Sallies. Helen McArdle recalls, 'Kate and William were by far the most approachable of the Sallies "Yahs".' Will Wales, as he was known, could often be found in the communal TV room watching the dreadful S Club 7 shows because, according to Helen, he fancied Rachel Stevens, who, blonde and petite, couldn't have been more unlike his new girlfriend.

The students often refer to the university as the 'bubble' because in this isolated part of Scotland they were cut off from the real world. Jules Knight, explains, 'We were all in a safe bubble at St Andrews. There was no intrusion.' Kate and William would often stroll to the popular student hang-out, Ma Bells in the basement of the St Andrews Golf Hotel. The bar had the affectionate nickname 'Yah Bells' because it attracted the public school crowd of undergraduates. One student who regularly saw William and his friends in the bar observes, 'My impression was that they were very confident, quite loud, even arrogant.'

Mostly though, Wills went there because he was left alone to enjoy Kate's company and sip his favourite pint of cider. Justin Hughes, who owned the bar at the time, said, 'They seemed very normal and were happy in each other's company. They could relax and that's part of the thing about St Andrews. They could go walking about the place, they could go down to the beach, and they could come for drinks here. They could just behave like a normal couple.'

After Ma Bells or, perhaps, the Gin House, another favourite bar, they liked to pop into the Anstruther Fish Bar. William had become very partial to their cod and chips. It was a simple routine enjoyed by thousands of students up and down the country. The town had no nightclub but every Friday the students' union held a 'bop' and William was quite at ease enthusiastically taking to the dance floor if the mood struck him.

William was concerned his student takeaway diet was piling on the pounds, especially as he also had a liking for pic 'n' mix

and couldn't pass Woolworths without popping in. He decided
he needed to get fit, so he took up rugby again, playing for a
local pub team, and Kate found herself on the touchline once
more – this time watching the prince instead of chatting to him.
As the weather improved, they started playing tennis together.
As Kate was very good at tennis and extremely competitive,
there was no quarter given in these matches. William also
joined his friends surfing in his bid to get fit and could be seen
marching along the beach with his surfboard under his arm.

Most weekends there was a ball to go to if they fancied ven-
turing out. Most of the clubs and societies would hold an
annual one, usually in a local hotel. Kate would invariably wear
a smart black cocktail dress and dance to the live bands. The
spectre of the May exams was soon upon them but both William
and Kate did well enough to go out and celebrate at Ma Bells.

For once Kate switched off her famous self-control button
and the residents of Sallies were granted a rare glimpse of a legless Kate being carried up to her room by Hairy Oli. One fellow
student recalled, 'She was so drunk she couldn't walk.' Helen
McArdle, who was studying for an exam the next day, remembers looking out of the window in time to see Prince William
staggering home later: 'Everyone was leaning out of the windows taking pictures because he had fallen into a bush outside
the front door. His bodyguards were trying to pull him out.'
Afterwards, a rumour went round that his security toured the
building confiscating everyone's film. Certainly no pictures ever
appeared of the night the future king and his bride were too
drunk to stand. William's reasons for giving Freshers' Week a
miss were probably correct after all.

Unsurprisingly, Kate and William decided that they wanted to
move in together as many couples do but, prudently, they
decided it would be too bold a step to start cohabiting – the
media storm would have been far too difficult to handle.
Instead they asked Fergus Boyd and a mutual friend called
Olivia Bleasdale, who was on Kate's course, if they would like to

join them in renting a maisonette in Hope Street for the coming year. Livy Bleasdale was a friend of Rose Farquhar in Gloucestershire and mixed with William's old crowd. It was a good move to share as the press still didn't click that there was anything going on between William and Kate.

One newspaper suggested that it was actually Fergus who was the object of Kate's affection. She was dismissed as just being a 'down-to-earth friend to William'. A fellow student was quoted: 'Kate isn't going out with William or anything like that. They are good friends but I think she's closer to Fergus.'

Their final social act of an eventful first academic year was to attend the Valedictory Dinner in June 2002 in Sallies' dining room. Afterwards, everybody piled into the common room for the annual awards ceremony. It was rather like the old *Smash Hits* awards where you could vote for, among other things, most fanciable star and best haircut. In this case, hall residents decided who would receive the special wand with a star stuck on the end. William failed to win 'most handsome man' and had to make do with being crowned 'King of Sallies', which led to much laughter. Kate was voted 'prettiest girl'.

9

Turning Twenty-One

Kate and William's ruse to play down their relationship worked a treat. They could look forward to moving in to the flat in Hope Street without public scrutiny. Kate enjoyed a summer holiday in Barbados with her parents without a paparazzo jumping out from behind a palm tree to try and photograph her in a swimsuit.

Kate needed to find a summer job and signed up for some temporary waitressing at the Henley rowing regatta, the annual society get-together on the Thames. Her parents could obviously pay for anything she needed as a student but that was not part of the plan for their children growing up – you have to work to get what you want. So Kate got a job working for the oddly named upmarket caterers the Snatch Bar, earning £5.25 an hour serving champagne. Her enthusiastic boss, Rory Lang, recalled, 'She was fantastic. She is just Berkshire's most beautiful woman, a terrific girl.'

Berkshire's most beautiful was soon back in blustery Fife unpacking the groceries with Prince William. This time in her life was an extremely happy one, when she could enjoy a student love affair in peace. William played his part, gritting his teeth to give an agreed series of interviews to the media about his life at St Andrews as part of the agreement to leave him alone the rest of the time. He was very enthusiastic about everything – quite a change from the previous year when he was moping around. 'I'm just a country boy at heart. I love the buzz of towns and sitting and drinking and whatever – it's fun. But, at the same time, I like space and freedom. I like cinemas, bars, restaurants and the sport – just making the most of everything up here.'

He didn't reveal that he also liked shopping in Tesco with Kate. While the couple strove to be as normal as possible, Kate had to get used to one unavoidable aspect of royal life – the omnipresent security. Two officers were still sharing the responsibility of protecting the future king. They weren't interested in Kate when she was busy on her course; instead they would wait patiently for William while he attended lectures. Jules Knight recalls, 'The bodyguards generally sat in the kebab shop down the road from the lecture hall.'

Despite their low-key approach, they were ready to spring into action the moment there was a sniff of trouble. On one occasion William and Kate were having a party when the fire alarm accidentally went off. When Will switched off the power, he also turned off the security cameras. Jules remembers, 'Suddenly we were surrounded by security guards demanding to know what was going on.' They were also quick to react when the alarm was tripped by William slipping onto the balcony for what he hoped would be a quiet cigarette.

William and Kate's life of takeaways in Sallies began to change more towards dinner parties with friends. William was happy to take his turn at cooking, usually with a glass of wine in his hand. He was, however, by his own admission 'absolutely useless', despite having had cookery lessons at Eton, and tended to serve up pasta when his turn came round.

He had a reputation for being generous but not in a flashy way. He would always stand his corner at the bar, thinking nothing of buying a round of twenty drinks for his friends. Jules, who lived next door in Hope Street, would later tell the *Daily Mail* that their life at St Andrews had the 'feeling of one big private house party.' While Jules may have talked to the media after he left university, he was one of the couple's group of friends who never spoke to the press at the time.

The newspapers still hadn't cottoned on to the fact that Kate and William were an item but to the couple's friends it was obvious and no big deal. Often the papers tried to link William with other girls. One of them was the strikingly pretty Bryony Daniels, who was on William's course, lived nearby and was in their growing circle of friends. Ironically, William and Bryony were photographed walking in the town after they had bumped into each other in the supermarket. Kate and William, who did the same thing almost every day, were still managing to avoid having their picture taken together. William invited Bryony and about fourteen others to a post New Year's weekend party at Wood Farm near Sandringham, the Queen's Norfolk estate. The guests enjoyed a typical country house weekend of shooting, riding and heavy drinking. Kate was there but when reports of the party surfaced, it was again Bryony who caught the media's eye. She looked like a model and was the daughter of a wealthy Suffolk farmer. She was also revealed to be one of the students who would be taking part in the Don't Walk fashion show a year after Kate had paraded down the catwalk. Bryony's mother, Pauline, shrewdly observed, 'I guess people must be putting two and two together and making five. If there was any truth in it, I am sure she would have told me.'

There was no truth in it but the diversion suited Kate and William, who decided not to attend the fashion show that year, correctly forecasting that his presence would have turned the whole event into a circus. Other than the pictures of Kate at the previous year's event, only one photograph of her and William surfaced in 2003. They were strolling along the street, casually dressed and giving no indication that they were anything more than two students on their way to lectures. Kate and William had already drawn up guidelines to keep their relationship as private as possible and this involved not holding hands when they walked down the street, however much they might have been tempted.

They may now have had a larger number of friends than during their first year as members of the Sallies Yahs, but their inner circle was still small. Besides Fergus and Olivia, there was Fergus's pretty French girlfriend, Sandrine Janet, Bryony, Leonora Gummer, daughter of MP John Gummer, and Katherine Munsey, who was renowned for throwing lavish dinner parties – and, of course, the Old Etonians, Oliver Baker and Ally Coutts-Wood. The friends of William are like an orange: you peel off the outer layer and there's an inner layer of further protection. The girls in the group decided to get together to form an all-women's drinking club to rival the St Andrews male equivalent, the Kate Kennedy Club, which William had joined. The female version was called the Lumsden Club, named after Dame Louisa Lumsden, a prominent St Andrews figure during Victorian times in the world of education. Kate enjoyed planning fundraising events, all of which seemed to revolve around drinking, such as the Red Hot Martini Party and the Summer Pimms Party.

At weekends they had the option of going to stay with friends at country house parties or slipping away to a remote cottage called Tam-na-Ghar on the Balmoral estate that had been given to William and his brother to use as their own retreat. Occasionally they would travel to London, where Kate's parents had bought a pied-à-terre in Chelsea, which meant they could come down to London for parties without making an official song and dance of it. They would spend many romantic evenings there in the future.

One of the few times they ventured out for a big event was the 2003 May Ball in St Andrews, organized by the Kate Kennedy Club. For once they weren't as discreet as usual and, for the first time, rumours began to surface that they were more than just good friends. As a result her parents were confronted on their doorstep by a journalist demanding to know the truth. Michael Middleton handled it well: 'There are two boys and two girls sharing the flat at university. They are together all the time because they are the best of pals. We are very amused at the thought of being in-laws to Prince William but I don't think that is going to happen.'

His response was well judged but the paparazzi now had a sniff that there might be something there and were loitering with intent when Kate and William enjoyed a quiet moment together after a rugby match in St Andrews. The rumours escalated in the summer when William attended Kate's twenty-first birthday party in a marquee at her parents' house in Bucklebury. She had decided not to celebrate in January, when many of her friends couldn't attend. Instead she held a 1920s themed night and was thrilled when William slipped in quietly to wish her a happy birthday. By all accounts when she spotted him she gave him a look that was unmistakably filled with love. An eyewitness said Kate looked beautiful and happy as she chatted to William, a glass of champagne in her hand.

William decided to counter the rumours when he gave an interview to mark his own twenty-first birthday the following week. He said he was single and was clearly alluding to Kate when he said, 'There's been a lot of speculation about every single girl I'm with, and it does actually irritate me after a while – more so because it's a complete pain for the girls. These poor girls, whom I've either just met or are friends of mine, suddenly get thrown into the limelight and their parents get rung up and so on. It's a little unfair really.

'I don't want to put any girl in an awkward situation, because a lot of people don't understand what comes with knowing me and, if they were my girlfriend, the excitement it would probably cause. Only the mad girls chase me!'

If this was a statement designed to take the heat off Kate and her parents, then it worked, especially when Jecca Craig flew in from Kenya for his big party at Windsor Castle, aptly themed 'Out of Africa'. Poor Jecca has always been around to deflect attention from Kate or, in some instances, to fuel gossip that Kate is seething with jealousy at her relationship with William. At the birthday, nobody seemed to notice William's real girl-friend as he seemed to be paying Jecca such close attention. The press were convinced that they had unearthed William's secret girlfriend. They were right that he had a secret love but they had the wrong young woman. Some even suggested that Jecca was going to be guest of honour at the party, which was slightly ludicrous as the Queen would be attending.

The party itself proved to be memorable for an incident that took place when William was giving his 'thank you all for coming' speech. Aaron Barschak, a man known as the 'comedy terrorist', jumped up on stage dressed as Osama Bin Laden and kissed a flabbergasted William on both cheeks before being arrested by shame-faced security. They had assumed he was one of the guests in fancy dress. It was all very amusing except nobody saw the funny side afterwards. The Home Secretary, David Blunkett, told the House of Commons he was 'deeply concerned' at the security breach.

William had chosen the fancy dress theme himself. He explained, 'I thought it would be quite fun to see the family out of black tie and get everyone to dress up.' More than 300 guests entered into the spirit of it all, drinking vodka from an ice sculpture and dancing to a Botswana marimba band called Shakarimba, which William had heard on his first trip to Africa. He has loved their music ever since and enthusiastically jumped up on stage to play drums with them.

Even the Queen dressed up. She went as an 'African Queen', although she was said to be rather apprehensive about her cos-tume. She wore a glittering white dress complete with a giant fur wrap and an African tiara. She was, she told guests, the Queen of Swaziland. Camilla Parker Bowles wore a bright red tribal dress with dramatic matching headdress. Her striking costume was matched by Tara Palmer-Tomkinson, who sported a golden headdress and a shocking green party dress. Fortunately nobody decided to go as Tarzan in front of the Queen, although someone had chosen a full-length lion costume topped off by a crown that completely hid their identity. There was no truth in the rumour that this lion king was Prince Philip.

The media were not invited and could only loiter outside the gates. They were obsessed by Jecca and barely noticed a battered white minibus that arrived bearing the banner 'St Andrews on safari'. Jecca was yet again a smokescreen. His real girlfriend, Kate, was inside along with Fergus, Oliver and the rest of his university crew. The oldies were ushered out of the party by 11p.m., giving William, Harry and their younger friends the chance to let their hair down. 'P Willy' was in the house.

That summer Kate was invited to a number of weekends at Highgrove, including a big Sunday barbecue when she met both Charles and Camilla. She stayed in William's room. The arrangement would be the same when his brother Harry brought his first serious girlfriend, Chelsy Davy, to stay: they too would share a bedroom. A friend explained, 'Charles is thoroughly modern on this aspect of things.'

Relations between William and his father had greatly improved over the years. He spoke about him warmly on his twenty-first: 'He does so many amazing things. I only wish people could see that more because he's had a very hard time and yet he's stuck it out and he's still very positive.' As Kate's old friend Jessica Hay observed, 'Charles is so much more fun than he is given credit for.'

When they returned to St Andrews in the autumn, William and Kate decided to move out of Hope Street and into a house. They wanted somewhere more private, away from the bustle of the town. If their relationship continued to flourish, then inevitably there would be more interest in them from a curious media and public. Fergus and Olivia decided to stay on in Hope Street so two other close friends, Oliver and Ally, moved in with them. Kate trusted their discretion. They chose Balgove House, a secluded four-bedroom farmhouse in the grounds of the opulent Strathtyrum estate, a bad tee shot from the famous 17th hole of the Old Course at St Andrews and about a mile past the outskirts of the town. William's security team moved into the cottage next door, where a state-of-the-art 24-hour surveillance operation had been approved. Kate's new home was bomb-proofed, full of CCTV cameras – except in the bedroom and bathroom – and panic buttons. Kate was discovering something many celebrities have to face: the greater the fame, the smaller their world.

At least it was an idyllic prison, with a long gravel driveway winding past beds of orchids, fruit trees and rhododendron and acacia bushes. At the back of the house were two acres of pasture ideal for private walks and picnicking away from prying eyes. This was a house where you wished for time to stand still.

William and Kate were seen out and about in the town but less so than when they lived in the centre. More often Kate could be seen perched on the back of William's old motorbike. He had been hoping for a new one from his father for his twenty-first but had to make do with a new polo pony, costing an estimated £100,000. Kate mostly kept the company of her friends, except when she made regular trips to the Sophie Butler hairdressing salon in the centre of town. Sophie had styled Kate's hair for the famous Don't Walk fashion night and Kate continued to go there throughout her university life. Sophie echoes what many said of Kate at the time: 'She was reserved but very sweet. She was well brought up with nice manners.'

Kate's successful introduction to William's Highgrove world as well as the absolute discretion of her parents convinced William that it was time to be a little bolder about his relationship with Kate. They were never going to be seen snogging in the supermarket but, among friends on weekends away, he would happily introduce her as his girlfriend, which was a step in the right direction.

The press still hadn't realized what was going on but that changed when William joined his father for the annual family skiing holiday in the fashionable Swiss resort of Klosters in April 2004. He asked Kate to join him, which was a huge deal for her. At least she was a superb skier and would be able to put up a good show on the slopes. Once again they were among a group of friends that included Old Etonian cronies Guy Pelly and William van Cutsem. Guy was always the life and soul of the party and apparently did a party trick in which he lit his own farts. He has always been close to William and Harry, despite being accused in the media of being a bad influence on them.

The trip was a huge success, with William feeling relaxed enough to sing at a local karaoke bar. Everything changed, however, when Kate and William were photographed sharing a tender moment on a t-bar lift bound for the slopes. Kate was wearing a red jacket over a black ski suit. The picture appeared in the *Sun* under the banner headline 'Finally . . . Wills Gets A Girl'.

Both William and Charles were incensed at what they saw as breaking the agreement not to use paparazzi shots of William while he was at university. The private office at Clarence House responsible for Prince Charles and his sons reacted to the *Sun*'s revelation by banning their photographer from future events involving William and Harry. The royal reaction suggested that there was something more to be annoyed about than the breaking of an informal embargo. In retrospect Kate and William were very lucky to have fooled everyone for so long. Kate had even found it quite exciting being the secret girlfriend. But now the genie was out of the bottle.

10

Graduation

Kate and William were still very young when they became a famous couple. He was twenty-one and she had just turned twenty-two. They lived a settled enough existence in their secluded farmhouse, but William didn't want to spend every waking moment with her. He was a lad who wanted to go out with his mates once in a while and let off steam. He liked nights when he could be boisterous and loud – like a million other young men up and down the country on a Friday night. Kate wasn't built like that. She had her moments of getting legless and she loved to dance, play games and laugh with her friends but she was never going to have any 'ladette' moments.

Kate had to learn to cope with a boyfriend who didn't want to be tied down. She knew that occasionally she would have to read about his antics in the newspapers. That had already happened in September 2003, just before they moved into Balgove House together. William and Harry were on a boys' night out to Purple nightclub, next to Chelsea Football Ground, when they met a nineteen-year-old model called Elouise Blair. William, in particular, seemed to pay the girl a lot of attention – something she couldn't wait to tell her mother back in Australia. She phoned her mum from the club. Incredibly, Mrs Blair ended up on television telling the world all about her daughter's evening with William. She said they had spent four hours together in the club and had kissed during that time. Her mother continued, 'Elouise said William was a really normal, sweet guy and she really liked his company.' Apparently Elouise told her mum she would like to see William again.

The incident was an interesting one. William is like a footballer or a pop star when he goes out to a club. He needs to be careful or anything he does will be blown out of proportion, as it was at the beginning of April, the week before he and Kate flew off to Klosters. Again, the venue was the VIP area of Purple, a favourite haunt at the time, which has since closed down. It was 'dirty disco' night and William was sitting with his bodyguard and some friends when an attractive blonde called Solange Jacobs came over and struck up a conversation with him.

Their subsequent three hours of chat became a big story when the 'cheeky Chigwell babe', a single mum, aged twenty-eight, told a Sunday newspaper that William was a 'real Prince Charming'. The following week, after it was revealed that Kate was really William's steady girlfriend, Solange said, 'Wills looked very much on the prowl, so Kate had better watch out if she doesn't want to be made a fool of.'

By kiss-and-tell standards this was pretty insignificant, and Kate was smart enough to know all about chatting up in nightclubs: it meant nothing as long as it stayed in the club. She realized similar stories might surface in the future. For the moment, however, she had to come to terms not just with being finally outed as William's girlfriend but also, the very next day, with rumours implying he was already dumping her.

William reportedly had arranged a summer visit to Kenya, where he would be meeting up with Jecca Craig again. A 'well-placed source' was quoted as saying that 'all this attention on Kate is misplaced'. The trip, unsurprisingly, never happened but not without speculation that Kate had put her foot down in a sort of 'her or me' fashion.

The gossip in the media was intensified when Kate was allegedly seen arguing with William at a polo game. They reportedly had a row beside his black VW Golf after a match at Coworth Park in Berkshire. One argument, as far as the press was concerned, was grounds for a split. Nobody told the couple: they jetted off for an idyllic summer holiday on Rodrigues in the Indian Ocean, where William was able to show his girlfriend around the island he had so enjoyed visiting on his gap year.

They travelled with half a dozen friends, as was their usual practice. They enjoyed going with their friends because it made the holiday more fun, but it didn't make them any less of a couple. Kate sunbathed while William whizzed around the tiny island on a motorbike. They both went snorkelling in the beautiful turquoise waters and took romantic walks along the white sandy beaches. In the evening they could hit the beachfront bars for cocktails with their chums before heading back to their guest house, which cost a princely £25 a night. There was a more serious point to this holiday: William had decided to write the dissertation for his degree on the coral reefs of Rodrigues.

William, it seemed, was on a mission to win a place in the Guinness World Records for the most number of holidays in one summer. No sooner had they landed in the UK than he was boarding a flight bound for Tennessee as a guest of a glamorous blonde American heiress. The girl in question, Anna Sloan, had met William through mutual friends while she was studying at Edinburgh University. They never dated but became friendly under tragic circumstances when Anna's father, George Sloan, died in a shooting accident on the family's 360-acre estate near Nashville. William's own experience of sudden parental death enabled him to offer Anna sympathy and insight. The invitation to stay at the farm outside the scenic village of Leipers Fork was one that William had always wanted to take up.

If you read the small print about William's visit, you would have seen that there were fifteen other guests invited for the week. William had a great time discovering American life for the first time and spent most of the week out and about. One minute he was scoffing waffles at the Country Boy diner; the next he was shopping in the local mall. He discovered an Abercrombie & Fitch store and bought a pair of jeans. Shoppers in the store hung around the racks to get a closer look, which caused a bit of a commotion. A shop assistant observed, 'I didn't even realize who he was until a couple of his friends with English accents wanted the clothes off the mannequins and I told them no. They were really cute and all the girls wanted to serve them.' As William left, one of his gang was heard to say, 'See, we can't take you anywhere.'

William dined out at a Nashville restaurant called Sperry's, where his party of fifteen ran up a $600 bill, which included twelve bottles of red wine. William ordered a fillet steak stuffed with blue cheese and wrapped in bacon with a side order of creamed spinach. A barmaid, LuAnn Reid, recalled, 'There was a constant stream of people going to the bathroom so they could walk by his table. Everyone was phoning family to tell them to get on over to see him. You should have seen the teenage girls coming in.'

Anna, who is worth millions, has been linked with William since this holiday but they weren't romantically involved and she has remained on friendly terms with him. She moved to London after university and set up in business with Emilia d'Erlanger, Kate's old school friend from Marlborough, who also studied at Edinburgh. In the small world of William and Kate, the same people keep popping up at weddings and week-ends.

When William returned to the UK he whisked Kate off to Tam-na-Ghar. It was the last she would see of him for a while because he was set to go on another boys' holiday – this time sailing around the Greek islands. William and six friends had hired a yacht, reportedly with an all-female crew found by Guy

Pelly. William may have had several reasons for treating his long-standing girlfriend in such a cavalier way: he may have wanted to show he was boss and could do as he pleased; he might have wanted to continue the old pretence that there was nothing serious going on between him and Kate; or he might just not have realized that there was anything out of the ordinary about his summer gallivanting around the world. He had only just celebrated his twenty-second birthday in June.

The rumours kept on coming. William reportedly spent time in pursuit of a young heiress called Isabella Anstruther-Gough-Calthorpe. She was the younger sister of one of William's polo-playing friends, Jacobi Anstruther-Gough-Calthorpe. When she was nineteen, her father complained to the PCC (Press Complaints Commission) about reports describing her as William's future bride when she hadn't even met him at that point. Isabella Calthorpe, as she prefers to be known, is a strikingly pretty blonde girl who apparently was seen with William in a London nightclub in 2004. A friend observed, 'The rumours about Isabella and Wills are nonsense. She hardly even knows him.' The gossip continued to follow her – even suggesting that William's infatuation was the cause of a rift between him and Kate.

Kate, however, is no weeping willow in their relationship. When friends suggested she should make the best of it because William was such a catch, she replied: 'He's lucky to be going out with me.' It has become her most famous quote. If the rumours were to be believed, William was getting more action than a Premiership footballer but Kate seemed very certain of her own status in their relationship. The only indication that seriously suggested she might be having second thoughts came in 2004 when she reportedly joined a female friend to look at new places to live in St Andrews.

Much was made of her absence from two society weddings that William attended: the first that of his former flame Davina Duckworth-Chad to Old Etonian Tom Barber; and the second of Prince Charles's godson Edward van Cutsem to Lady Tamara Grosvenor. At the latter, held in Chester Cathedral, Jecca Craig, who had once dated the groom's younger brother, was seen wearing her trademark cowboy hat. Her appearance and Kate's absence yet again got tongues wagging.

Now that Kate was in the public eye, she was learning a lesson that every celebrity has to grasp: you will be involved in stories that are rubbish. There was no real evidence that William had let her down at all during 2004, that they had split or even had a cooling-off period. Kate, however, must have choked on her muesli when she opened up the morning paper and saw herself described as 'William's ex'.

At least she could look forward to a sense of normality when they returned to St Andrews. It was their final year and one in which they needed to work hard to achieve a good degree. Kate had to attend seven lectures a week and prepare her dissertation. She found the quiet of the farmhouse ideal for working on this essential part of her degree. She had chosen to write about the author of *Alice in Wonderland*. Her title was 'Angels from Heaven: Lewis Carroll's Photographic Interpretation of Childhood'.

She found the time to attend Prince Charles's fifty-sixth birthday party at Highgrove in October – further evidence that she had been readily accepted by her boyfriend's father. She and William were apart for Christmas: she was with her family at Bucklebury and he with his at the traditional royal gathering at Sandringham, the Queen's country estate in Norfolk.

They were together again for a long weekend skiing in the fashionable Swiss resort of Verbier towards the end of February. Then it was more hard work and another Easter holiday to Klosters. The latter was a significant event for Kate because Prince Charles was marrying Camilla the following week and this was his last chance for some holiday time with his two sons. Harry brought along Guy Pelly to keep everyone cheerful while William escorted Kate. Camilla, who is afraid of heights, had never learned to ski and was happy to stay behind at Highgrove, sorting out the arrangements for her big day.

Once again the trip showed Kate what a merry-go-round life with the royals was. From her personal point of view it was a great success. A year after she had been exposed as William's girlfriend, she was back, clearly integrated into his family and enjoying their company. She perched on William's knee at lunch and was seen chatting away happily to Prince Charles and sharing a cable car to the slopes with him. That evening the younger members of the party went to Casa Antica nightclub, where everyone was in high spirits, particularly Harry and Guy.

Harry loudly announced that he was going commando that night, which prompted Guy to strip down to a gawdy pair of gold boxer shorts and start madly rushing around the club pursued by a pack, including William and Kate, intent on pulling them down. Guy ended up in the lap of someone he clearly thought was a member of the security team. Unfortunately, he was the *Sun*'s new royal reporter, Duncan Larcombe, which everyone found hilarious except Guy, who quickly disappeared.

At that point William ambled over to the reporter to chat. He told him that he had enjoyed a great time at St Andrews thanks to the agreement with the press. He asked Duncan why there were so many photographers – at least forty – on this trip. Duncan told him it was because of Kate and the thought that one day they might marry.

'Will you be following in your father's footsteps?' asked Duncan.

William laughed before replying, 'Look, I'm only twenty-two, for God's sake. I am too young to marry at my age. I don't want to get married until I'm at least twenty-eight or maybe thirty.'

And with that remark, William left to pursue the more pressing business of the night – joining Kate and the others in trying to get Harry's trousers off.

William knew he was talking to a reporter and that it was not off the record. The quote has followed him around ever since.

Perhaps he had been hoping that his statement would mean that he and Kate wouldn't have to suffer tedious questions about whether they would be getting married every time they ventured out. William, as future events would prove, was being entirely truthful. He did not want to marry young, preferring to put his career on track first. His intentions in speaking up may have been worthy but the quote backfired when it became a millstone – not around his neck, but around Kate's. She would forever be perceived as waiting for her man.

The very next morning, typically, William was asked at an official press conference if there was likely to be a second royal wedding soon. Aagh! His grin was a little more fixed than previously as he scoffed, 'Er, no, I don't think so.' The press conference was the usual one that William, Harry and Charles always agree to on their holidays together so they could be left alone to enjoy their skiing. It became notorious on this occasion because Charles was in a grumpy mood. The main topic was his forthcoming wedding to Camilla. The BBC's royal correspondent, Nicholas Witchell, asked how the young princes felt about the marriage. William responded innocuously, 'Very happy, very pleased. It will be a good day.'

Forgetting his mic was still on, Charles was heard referring to the assembled media as 'these bloody people'. He also gave his opinion of Nicholas Witchell: 'I can't bear that man. I mean, he's so awful, he really is.' It was a blunder from Charles, who needed the media on his side at this point, when he was trying to win the support of the British public for his marriage to Camilla. If Kate needed further proof that she needed to be continually on her guard where the press was concerned, then this was it.

Kate wasn't asked to the civil wedding at Windsor Guildhall on 9 April, apparently because it would have breached protocol, although it was never properly explained exactly what this meant. William was a ring bearer along with Camilla's son, Tom Parker Bowles. Their mother had died seven years before and both William and Harry had accepted that Camilla was now part of the family. In a joint statement they said, 'We are both very happy for our father and Camilla and we wish them all the luck in the future.' Harry, in typical cavalier fashion, also said, 'We love her to bits.' William gave his new stepmother a kiss for the photographers.

William returned to Scotland to join Kate for some furious revision for their finals, barely a month away. In the end, both he and Kate did well, each obtaining a 2:1 degree – a more than respectable result. After Kate had finished her last exam, William and her other friends showed up to give her a 'soaking', a St Andrews tradition that is a bit like the end of a Formula One grand prix when the winner gets champagne sprayed all over him. This was student life, though, so instead of champagne Kate was soaked with fizzy pop. The final month of university life was a bit like the beginning: a chance to go to parties and bars and drink happily with friends.

In June Kate also joined William for the first time at a society wedding when his friend Hugh van Cutsem married Rose Astor at a church in the Cotswold village of Burford. It would be the first of many such occasions when Kate would be the main focus of attention, especially after William's remark that he wouldn't be getting married any time soon. Kate, William and their friends would attend so many weddings over the subsequent years that it became almost a pastiche of the film *Four Weddings and a Funeral* except in this case it would be more like a dozen weddings.

The principal interest on such occasions was what Kate was wearing. Her sense of fashion was moving on from her student days and she was beginning to find her own style. Kate wore a fitted cream jacket over a black and white lace patterned skirt with a jaunty black fascinator in her hair. Alison Jane Reid observes, 'I think it's a very chic elegant outfit. I liked the fitted pencil skirt because it accentuated her slim body and her fabulous legs.'

Training on the Thames – Kate joined the all-girl rowing crew, The Sisterhood, for a charity race across the Channel. Disappointingly, she pulled out before the event.

William shows off his moves on a crowded dance floor in a tent at the Beaufort Polo Club on his twenty-sixth birthday.

Well, that got rid of them . . . William and Kate's jiving clears the floor.

Kate and Prince Harry always have a laugh together. They giggled at the sight of William when he became a Knight of the Garter in June 2008.

Kate and Harry's girlfriend, Chelsy Davy, have never really hit it off and had little to smile about watching a polo match at the Beaufort Club.

It's a myth that Kate doesn't know how to enjoy herself: she cheers home a winner at the Cheltenham Festival in March 2008, next to the renowned amateur jockey Sam Waley-Cohen.

She loved the Boodles charity boxing night. Jecca Craig is standing up in black to the right. Guy Pelly is in the left-hand corner, sticking his tongue out.

Kate is rubbish at roller skating and needed some advice on how to stop herself from falling at a roller disco in September 2008.

Fascinating Kate: she was always the centre of attention at other people's weddings and had a new fascinator for every occasion. She wore black to Hugh van Cutsem and Rose Astor's wedding.

She chose a fascinator with pheasant feathers when Laura Parker Bowles married Harry Lopes.

She was all in red – a bold choice for a wedding – when Emilia d'Erlanger married David Jardine-Paterson in April 2010.

Kate's last wedding day before her own was the marriage of old friends Harry Meade and Rosie Bradford in October 2010. She knew the announcement of her engagement was only days away.

The day the world knew her great news. In her Issa engagement dress she posed with her fiancé at Clarence House on 16 November 2010.

Now the pressure was off, Kate could let everyone see how happy she was on her first public engagement – naming a new lifeboat in North Wales.

The signs are promising that Kate can make a connection with the public. She chatted happily to a pensioner during a return to St Andrews in February 2011. Below, she is a picture of concentration, showing a little girl how to toss a pancake on Shrove Tuesday in Belfast.

Elegant, confident and fashionable – the iconic Kate.

Afterwards, Kate and William spent the night at the King's Head Inn in nearby Bledington, where they stayed up chatting and drinking with their friends well after the reception had finished. They slipped away after breakfast in William's much travelled VW Golf. A couple of weeks later she joined him for the Argentine Club Cup at the Beaufort Polo Club and, according to an eyewitness, held his hand and stroked his leg – an unusually bold display of intimacy in public.

They were back at St Andrews for the final time as students to attend their graduation on 23 June 2005. Kate's parents had been invited to dinner before the ceremony by Prince Charles and Camilla, now the Duchess of Cornwall – an indication of how seriously Prince Charles was taking his son's relationship. A family friend observed, 'The Prince of Wales thinks the time has come for the two families to get to know each other better.' The meeting also rewarded the Middletons for being completely discreet, even though they may have been chuffed to bits and secretly wanting to tell the world.

The Middletons travelled up to Scotland to support Kate. The occasion was made more memorable by the attendance of the Queen even though, as William later revealed, she was feeling 'under the weather'. For the ceremony Kate was dressed in the traditional fashion – a simple white blouse and black skirt underneath her black silk graduation robe. She and William entered Younger Hall together before making their way to their seats. They couldn't sit by each other as the seats are arranged alphabetically on these occasions so Kate ended up five rows in front of William Wales. She smiled when the name Catherine Middleton was called out and she made her way to the Chancellor's wooden pulpit.

The Chancellor, Sir Kenneth Dover, tapped her on the head with a scarlet cloth cap, which, according to St Andrews tradition, contains a scrap of breeches worn by the religious reformer John Knox, who preached in the town in the sixteenth century. Sir Kenneth then muttered '*Et super te*', which translates as 'and upon you', while another official placed a silk-lined hood over Kate's head. The procedure was the same for the 260 graduates, including William some forty-five minutes later. The Queen, Prince Philip, Charles and Camilla all looked on approvingly. William declined the option of wearing a kilt for the ceremony, sparing everyone a glimpse of the royal knees.

During his speech, the University Principal and Vice-Chancellor, Dr Brian Lang, made some prophetic remarks: 'You will have made lifelong friends. I say this every year to all new graduates: you may have met your husband or wife.' He described St Andrews as the 'top matchmaking' university, a claim that was backed up by figures that showed ten per cent of students married each other. William and Kate's friends Fergus Boyd and Sandrine Janet, Oliver Baker and Melissa Nicholson were among them.

One fellow graduate explained, 'There is no escape in St Andrews. You spend so much time with your partner, the relationship becomes stronger faster than if you were in a different student environment.' Kate and William were able to flourish in this small town in a way that might have been impossible in more hectic big city campuses.

Kate had grown up. She arrived from Berkshire a student facing four years of relative remoteness on the east coast of Scotland. She left an accepted member of royal circles.

William had grown up too. After the degree ceremony, he again revealed how accomplished he was becoming at handling the media. He said, 'I have thoroughly enjoyed my time at St Andrews, and I shall be very sad to leave. I have been able to lead as "normal" a student life as I could have hoped for and I'm very grateful to everyone, particularly the locals, who have helped make this happen.' He added, more revealingly, 'I'm going out into the big wide world – not just essays now.'

The Queen, who had missed her son Charles's graduation from Cambridge, gave William a pat of congratulation as she left. She wasn't introduced to Kate. If she had been, in such public surroundings, it would have been seized on as giving Kate some sort of royal approval, which wasn't appropriate at that time. Who could say for sure what would happen to William and Kate's relationship in the 'big wide world'.

After all the parents and families had left, it was time for the new graduates to get down to the more serious matter of the graduation ball, held in a large marquee behind Sallies. It brought the curtain down on a truly happy time in William and Kate's lives. For once, William was relaxed enough to show his affection for his girlfriend publicly: as they queued to be served at the bar, he pinched Kate's bottom.

11

The WAG Years

Kate looked utterly miserable staring out of the window of a number 19 London bus. Just a couple of months before, she was in Kenya with William, enchanted by Lewa Downs. Now she had to cope with the congestion charge and the attentions of the paparazzi while William hopped from one thing to the next as if he were enjoying his second gap year. He seemed to have every day of the rest of his life mapped out, while she had slipped back to square one. Like the majority of graduates, she left university unsure of where to settle and what job she might find.

William's feet hadn't touched the ground. His graduation ball hangover had barely cleared before he flew to the other side of the world to support the British and Irish Lions on their rugby tour of New Zealand. Ostensibly, he was undertaking his first solo overseas visit, representing the Queen at a number of events marking the sixtieth anniversary of the end of World War Two. He laid wreaths at memorials in the capital, Wellington, and in Auckland. He also ticked off a number of royal firsts, which included all manner of everyday events in the life of a member of the Royal Family: he inspected a guard of honour, took his first royal salute as troops marched by, planted an official tree, visited a hospital and went on a walkabout. He will have to take part in hundreds of similar events in the years ahead. But the opportunity to watch the most famous rugby team in the world, the New Zealand All Blacks, made the trip more holiday than duty, even if they did beat the Lions easily. William was asked by an All Black about the relationship with Kate and was heard replying, 'It's going well.'

Kate, meanwhile, was back in Bucklebury packing for their holiday to Africa. It would be her first visit to the country William loved and, once and for all, it would squash the tiresome rumours about William still carrying a torch for Jecca Craig. As usual, it was a trip with a few friends, including Thomas van Straubenzee, who had been William's mate since they were at Ludgrove together. Thomas, whom the prince calls 'Vans', didn't grab headlines like mutual friend Guy Pelly but he was a constant presence in William's gang. William paid £2,000 for a week's hire of the Il Ngwesi Lodge on the estate, complete with a stunning saltwater swimming pool.

William wouldn't have chosen to bring Kate to this uplifting place if there was any chance of painful scenes involving Jecca. The reality was that Jecca had become a very good friend of both William *and* Kate. While William spent some of the time working with the conservationists he had first met on his gap year, there was always someone around to play tennis with Kate or hang out by the pool. She could have hired a horse if she had wanted to but, at this stage, Kate showed no inclination to learn how to ride because of her allergy to horses.

On her return from Africa, Kate began to live a strange existence. She moved into her parents' flat in Chelsea. During the day she polished her CV, went shopping – sometimes with her mother – and waited for a call from William from wherever his busy life had taken him. Every so often his diary would allow them to meet up, often for a social event to which they had both been invited. She was like a footballer's wife who struggled to fill her time with aimless pursuits while her man was busy training, travelling to away games, playing internationals and generally being a star.

At least Kate was trying to get a job. Her most obvious path was to use her degree and look for work in the art world. Camilla's daughter, Laura Parker Bowles, who studied history of art at Oxford Brookes, had been faced with the same decision and was opening her own gallery in Belgravia. Kate sent her CV to a number of art galleries and was seen leaving a dealer's in Savile Row but nothing came of it. Perhaps she could follow her parents' example and set up her own business. She too thought there was an online market for goods aimed at children. Her parents had exploited a gap in the party market and she hoped to do the same with clothes. It was something to have on the back burner in case nothing else came her way so she put out some feelers to see if she could interest an established company in her idea.

Kate's frustration at the way things were turning out for her suddenly focused on the paparazzi. She hadn't seemed to mind too much when she was photographed walking down the street with her mother, both laden with carrier bags, and even managed a smile for the cameras. She had politely turned down a request to allow photographs to be taken at the Gatcombe Horse Trials in August by explaining, 'If I pose for you, I'll have to pose for everyone wherever I go, when I'm skiing and so on.'

She looked less pleased when she was photographed job hunting but a picture taken of her on the number 19 bus prompted a dramatic change of mood, not just from Kate but from more powerful royal forces. The picture appeared the same day it had been taken in the London *Evening Standard*, prompting a speedy response from Prince Charles's lawyers, Harbottle & Lewis, who, on Kate's behalf, claimed that this was an unjustified intrusion into her privacy – a line of both attack and defence becoming increasingly popular in celebrity circles. They appealed to editors to leave Kate alone. It could be argued that publication was a security risk as it revealed the Prince's girlfriend travelled on public transport with no police protection. Both Kate and the photographer who had taken the picture were in public places, which made privacy harder to argue. *Hello!* magazine ran the picture over two pages with the headline 'Kate Stands at a Crossroads' and used it to prompt discussion of whether she should wait around for William or try and make something of her life.

Kate – and, indirectly, William who loathed this sort of picture – ran the risk of taking photographic intrusion too seriously. The intention may have been to set the goalposts as early as possible so that Kate could at least try to lead a normal life in London. The city was not the best choice for that. As yet Kate was not facing the daily nightmare that William's mother, Diana, had to bear. There's a world of difference, though, between an accredited press photographer and the often untrained opportunist. Being pursued is a joyless experience that Kate hadn't experienced fully but she would soon enough.

William was away from all that. The first task of his summer travels was to pass the arduous selection process for Sandhurst, the Royal Military Academy in Surrey where he hoped to start his officer training in the new year. That proved to be no problem.

He then donned the garb of a young squire, complete with compulsory tweed cap, to work at Chatsworth, the Duke of Devonshire's Derbyshire estate. William's 'work experience' was always great fun. He stayed at the estate's hunting lodge, which costs more than £1,000 a week to rent and would be well out of the financial reach of the average farmhand. William did drive a tractor and help deliver a calf but working in the magnificent 35,000 acres of grounds was rather like a trip to the English equivalent of Lewa Downs.

Next, he put on a smart suit and tie for three weeks of work experience in the charity services division of HSBC in St James's Street, a short walk from Clarence House. He was able to spend some proper time with Kate before heading to Anglesey for training with the Royal Air Force Valley Mountain Rescue Service. William never forgot how much he enjoyed his brief time with the brave team. He wasn't allowed onto the front line, rescuing climbers in trouble, because of unintentionally humorous concerns that young women might feign injury so they could be rescued by the prince. But he was able to observe the complex work that would help with his own training later – compass work and navigation, handling casualties, communication during rescue and advanced first aid.

Kate didn't need rescuing from the Peter Jones department store in Sloane Square or from the chic boutiques down the King's Road, Chelsea, where she would spend her afternoons popping in and out to browse the latest fashions. Sometimes she would get the bus to Kensington High Street for a change of scene and a look around Topshop. With the photographers constantly near, she couldn't mooch around town in jeans and an old jumper. And she would continue to be in the front line when William disappeared from view to start life as an officer cadet at Sandhurst in January 2006.

After spending her first Boxing Day with William at Sandringham, she was his guest for the third time at Klosters. The *Sun* once again was there to record the event. Their photographer, Scott Hornby, spent most of the time in vain pursuit of the couple, who were, as he later described, 'like Olympic skiers'. Halfway down a slope on Casanna Alp he got lucky: 'They had stopped to take in the great view of the mountains. I whipped out my camera as I went past them and took a shot on the move. They were kissing!'

Every year something happened in Klosters. The first time, Kate was revealed to be William's girlfriend. The second year, William announced he wasn't marrying until he was twenty-eight or thirty and now they were caught having a snog halfway up a mountain. They really needed to find somewhere else for their winter sport. On their return, Kate organized a farewell drinks party for William at Clarence House and he gave a thank-you speech in which he referred to his girlfriend as 'my adorable Kate'.

Sandhurst was worse than boarding school. The first five weeks of basic training were the hardest. William struggled to answer the 5.30 alarm – the bashing together of dustbin lids outside the barracks – and reportedly started sleeping on the floor so he didn't roll over and go back to sleep, which would incur the wrath of his sergeant. After basic training the regime eased a little and William had more time to travel up to London to see Kate. He had been furious when a German magazine published photographs that revealed where she lived and so, for security reasons, they usually spent the night together at his private apartment in Clarence House.

Kate liked the nightclub Boujis because she could go there with William, usually on a Tuesday night, and be reassured that they would be looked after and unbothered in the VIP area. She could walk from her flat to the club, which had opened in 2002 in a building opposite South Kensington underground station. It had always attracted a fashionable crowd. Kylie Minogue, who once lived down the road, hired it for a party and Usher had been known to pop in when in town. A smattering of Premiership footballers would be there every night. Britney Spears was rumoured to have clattered down the stairs once after sampling the club's famous house cocktails, a lethal concoction known as 'Crack Baby' shots – just combine vodka, passion fruit, raspberry liqueur and champagne in a test tube and down in one. Prince Harry loves them and even Kate has been known to knock one back.

Boujis very cleverly nurses its exclusivity. Celebrity PR Stuart Watts explained the appeal: 'It's like a local club for celebrities.' The capacity is limited to 120 and membership, which is by personal recommendation, is more difficult to obtain than the most exclusive of golf clubs. Four bouncers on the door make sure there is no infiltration from either press or public. A young woman with a clipboard checks the guest lists before anyone passes through the velvet ropes. For a small select crowd in this part of London, Boujis was the local just as if one were popping into the Queen Vic for a pint. The style writer Peter York observed, 'The lure of Boujis has nothing to do with the DJs or the music, it's about belonging to "Our Crowd" – that's the point of it.'

The club hit the jackpot with the patronage of William, Harry and Kate. If they were coming down, then the Brown Room, one of the suede-lined VIP rooms, would be cleared and the area would become a grown-up version of the old Club H at Highgrove for the night. The boys would order champagne and Grey Goose vodka and entertain their friends for the evening, confident in the knowledge that a security guard was on the door and nobody from the club would blab about their night out.

Keeping the young royals happy was the number one priority of the manager, Jake Parkinson-Smith, who had cannily developed the club's reputation over the years. He spoke only once of his most famous clients: 'They are very ordinary, nice guys. They feel very safe here because their pals come with them and they all know each other.'

The publicity value of attracting the princes was immeasurable – so much so that in 2006 the club stopped charging them, putting their drinks on the 'royal comp'. The two princes are millionaires, of course, but it's still nice to get a £340 bottle of vodka for nothing. The minimum spend for a table in one of the VIP rooms is £2,000.

The only drawback to a fun night at the club was getting past any waiting cameras on the way home afterwards. When it was time to leave, Kate would announce that she was just 'popping to the loo' and disappear to touch up her make-up just in case an unwelcome photographer sneaked her picture. On her way out of the ladies' she would pass a prominent sign on the door that declared: 'Drugs are not tolerated here. Any drug use will be reported to the relevant authorities.' Ironically, the manager fell foul of his own zero tolerance rule in 2009 when he accepted a caution for possession of cocaine and was promptly sacked.

Kate would invariably leave the club before William and dive into a waiting car to be driven home. Sometimes William would stay later in a bid to outlast the paparazzi. The couple's favourite trick was to leave by separate entrances. If Kate, looking immaculate, was being pictured leaving by the front, then you could bet that William, looking the worse for wear, was staggering out the back.

Boujis was not everybody's cup of tea. The *Daily Mail* journalist Tanya Gold memorably described it as reminding her of a 'Tufnell Park squat'. But Kate liked it and she was only twenty-four. It would be wrong to assume she was in Boujis every night. On Thursdays she was more likely to be in Mahiki in Dover Street while on other nights there was always Kitts in Sloane Square or Raffles on the King's Road.

The nightclubs provided happy ways to spend an evening but Kate was no nearer to settling on a job. She just seemed to be waiting around for William all the time to the extent that an unwelcome nickname sprung up in the press – 'Waity Katie' – the last thing she needed. She was still hopeful that her online idea might come to something. One of the unforeseen drawbacks to employing Kate was that, as Prince William's girlfriend, she would bring a lot of attention to her employer. The publicity might be attractive but it could also cause a great deal of disruption.

Kate once more tried to develop her clothing idea. This time, she managed to interest Viyella in her plan for a mail order company selling children's clothing. A business plan was worked out but again nothing came of it. Kate also investigated setting up under the umbrella of her parents' company but abandoned the notion when it became clear it wouldn't be financially viable.

Even William was getting concerned that if Kate didn't have a job, the media would begin to turn her into a figure of fun. To be called 'Waity Katie' was irritating but if that changed to 'Lazy Katie', then she would be in trouble with public opinion.

She seemed unworried as her social life progressed more smoothly than her working one. She was seen wearing a Russian-style fur hat at Cheltenham races to watch the Gold Cup in March. She was escorted for the day by Thomas von Straubenzee and during the afternoon she joined Charles and Camilla for drinks in the royal box. William was still at Sandhurst, where his officer training would last forty-four weeks.

Then she was packing again for a holiday in the Caribbean with William, who would be getting his first proper break from Sandhurst. Once more it was a trip spent with their close friends and they were given a villa on the glorious island of Mustique free for a week. Normally it could cost as much as £24,000 to rent Villa Hibiscus, the luxurious hillside mansion belonging to clothing tycoons John and Bella Robinson, the founders of the highly successful Jigsaw fashion chain, but he waived the charge to William after being approached by a mutual friend. John told the *Mail on Sunday*, 'To be honest with you, I don't know him. He is making a donation to a hospital in St Vincent. I'm not 100 per cent sure how much he's giving.' The charitable donation is a good wheeze when taking advantage of a freebie. The former Prime Minister Tony Blair also used this arrangement when Sir Cliff Richard lent him his villa on Barbados.

William and Kate went on a cruise on Richard Branson's yacht and played tennis with the boss of Virgin. They joined their friends to play volleyball on the beach every day and also challenged a group of locals to a game of frisbee. At one point Kate climbed on William's shoulders for a piggyback. Fortunately, the prince is 6ft 3in and can manage to carry a 5ft 11in girl without looking ridiculous. In the evening they had cocktails at Firefly, which had been recommended by William's cousin Zara Phillips, who had once stayed there. They also dropped in to Basil's Bar, a waterfront bistro, where William got up and sang Elvis Presley's 'Suspicious Minds' on the karaoke. One of the staff there revealed that Kate favoured pina coladas.

The holiday did provide an unexpected bonus for Kate. Through the contact with the Robinsons, she landed her first proper job as an accessory buyer for Jigsaw and their younger brand, Jigsaw Junior. The appointment had the air of a shrewd business move for the High Street chain, as Kate's was already the most prized photograph in town and it would be a publicity bonus if she were seen wearing a Jigsaw outfit.

Mostly Kate would set off for work in the morning in the black VW Golf she had inherited from William – he now had a spanking new Audi – and spend the day at the Jigsaw offices in Kew. Exactly what her job entailed has never been revealed but, at least to begin with, it provided training for a career in fashion – a sort of extended work experience. At one fashion shoot in Shepherd's Bush Kate was happy to make the tea for everyone and run errands. She still harboured ambitions to be a photographer one day but slowly over the following months it began to dawn on her that if her relationship with William continued, she could never have a real career.

For the moment at least the public loved Kate. When she and William arrived at the wedding of Laura Parker Bowles to former underwear model Harry Lopes in the Wiltshire village of Lacock in May 2006, they were given the biggest cheer of the day. It was their first appearance together at a 'family' wedding. Every time she went to a wedding, Kate had to bear intense speculation about when William might pop the question. The renowned royal commentator Judy Wade observed: 'Kate may find that she must forget her career plans to become a royal wife.'

And so she joined William on her fourth fabulous holiday that year: after Kenya, Klosters and Mustique – not forgetting trips to Norfolk and Scotland – they flew to Ibiza to stay with

Kate's millionaire uncle, Gary Goldsmith, at his villa La Maison de Bang Bang in Cala Jondal on the south side of the island. He had apparently wanted to call the house Cumalot but was talked out of it on the grounds of taste.

Gary, who had just made an estimated £25 million by selling his stake in an online recruitment agency, was an ebullient character who was enjoying the high life on the Mediterranean island. He had his initials GG tattooed on his shoulder and the words 'Nouveau Riche' inked between his shoulder blades. He greeted William with the immortal first words, 'Oi, you fucker! Did you break my glass pyramids?' William apparently had been mucking around with a ball and had accidentally broken some of the ornamental glassware in the garden.

Life with Gary was certainly different. He invited his mates round and some of them taught William how to mix on the latest music tunes. They told the prince that as a DJ he needed a 'shout', an individual greeting for his audience, and recommended 'The King's in da house'.

On one gloriously sunny day, William hired a yacht and they were seen sunbathing and larking about. Kate wore a skimpy white bikini like the one Mylene Klass famously wore in the shower on *I'm a Celebrity Get Me Out of Here*. Kate too was photographed wearing it to cool off under the shower in a series of shots taken by a holidaymaker on a mobile phone. The pictures, though a bit fuzzy, have become online favourites. Fortunately, Kate looks in great shape but it must have been galling to realize she was a target for pictures wherever she was and whatever she was doing.

12

A Lovers' Tiff

Speculation about a royal engagement was so strong towards the end of 2006 that Woolworths produced a line of commemorative mugs. Someone at the now defunct High Street store should have read *Hello!* magazine which, in October 2005, predicted that Kate would have to wait five years before an engagement announcement. The precedent, it said, was the path to marriage of William's uncle, Prince Edward, who waited that long before putting a ring on the finger of his long-term girlfriend, Sophie Rhys-Jones. If *Hello!* was to be believed, then Kate would have to wait until October 2010.

The expectation had been heightened when it was revealed that Kate would attend William's Passing Out Parade at Sandhurst in front of the Queen. The ceremony, on 5 December, was a day after an inquiry into Princess Diana's death concluded that it was an accident. Conspiracy theories will always surround the circumstances of the crash but this inquiry offered William some sense of relief and closure.

The Passing Out Parade is similar to a graduation at university in that it is a ceremonial conclusion of one's training. All the early mornings of intensive drill, running, polishing his boots and ironing his own shirts had paid off: William had passed and would receive a commission as a cornet, equivalent to the rank of second lieutenant.

Kate was there as a friend of the prince and not as a member of the royal party. She was, however, attending a significant royal event for the first time. Prince Philip, Prince Charles and Camilla were also there. Kate chose to bring her parents along to help her through the day, which might prove to be nerve-racking with the eyes of the world upon her. She didn't shy away from the attention. Instead of walking informally from the car park to her seat in the stand with the other families, Kate nonchalantly strode down the ceremonial walkway lined with troops awaiting the arrival of the Queen. She was escorted by William's private secretary, Jamie Lowther-Pinkerton. She didn't dress as if she wanted to hide away from the cameras, wearing a bright red coat and a wide-brimmed black hat. She looked more as if she was there to have her picture taken for a glossy magazine than to support her boyfriend on his big day.

William looked the part in his uniform, complete with a red sash, which signified that he was an escort of the sovereign's banner. It was a special honour won by his platoon for the best performance in training. He was also acting as a marker for the day to ensure that the cadets kept in a straight line as they marched slowly by the Queen to the traditional strains of 'Auld Lang Syne'. As he passed smartly by, carrying his SA80 rifle, Kate pointed at him excitedly and turned to her mother, exclaiming, 'I love the uniform. It's so sexy.' He certainly looked very serious, revealing just how hard he was concentrating. He, of all people, could not afford to make a mistake. The Queen cheered him up when she walked down the lines of cadets and paused to have a special word with her grandson, who broke into a broad smile.

Neither Kate nor her parents met the Queen that afternoon. After the event, Kate's mother received unwelcome media attention when reporters spotted her chewing gum, which, in a rather po-faced manner, was described as a breach of royal protocol. The press sneered that she was overheard using the word 'toilet'. The implication was that she lacked good manners. Carole Middleton had to get used to the papers making little digs at her expense. The worst was the joke that William's friends would whisper 'Doors to manual' whenever they saw her, an unfunny reference to her previous job as an air hostess. A friend observed, however, 'William is not a snob and would never stand for that. I don't believe it was ever said.'

Through it all, Carole Middleton refused to speak about her daughter. The only time she has let her true feelings slip was an off-guard moment at Newbury races when she said, 'I'm not a celebrity and don't want to be one. Celebrities have minders and PR people. I don't want a PR person and wouldn't want to have to pay to employ one. I haven't asked for all this.'

Behind the scenes Kate's family had suffered two losses that had greatly upset her: both her grandmothers had died within three months of one another. The formidable Dorothy Goldsmith died from cancer, aged seventy-one, in July 2006. Kate read a poem at the funeral. Then Michael's mother, Valerie Middleton, passed away in September from lymphoma at the age of eighty-two.

Her parents had decided that the family should holiday together for Christmas and rented a splendid eighteenth-century mansion called Jordanstone House in Perthshire well away from prying photographers. They asked William if he would like to join them for Hogmanay but he failed to show, which was a huge disappointment for everyone. Kate was reported to be in tears when he phoned up to tell her he was staying at Sandringham after all.

Kate barely saw him when she returned to London because he had to report for duty in Windsor with the Blues and Royals, one of two regiments that form the Household Cavalry, and she was due back at Jigsaw. The media continued to be in a frenzy of anticipation. Patrick Jephson, Diana's former private secretary, wrote an article for *The Spectator* that had a superficial air of authenticity. The headline proclaimed 'The next People's Princess', which was all Kate needed. It suggested that Kate's twenty-fifth birthday would be a good day to make an 'announcement'. 'The smart money now says that brand Windsor is about to get a much-needed injection of fresh young glamour to complement its established octogenarian market leader.' The smart money would, of course, have lost. William had made it perfectly clear that he didn't intend to marry until he was twenty-eight or maybe thirty and he hadn't changed his mind.

The serious nature of the article heightened excitement as Kate's birthday approached. William was at his barracks in Windsor when she stepped out of her Chelsea home on the morning of her birthday, 8 January 2007, to go to work. She was greeted by pandemonium. Kate had no staff, no PR and no protection to try and help her through the squabbling, elbowing hoard of paparazzi that had gathered outside. Finally she could understand for herself what William had been talking about when he described the hounding and misery of Diana. She hated it. Usually Kate could manage a smile for the photographers if she was caught leaving a nightclub, but this was completely different – it was her birthday.

Her face was set in stone as she battled her way into her new dark blue Audi A3. William was furious when she told him what had happened and was on the phone to Paddy Harverson, the respected Communications Secretary at Clarence House, insisting that he issue a statement: 'Prince William is very unhappy at the paparazzi harassment of his girlfriend. He wants more than anything for it to stop. Miss Middleton should, like any other private individual, be able to go about her everyday business without this kind of intrusion. The situation is proving intolerable for all concerned.'

Making the statement was literally all William could do to help. The couple weren't engaged so Kate was not entitled to protection. She had been given some advice about how to deal with the paparazzi but it didn't prepare her for this invasion. One celebrity explained, 'These people are horrible. They are not civilized. They are just people who have got cameras who hang around her door in the hope of making some money. So they spit on her, they shout at her, they get in her way because all they want is for her to crack. The stress is immense.'

All the media speculation about a royal engagement was only making the situation worse for Kate. William didn't like it either and felt trapped, especially as he was now spending more time with a bunch of new army pals than with Kate. He had made it perfectly plain that he was not ready for marriage and was sick and tired of being tied down by the media. His days were demanding and sometimes he wanted to let his hair down with his friends rather than settle in for the evening with Kate.

Their relationship was not on the rocks, however. They went for drinks at Boujis just before Valentine's Day and William surprised Kate with a beautiful gift – a green enamel Van Cleef & Arpels diamond-framed compact, featuring a polo player about to hit a pearl. The 1927 antique was worth £10,000, although nobody knows if William bought it or if the piece was already in the family collection. It was thoughtful and just the gift Kate needed to take into the ladies' with her to touch up her make-up before leaving the club.

They revisited their early courtship when Kate joined William and Harry to watch the England rugby team beat Italy in the Six Nations Championship at Twickenham, although the occasion was somewhat grander than the touchline at St Andrews. Kate cheered enthusiastically when Jason Robinson scored a try for England in the first half.

A few nights later, William was out with his mates in Boujis when, unusually, the ring of silence around him broke down. His eye had been taken by a foxy blonde PR girl called Tess Shepherd, who knew one of his friends. After chatting at his table, William suggested a dance. Tess explained that there

were actually three girls dancing with William. 'It was very flattering. He was twirling me around.' William and Tess did kiss,
fuelled in his case by a Crack Baby cocktail or two but Tess
maintained they didn't swap tongues: 'It's not true that I
snogged him – it was an embrace but not a French kiss.'

To her credit Tess was embarrassed by the press interest in
the evening, adding, 'It's not even like I fancy him – and I'm
kind of seeing someone' – not something to boost the royal
ego. Kate could cope with this sort of incident, realizing nothing much happened. She had herself been pictured with a
good-looking blond man, who had his arm round her while
queuing to get into Mamilanji. He bore a striking resemblance
to William but turned out to be a well-connected Oxford graduate called Freddie Sayers. He had played William in a
television film called *Diana: A Tribute to the People's Princess.*

Freddie, who was well known on the London social scene,
had met Kate for the first time at a private birthday party at the
Chelsea Gardener in Sydney Street before half a dozen of the
guests, including Kate, decided to walk to the club to continue
the evening. Kate had no coat and was wearing a black floral
print dress with short sleeves. She was freezing so Freddie gallantly put his arm around her and gave her his coat to put on
while they spent ten minutes waiting outside. Kate left
Mamilanji alone at 2.30 and hailed a taxi to take her home.

Afterwards, Freddie said, 'We share a mutual friend and we
were at the same party together. She seemed really nice but
obviously nothing happened between us. She was cold in the
queue so I lent her my coat and I might have passed my arm
around her briefly as I was ushering people into the club.
There's nothing more to it than that.'

Even something as innocent as this encounter became a big
story in the newspapers. More importantly as far as Kate was
concerned, she and William flew off with the usual crowd of a
dozen friends, including Thomas von Straubenzee and Guy
Pelly, for a skiing holiday in Zermatt. After a morning racing

each other down the slopes of the famous Matterhorn, they all retired for a long, lazy lunch at Blatten's restaurant, where Kate and William kissed and cuddled and, at one point, spent more than a minute in a tender embrace. They didn't look like a couple on the verge of splitting up, although there was much unfounded speculation that it was on this holiday that they had decided to split. This was another occasion when two and two made five.

They were, however, at different points of their lives. A friend observed, 'They were going through a stage when they both felt they were in a bit of a rut. William was enjoying the buzz of his new career, while Kate felt she was going nowhere and the whole eyes of the world were watching her struggle.'

On their return to the UK, they joined William's cousin Zara Phillips for a day at Cheltenham Races, which had become a firm favourite in Kate's social calendar each March. Experts thought their body language was strained, although that may have been more to do with William's general apathy where racing was concerned. He didn't share the girls' enthusiasm for the sport, although he cheered up when he won £30 on a bet. That afternoon would be the last time the couple were seen together in public until the day of the Concert for Diana on 1 July.

William left three days after their trip to the races for a ten-week tank commander course at Bovington camp near Wareham in Dorset. Kate didn't look like she was upset about anything when she went back to Cheltenham that afternoon to watch the Gold Cup. She was chatting merrily with Thomas van Straubenzee and others before the big race. She clearly had a winner because she was seen jumping up and down with excitement.

William settled in quickly at Bovington and joined his new soldier mates for a boozy night out at Elements nightclub in Bournemouth. This wasn't Boujis or Mahiki or one of his more discreet London haunts, and the prince wasn't protected by his usual coterie of cronies. But William, as he admits, likes to feel he has control of his life and if he fancied a piss-up with his mates, then he was jolly well going to have one. He meant business as he drank several pints of lager. Eyewitnesses said that with every pint he also sank two sambuca chasers, which he downed in one, while his friends urged him on by shouting 'One, two, three.'

Word quickly went round the club that a drunk prince was in the house and William didn't seem to mind when a number of girls fished out their mobile phones to have their picture taken with him. One of them was a petite brunette, Ana Ferreira, an eighteen-year-old student from Brazil, who spotted William dancing to some 'cheesy' eighties music in one section of the club. She would subsequently tell the *News of the World* all about her brush with the prince: 'There were a lot of girls hanging round him and he was posing for pictures. He had me on one arm and my friend Cecilia on the other. I really didn't know what to do so made a big peace sign with my hand. William clearly knew what he was doing with his hand!'

It was groping Ana's right boob. Ana continued, 'He has big manly hands and certainly knows what to do with them'. Before speaking to the *News of the World*, Ana did what any self-respecting girl would do under the circumstances – she emailed the picture of the groping, glassy-eyed prince to her mum back in Brazil: 'My mother thought it was very funny. She is pleased I met Prince William even though he was a little naughty.'

William's night was far from over, however, as his attention was then caught by a six-foot tall young blonde woman with a ring through her bottom lip. He hauled Lisa Agar, nineteen, on to a small dance platform and declared, 'Come on, show us how it's done.' Lisa, who was wearing a tight pink top, black leggings and high heels, also told the *News of the World* all about it: 'He was being very flirty and I was quite taken aback but just went for it. He was very close to me, shaking it all about. One of his mates started gyrating behind me and I was caught in a bit of a sandwich between them.'

She stayed with William's party until 3a.m., when one of his friends asked her back to the barracks, an invitation that William endorsed. Once there, however, the evening went a bit flat and William took himself off to bed, leaving Lisa to chat to his friends in the officers' mess. She said, 'I think he was pretty wasted and he told me he had to be up early the next morning. I think he was close to passing out and wanted to get upstairs before he was sick.' She only stayed a further twenty minutes, telling the newspaper that she didn't fancy William.

If this had been a night out at Boujis, then the world would almost certainly have never heard of it – nor would Kate. It was a night of high jinks and nothing more. When Chelsy Davy, Prince Harry's long-term girlfriend, complained of Harry's laddish behaviour and girl chasing, Kate tellingly told her, 'It comes with the territory.' But only very rarely did Kate have to read about it in the Sunday newspapers. The thing that made this particular evening rankle for her was the breast-groping photograph. The picture was a step too far, especially as Kate was trying her best to remain in control when under constant siege from the paparazzi. She couldn't put a foot wrong. Now, here was her boyfriend having a grope for the entertainment of the masses.

The *Sun* found a royal source who said William would have to grovel when he and Kate met up again the following weekend: 'They have a mature relationship but this is very embarrassing for both of them.' William is not the sort of man to grovel even if Kate was expecting an apology. They went out for dinner at the King's Head in Bledington with newlyweds Hugh and Rose van Cutsem but there was no particular clue that they were on the verge of breaking up.

William was in good spirits when he went out drinking with his officer mates to a Bournemouth wine bar, where a musician called Dan Baker was playing an acoustic set. One of William's group astonished the 200 fans watching the gig by jumping up on stage and reportedly shouting, 'Please stop playing these crap songs – the prince wants dance music.' William, according to reports, raised his glass to acknowledge his friend's initiative. One of the crowd said, 'William and his mates were a disgrace. They were drinking heavily and loudly and showed no respect.' Dan was equally unimpressed and called the intervention 'the rudest thing I've ever experienced. It clearly said acoustic performance on the door.' Again Kate had to learn about her boyfriend's escapades in the daily newspapers.

The trigger for the tiff that launched a thousand headlines is something Kate and William have kept to themselves. It may have been a throwaway remark by Kate that William seemed to be drinking too much. He wouldn't have appreciated that nor would he have enjoyed the observation that he seemed to be behaving like a bachelor. Kate left work at Jigsaw abruptly on Wednesday, 11 April and went to her parents' house. She had apparently taken a phone call from William and hurried out to the car park so that their conversation couldn't be overheard. A colleague who witnessed the scene said, 'She was walking up and down and looking upset as if she was having an argument. When she came back into the office she didn't say anything but grabbed her bag and left straight away.'

Two days later William appeared to be celebrating his freedom in style at Mahiki, his favoured alternative to Boujis. This was the infamous evening when he suggested to his group of friends, 'Let's drink the menu.' He ordered Dom Perignon champagne before they began to work their way through the cocktails. If you can finish all eighteen on the menu, the club gives you the infamous Treasure Chest – literally a wooden chest containing brandy, champagne, peach liqueur, lime and sugar. William, it was said, was in high spirits and shouted out 'I'm free!' before launching into his version of the then popular robotic dance used by footballer Peter Crouch when he scored a goal. Reports vary as to how much William spent on his first 'free' night but about £5,000 would be about right.

The following day the world woke up to the split when the national press told everyone. Twenty-four hours later it was deemed of such national importance that Tony Blair commented on the *Politics Show* on BBC One: 'They're a young couple. We've had the announcement. Fine. They should be left alone now without reams of stuff being written that I can assure you, from my experience of royal stories, most of which will be complete nonsense. I think, now it has been announced, they should be allowed to get on with their lives.'

The Prime Minister was quite right when he said they were young. William had, with hindsight, acted with youthful haste in telling his family that it was over between him and Kate. Clarence House refused to comment, pointing out that they never did anyway. The break-up gave the press the opportunity to examine the relationship forensically. Every columnist suddenly became an agony aunt. Sue Carroll in the *Daily Mirror* said, 'In preserving his freedom the prince has liberated Kate from a world of overbearing courtiers, whispering flunkies and a miserable goldfish bowl existence.' Sue, while understandably swept along by the media stories of the split, had been right about one thing – Kate's life really *was* a miserable goldfish bowl existence and she needed to do something about it.

Everyone had jumped the gun, however. The great break-up of 2007 was no more than a lovers' tiff. 'It lasted about a week,' said Jessica Hay. Few realized it at the time but just as everybody was getting used to the idea that they were single, they were back together.

13

Starting Over

The decision to split was a shock to both of them. Kate found herself back home with her mum and dad trying to make sense of how it had happened. Her job was proving unsatisfying. She had photographers in her face every minute of the day and she couldn't even put her weekly rubbish out for the dustman without it being recorded for posterity. When she went to the supermarket, someone would be hiding behind a distant parked car taking pictures of her shopping bags. When she received a parking ticket, she was photographed grabbing it off the windscreen. She had no royal status, no protection from the media and public and she hadn't even met the Queen. She had shared her life with the same man for five years and now that had finished abruptly. She would later describe her feelings: 'I wasn't very happy about it, but actually it made me a stronger person. You find out things about yourself that maybe you hadn't realized. I think you can get quite consumed by a relationship . . .'

Kate needed to come to terms with the fact that she didn't have much of a life. Far too much of her time and energy was being channelled into what William was doing. She did what she always did in times of personal difficulty: she asked her father what she should do. Jessica Hay observes, 'Her father is a huge part of her life. She absolutely adores him and he is very quiet but he has got a very good head on his shoulders. She always listens to her dad.'

His advice was that she needed to take charge of her own life, whatever might happen with William in the future. Even though the couple realized almost immediately that they had made a dreadful mistake and their love was as strong as it had always been, she understood that she needed to re-evaluate things. William agreed, 'We were both very young. It was very much trying to find our own way and we were growing up. It was a bit of space and it worked out for the better.'

Kate was quickly reassured that she was still William's girl despite all sorts of rumours that he was back on the prowl among the Gloucestershire polo set. Jessica Hay explains, 'The split was about a week really. But the press didn't know. They said he was seeing somebody else and she was heartbroken and everything else. I think they just wanted to figure stuff out during this period so it suited them to keep the press in the dark about the real situation to avoid any more intrusion.'

Clearly, if the couple had split up, they weren't getting engaged, so the paparazzi would soon tire of hanging around outside Kate's door. Royal expert Christopher Wilson believes the wool was pulled over our eyes: 'They took full advantage of something that was very minor indeed. As a consequence of the press announcement, the paparazzi stopped pestering her and gave her a break.'

The key figure behind the scenes was Paddy Harverson, who had become used to all manner of scandal, bad news and media frenzy when he presided over communications at Manchester United. He had, for instance, been at the centre of the storm over Sir Alec Ferguson kicking a boot that hit David Beckham in the face. The BBC journalist Michael Crick observed, 'Being the PR at Manchester United is the toughest PR job in the country.' At Clarence House, he had the opportunity to shape public opinion as far as William and Kate were concerned. This was an opportunity to undermine the media opinion that Kate – 'Waity Katie' – was wasting her life waiting for William.

The signs that Kate was feeling a great deal happier about life came within just a few days of their tiff. She swept out of her parents' house, drove to London and was pictured smiling as she collected her tennis racket from her Chelsea flat.

While over the moon that they had kissed and made up, Kate was aware that she needed to take charge of her own destiny and not allow the old situation to continue. It would be three months before the press realized they were back together – plenty of time to change things. She decided to live a little. She always seemed to be with William's old crowd so perhaps it was time to form her own girl posse. She already had the perfect partner in crime, her high-spirited sister Pippa, who completed her finals in English literature at Edinburgh University in May and arrived in London with the intention of enjoying herself.

Pippa had shared a flat in Edinburgh with two young aristocrats, Ted Innes-Ker, son of the Duke of Roxburghe, and George Percy, son of the Duke of Northumberland. This led to many catty suggestions that she was socially ambitious. A fellow student was quoted in *The Scotsman* newspaper: 'She was very charming about it but quite ruthless in cultivating the "right" friends. If she found out that someone had impressive social credentials, she would immediately pay them a lot of attention.'

Growing up in Berkshire, it was Pippa who seemed destined for great things. She was equally sporty, especially at tennis, in which she excelled, achieved more academically and was well regarded at her schools. Pippa was head girl at St Andrew's preparatory school and won a scholarship to Marlborough, where she had a reputation for being more outgoing than her sister. Jessica Hay thought Pippa probably took after her vivacious mother, while Kate had inherited the more measured, quieter personality of her father. Another former school friend recalls, 'Kate was always very protective over her sister.'

Each sister is said to be jealous of the other. They could be very competitive, especially over the question of who was the thinnest. Kate envied her sister's bubbly personality that always threatened to eclipse her. Pippa didn't like losing the spotlight after Kate began dating William. A family friend observed, 'The two sisters are certainly close but there was always a real sense of rivalry between them.'

Pippa is four inches shorter than Kate but shares her athletic frame, although it is perhaps more curvy. She too has glossy, flowing brunette hair. She started visiting the same fashionable celebrity stylist as Kate – Richard Ward, whose salon is just off Sloane Square. Sometimes their mother would come up from the country and join both her daughters for the 'couture hair experience' as the salon calls it. Pippa persuaded Kate that they would both look healthier with a spray-on tan so she arranged for a mobile tanning service to visit the Chelsea flat regularly. Pippa was single, having just split from her long-standing boyfriend, JJ Jardine-Paterson, an eligible Old Etonian and a member of a prominent Hong Kong banking family. They had been going out for three and a half years but their relationship didn't survive after Pippa left university. Pippa was said to prefer the same type of young man – 'squeaky clean, handsome, well connected and from a moneyed family'.

For a summer she and Kate became known as the 'sizzler sisters', hitting the clubs in a collection of eye-popping designer dresses and short skirts. It made a welcome change from their previous, less flattering nickname, the 'wisteria sisters': 'highly decorative, terribly fragrant and with a ferocious ability to climb'. The younger sister often seemed to have a little more spark and oomph. Jessica adds, 'Pippa is a little bit more of a party animal. She just lasts a bit longer. Prince Harry is the more boisterous of the two brothers and it's the same with Pippa and her sister. Pippa is still growing up and she wants to go out and have a good time. She is more spontaneous.'

When Pippa, or Pip as Kate calls her, hit town, it was she

rather than her older sibling who led the way. They first caught the eye as a society double act at a book launch in May 2007. They held hands and grinned broadly as they strode into Asprey for the party to celebrate the publication of Simon Sebag Montefiore's biography of the young Stalin, which didn't sound like a subject to get you in the mood for dancing. Pippa seemed to give Kate a youthful energy but that may have been a result of the mobile tanning service. 'It's our first book launch,' she announced as they mingled easily among the academics and celebrities.

Four nights later they donned their glad rags again for a night at Boujis. There was no shortage of invitations for the girls and, with William at Bovington, it was ideal for Kate to have her sister beside her. Guy Pelly, who enjoyed Pippa's youthful exuberance, arranged for them to be guests at a Johnny Cash-themed night he was throwing at Mahiki, where he was in charge of entertainment. Pippa was rumoured to have dated Guy a few times but nothing came of it and they settled for being friends. There was also polo to watch and Wimbledon and Henley to attend.

The girls accepted an invitation to a rather unusual party at Kitts club to mark the DVD release of a film called *Rabbit Fever*, which recounted the story of the Rampant Rabbit, the successful sex toy. Kate wore a pair of Playboy bunny ears and 'worked the room', according to other guests. Kate and her sister left at 1.30p.m., slightly tipsy and clutching a goody bag containing, apparently, one of the products that starred in the film.

Kate was moving on from Old Etonian drinking nights to a more varied and racier crowd. One of her new friends was Emma Sayle, who achieved a certain notoriety through her connection with sex parties. After she left Downe House school, she began working for Club Fever, a company organizing orgies for 'liberated couples and single women'. She went on to start her own company called Killing Kittens, which advertised on its website £120-a-couple sex parties at a private London house for 'strictly good-looking couples and single girls only'. It was a thriving business. Emma didn't personally participate in any of the nights. She told the *Daily Mail* that by the time she met Kate she had sold part of it and was no longer involved in the management side of things.

Kate was introduced to Emma through a mutual friend, Alicia Fox-Pitt, who had been at Marlborough and was helping recruit girls to take part in a boat race Emma had organized for charity. Alicia noted that Kate was a 'very gifted sportswoman'. The nineteen-strong all-girl crew, called The Sisterhood, were going to race across the English Channel against an all-male boat in August 2007. Kate jumped at the chance to become involved in something sporty that was also supporting a good cause. CHASE Ben Hollioake Fund, the children's hospice charity, and Babes in Arms, which sponsors research into newborn abnormalities, both stood to benefit by £100,000.

The Sisterhood described themselves as 'an elite group of female athletes talented in many ways, toned to perfection, with killer looks and on a mission to keep boldly going where no girl has gone before.' They provided an eye-catching sight as they trained hard on the Thames each day. Emma was not the only colourful character in the boat. When news leaked out that Kate was among them, the *Daily Mail* did some digging into the others in the crew and described them in quite creative terms. They included The One Who Seduced Her Teacher, The Fetish Party Artist, The Nightclub Podium Dancer, The Posh Masseuse, The Kick-Boxing Actress, The Sex Toy Marketeer and, somewhat incongruously, The Friend of Prince Philip.

It was good fun, although probably not the kind of publicity any of the young women wanted. Media interest ruined it for Kate and she dropped out reportedly under pressure from the Palace. It's never quite explained who 'the Palace' is under these circumstances. The most likely explanation is Kate decided her involvement was making life difficult for the other girls, which wasn't fair on them and detracted from the purpose of the venture – to raise money for charity.

Spreading her social wings a little did Kate no harm. It was suggested that she was showing William what he was missing but that's not quite as it was. Looking more closely at the male company she was keeping, they were mostly friends of William. As well as Guy Pelly, she danced at Mahiki with entrepreneur Jamie Murray Wells, chatted to estate agent Charles Morshead and was pictured with Henry Ropner, the former boyfriend of Jecca Craig and heir to a £30 million shipping fortune. There was nothing untoward about enjoying a drink with some of William's oldest friends.

All Kate was doing during the summer of 2007 was setting new guidelines for a relationship that was still very much on. William and Kate continued to meet in secret, usually at Clarence House, whenever he was able to get away from Bovington. They were first seen together again at a party arranged by the renowned amateur jockey Sam Waley-Cohen and held at his parent's mansion in Oxford. Sam had been at Eton with William, while his brother Tom had been at school with Kate. Sadly Tom died, aged twenty, in 2004 after a grim ten-year battle with bone cancer. At the party, Kate and William were seen chatting away, happily prompting rumours of a reconciliation when, of course, they had been together again for a couple of months. Sam disarmingly laughs off the idea that he was matchmaker: 'I don't think it was me with my Cupid's arrow.'

Privately, however, Kate was more carefree. William had been keeping his head down at camp, determined to get his career and his relationship back on track. He wasn't going to be photographed grabbing a young woman's boob any time soon. He was happy to see Kate in a better frame of mind and they enjoyed quiet weekends at Highgrove, where they rediscovered how much they enjoyed spending time together. He couldn't resist the opportunity to invite his girlfriend to a fancy dress party at his barracks, however, to see for himself her new carefree spirit.

The theme was 'Freakin' Naughty' and the organizers hung blow-up dolls from the ceiling to set the tone for the night. Kate dressed as a naughty nurse, while William was a sight in hot pants, a muscle vest and a policeman's helmet. An eyewitness noted how tactile they were with each other. They spent much of the night dancing before stumbling back to his quarters. News of their evening together reached Katie Nicholl of the *Mail on Sunday*. She was able to tell the world that the couple were back together on 24 June 2007. The secret was now out but keeping their reconciliation quiet had served its purpose.

Kate was much happier and had enjoyed the best three months since she'd moved to London. William, meanwhile, was dealing with a major event in his life – the tenth anniversary of the death of his mother. Together with his younger brother he had organized a memorial concert at Wembley Stadium to celebrate her memory and raise money for charity. Ticket receipts alone would come to more than £3 million.

The princes met with the NBC anchorman Matt Lauer to talk openly about their mother and how they had always wanted to do something for her. Harry said, 'It still upsets me, the fact that we didn't have as much of a chance as other children to spend time with her.' William hoped those coming to the concert would think of Diana as well as the music: 'I really hope that everyone just leaves with a nice, warm feeling and are going, "Yeah, that was the Princess of Wales I remember, that's her. That was the Diana I remember."'

The boys had assembled a stellar list of performers for the big day, 1 July, which would have been Diana's forty-sixth birthday. Kate was going to be there, of course, but the big question was what to do with her? The night before, she parked her Audi discreetly in a Kensington hotel before making her way on foot to Clarence House. By the time a servant had been dispatched to collect the car she was behind closed doors discussing the plan. She and William decided that they shouldn't be seen side by side as that would get the photographers overexcited. The result might mean that Kate was the story in the news and not Diana and her two sons.

Kate agreed to watch from the royal box, next to her sister and brother, James, but a few rows from the front, where Harry and William would command the limelight. James was just twenty and still a student at Edinburgh University but mixed easily with Kate and Pippa's friends and was proving very popular. James, said a friend, is a 'real sweetie'. He was the ideal choice to escort Kate for the day.

The concert itself, while long at more than six hours, would have been a credit to Sir Bob Geldof. As well as benefitting the Princess Diana Memorial Fund and other charities close to her heart, such as the National Aids Trust. William and Harry were both able to nominate causes they admired. Harry, who had said he would have liked to live in Africa given the chance, put forward the charity he had founded, Sentebale, which supports orphans and vulnerable children in Lesotho. William suggested Centrepoint, which cares for homeless young people in London. He had become patron after Diana died.

Sir Elton John opened proceedings at 4 o'clock, not with 'Candle in the Wind 1997' but with the timeless 'Your Song'. Kate had always liked the classic, although later she would much prefer the Ellie Goulding 2010 version, which she would play constantly on her iPod. Elton sang the original in front of a giant photograph of Diana taken by Mario Testino, who a few years later would be asked to take Kate and William's official engagement pictures.

After Elton had finished, the two princes bounded on stage in their usual casual uniform of blazer, open-necked shirt and jeans. 'Hello Wembley,' bellowed Harry. They both looked nervous – understandably so in front of 70,000 people. Harry managed a good joke: 'When William and I first had the idea, we forgot we would end up standing here desperately trying to think of something funny to say. We'll leave that to the funny people – and Ricky Gervais.'

William was more serious. He told the crowd, 'The event is about all that our mother loved in life – her music, her dancing, her charities and her family and friends.' He had already written in the £10 programme that his mother would have been 'the first up out of her seat and dancing.'

The princes returned to the royal box to join the 200 or so family and friends who were there. Kate gave no indication that she was peeved at not being in the front row as she chatted happily to Zara Phillips and her boyfriend, the England rugby player Mike Tindall. Occasionally she glanced over to William, who watched the concert sitting between Harry and Thomas von Straubenzee. Chelsy Davy was on Harry's immediate right.

It didn't take long for Kate to jump up when Lily Allen came on to perform her hits 'LDN' and 'Smile'. William, too, was not shy about leaping out of his seat to treat the crowd to his personal style of dancing, which could clear a dance floor in ten seconds. All 70,000 people seemed to be turning as one to capture the royal movers on their mobile phones. The performers ranged from current favourites like The Feeling and Kanye West to the older Tom Jones and Rod Stewart, who performed 'Sailing' with a gospel choir. Nelly Furtado proved to be the unexpected hit of the night when her 'I'm Like a Bird' had everyone up on their feet. David Beckham appeared on stage to introduce Take That. He had become friendly with William, who was a keen football fan and when younger had watched Manchester United play.

A filmed tribute from Nelson Mandela was cheered, while another from the Prime Minister Tony Blair was not so well received. William's favourite moment came when rap superstar P Diddy came on stage and performed a moving version of his classic tribute song 'I'll Be Missing You' in which he changed the rap to embrace Diana's memory – 'She was so beautiful – so royal' he chanted while her sons danced.

At the after show party, Simon Cowell told them, 'You've put on one heck of a show. In the future, if you get tired of running the country, you can come and work for me producing *The X Factor.*'

Kate was thrilled that it had all gone so well for William. At least, on the day, they were able to have the last dance together. In retrospect, while the reasoning was understandable, it was a shame that Kate wasn't beside her man throughout one of the best days of his young life. The concert was in many ways a turning point in that William at last decided he was committed to a future with Kate.

A few weeks later, they left for a summer holiday on the paradise island of Desroches, one of the Seychelles in the Indian Ocean. They checked into the £5,000-a-week resort under the names of Martin and Rose Middleton. William flew in from Kenya, where he had been staying at Lewa, while Kate made the journey alone from London. Finally, they were on holiday by themselves in one of the most idyllic spots on the planet. The tiny island is just three miles long with one airstrip and the couple could stroll for hours along the ten miles of sandy beaches with nobody bothering them. They went snorkelling, sunbathed and discussed their future.

They returned home with an understanding that they would be married. It changed everything for Kate. They were not yet officially engaged but Kate now knew it was her destiny. As a friend observed, 'It's like they had written it on a piece of paper and stuck it in a drawer ready to bring out when the time was right. The only thing missing was the date.'

PART THREE

PRINCESS

14

Chelsy

While Nelly Furtado sang 'I'm Like A Bird' on stage at the Diana concert, Chelsy Davy, blonde and tanned in a simple black summer shift dress, kissed her boyfriend, Prince Harry. It was the most natural thing in the world – two young people enjoying their love. They were lost in the moment and oblivious to the 70,000 noisy people all around them. Sadly for Kate, she has never been able to show such affection in public. Her natural reserve would almost certainly have kicked in even if she had been sitting next to William that afternoon. Instead she and William have made do with stolen kisses, as if always looking over their shoulders to make sure nobody was watching or, even worse, taking their picture.

Kate and William, it seemed, were forever trying to keep their relationship under wraps, not revealing the depth of their feelings. Harry, by contrast, was very proud of his girlfriend and wanted the world to know how lucky he was. He loved it when she drew attention to herself with a daring choice of outfit. He was delighted when she chose a turquoise dress with a plunging neckline to wear to his graduation ball at Sandhurst. He explained, 'My girlfriend is somebody who's very special to me. I would love to tell everyone how special she is . . .'

Chelsy is not the sort of girl to hide away. She and Kate are very different, despite media attempts to make them out to be royal pals. In truth, they didn't get on. They aren't far off being polar opposites. Chelsy is a dynamic girl, a party animal, who was far better able to establish a rapport with Pippa Middleton, who is closer to her own age. A university friend of Chelsy observes, 'Chels is more friendly with Pippa because they are more alike. When she's in London, they party together. They like to party and shop. She finds Kate a bit stuffy.'

Chelsy Yvonne Davy is Zimbabwean born and bred and proud of it. She was brought up in luxury at the family farm in the Lemco Safari Area, now known as the Bubye Valley Conservancy, about 150 miles south of Bulawayo in a region called Matabeleland. She could play tennis on the court in the garden and then cool off in the swimming pool. In the evening she would join her parents and her elder brother Shaun to dine on the terrace surrounded by acacia trees. The Safari Area was a beautiful wilderness, where elephants and buffalo grazed by day and lions roared at night. Sometimes the family would travel to Northern Zimbabwe to visit her mother Bev's parents. They lived on a huge estate called Yeadon, where Chelsy would ride bareback through the veld or join Shaun to hunt snakes and kill them with her bare hands. It was a million miles away from the rural England Kate knew.

Chelsy's father, Charles Davy, made his money initially by running hunting safaris, charging customers £660 a day to track and shoot big game. His friends describe him as a 'very jolly guy' but he is a controversial figure who has made and lost fortunes over the years and has been heavily criticized in the press for his links with Robert Mugabe's government. He was one of the very few white landowners to keep their farms. He was spared the fate of many because of the American investment in his businesses. Chelsy's uncle, Ian Donald, explains that his brother-in-law has been hugely misrepresented by people who 'don't understand how Africa works.' Charles was labelled an undesirable by the power-sharing former opposition party, the Movement for Democratic Change (MDC), prompting him to move his safari business to the neighbouring country of Zambia.

Not everyone in the family was as fortunate. Chelsy's grandparents watched helplessly while Mugabe's men seized their farm and razed the house to the ground. Her grandfather was never the same again and died soon afterwards, while her grandmother lives out her days in a nursing home in Durban.

Chelsy's home is now in South Africa, where her millionaire parents own several properties, primarily in Cape Town and Durban. Despite being proud of their heritage, they decided their daughter should finish her education in England, first at Cheltenham Ladies' College and then as a sixth former at Stowe School in Buckingham. The fees of more than £25,000 a year put the latter firmly in the Marlborough College bracket. When Chelsy was in her last year there, in 2003, she was introduced to Prince Harry by a mutual friend. She joined the gang at Club H in Highgrove, where she enchanted him with stories about growing up in Africa. She stood out from the usual eighteen-year-old schoolgirls Harry met and he was bowled over by her good looks, her natural blonde hair, her vitality and her easy charm. She was also the best shot of any girl he knew. Her appeal, according to a South African friend, is 'She is a real African girl, almost tomboyish.'

Chelsy was happy to tell her friends that she lost her virginity to Harry. He had been linked with girls before but she was his first serious girlfriend, his 'first love' too and, as he would make plain to royal officials in the future, a non-negotiable part of his life. The friend explains, 'In the beginning their relationship was based on physical attraction but it grew into something very emotional, a deep love.' When he left Eton, Harry spent part of his gap year in southern Africa, working with children in

Lesotho, where he had the idea for his own charity, Sentebale. He told Chelsy that he would be in Cape Town at some point and she immediately invited him to stay at her parents' villa. Harry took her up on the offer and by the time he flew back to London in the spring of 2004 they were officially boyfriend and girlfriend.

When it became public knowledge that Harry and Chelsy were an item, the media immediately characterized her as a fun-loving blonde, a sort of colonial Essex girl. She was described as 'pneumatic', as if she were one step away from being Jordan or Kerry Katona. The press were right that Chelsy was fun-loving, but she had been expensively educated, is very intelligent and has a serious side to her. She was about to study politics, philosophy and economics at Cape Town University. She eventually graduated with a first class bachelor of commerce degree in 2006, despite partying hard whenever the opportunity arose.

Few of the students she met realized she had a famous boyfriend and she didn't flash her parents' wealth around, although she drove a silver Mercedes coupe at the time. She also avoided living in halls of residence and student flats, preferring to share a house with her brother in the upmarket Newlands area, near the famous rugby and cricket grounds and close to the university. Friends who visited to laze around the pool describe it as a 'big family home'. Like Kate, Chelsy wants to be left alone as much as possible. She 'freaked out', according to a friend, when she found a mobile phone stuck to the underside of her car so that someone, presumably a photographer, could track her movements: 'People always used to try and take pictures of her when she was at university and it really annoyed her. But this was very scary – thinking that someone was monitoring her.'

Chelsy became well known in South Africa because of her relationship with Harry and the house, hidden by trees behind electronic gates, allowed her privacy. Harry could also visit without any publicity. He would regularly make the twelve-hour trip to Cape Town – often to patch up a quarrel. They were forever splitting up and getting back together again. He would literally fly in overnight, say he was sorry and then fly out the next morning. He got on well with her easygoing parents and, in particular, with her brother, whom everyone thought he was very like. On these flying visits, Chelsy would cook a meal and they would stay in, enjoying each other's company. On longer visits they would socialize with Chelsy's friends. It was a relaxed, bohemian world.

When they ventured away from this environment, Chelsy and Harry were far more likely to be exposed to public scrutiny. The *Mail on Sunday*, for instance, alleged that Chelsy was seen smoking dope with friends on a beach on Bazaruto Island off the coast of Mozambique. The newspaper was told by an onlooker, 'They all looked totally stoned.' Chelsy refused to comment when the newspaper confronted her with its story. Harry had been on holiday with Chelsy but had left before her friends flew in. She also refused to answer the paper's questions as to whether she had used cannabis while she was with the prince. Harry, on the other hand, had a well-publicized encounter with drugs as a teenager.

In January 2002, he was reported to be enjoying drinking and drug parties at Club H, the brothers' Highgrove den. The story made the front page of the *News of the World* under the banner 'Harry's Drug Shame'. Harry was immediately summoned to Highgrove for an unsettling interview with his father, who has always been extremely anti drugs. Charles took immediate action and insisted that Harry issue an apology. He also sent him to Featherstone Lodge, a rehab centre in South London, to speak to former heroin addicts and learn firsthand the dangers of taking drugs. Neither Harry nor Chelsy have admitted any interest in drugs.

Kate and Chelsy met when she flew in to Britain to see Harry and went to watch him play polo in early 2005. Kate invited

Chelsy to go shopping and was reportedly miffed when the younger girl said no. It was said at the time that Chelsy didn't care for British fashion but she did enjoy some of the High Street stores that Kate liked, such as Topshop, River Island and Whistles. She also loved shopping in Selfridges.

Inevitably, when they were photographed together watching polo, stories began to appear, comparing the two girls' friendship to that of Princess Diana and the Duchess of York in the eighties. Chelsy, much to her annoyance, was perceived as the Fergie figure. Chelsy always seemed to come out worst in comparisons between the two women – even her name was said to ooze 'chavness', as if a Princess Chelsy would be the stuff of royal nightmares. Kate was nearly four years older than Chelsy, which is quite a significant gap at that age. She was leaving university just as the younger girl was beginning her student life. Kate had lived with her boyfriend in a settled domestic situation, whereas Chelsy and Harry lived on opposite sides of the world and had an entirely different, more volatile relationship.

While Kate happily spent her last evening as a student dancing with William at her graduation ball, Chelsy finished university in 2006 with an all-night bender at the Wadda Bar in Claremont, the student area of Cape Town. She staggered out into the South African dawn, went straight to the airport and caught a flight to London to be with Harry. Just a couple of months before that, she had been in hospital having her appendix removed. Two nights after the operation she was back in the Wadda Bar, smoking her favourite Marlboro Lights, knocking back vodka and Red Bull and chatting happily to her mum, who had come out with her.

From the very beginning stories would occasionally surface that Kate and Chelsy were frosty towards one another. Chelsy's friend observes, 'She is a force of nature and doesn't have time for Kate. She finds her boring and she also hates how Kate is seen as the angelic "Diana" figure. Chelsy wants a career for herself and doesn't want to be known simply as Harry's girl-friend. That's always been an issue in their relationship and a reason why she doesn't have much respect for Kate.'

The pair are not often pictured together, although they are friendly enough when they are out with the boys as a four-some. They never seem to be having a laugh. In some ways it's a pity Chelsy and Kate aren't better friends because their expe-riences as royal girlfriends have been uncannily similar over the years, as they progress through nights out clubbing, scrutiny of their dress sense by the fashion police, continued analysis of the state of their relationships and, of course, the attention of the paparazzi. And they have both had to deal with splits.

The only time Kate and Chelsy have made a proper connec-tion was in 2007 when they both almost simultaneously broke up with their royal boyfriends. Chelsy and Harry have a stormy relationship but this was more serious. She read in the papers in Cape Town about his nightclub antics, when he was linked with a procession of pretty girls and then photographed kissing and cuddling bar girls while on army training in Canada. Chelsy had previously called Kate when news of her troubles with William reached Cape Town and Kate returned the kindness to offer some words of encouragement. Speaking from her own experi-ence, she advised Chelsy it was something they had to put up with and to turn the other cheek. Chelsy, who wears her emo-tions on her sleeve, wasn't impressed and the exchange was said to have prompted yet more frosty relations between the two women.

After Chelsy finished her degree, she spent time travelling in the US before beginning a postgraduate course in law at Leeds University in September 2007. Inevitably she saw more of Kate, particularly when they attended the same royal events. They were 'cordial' to one another.

It was Chelsy and not William who was with Kate for one of the biggest events of her life: meeting the Queen for the first time. They were guests at a royal wedding in May 2008, when Princess Anne's son, Peter Phillips, married Canadian-born Autumn Kelly, a delightfully named management consultant. Peter was the first of the Queen's grandchildren to marry so the royal headcount was high at St George's Chapel, Windsor.

William was just about the only one to miss it. He had flown to Kenya for the wedding of Jecca Craig's elder brother, Batian, to his British girlfriend, Melissa Duveen. He had already accepted the invitation before the date of the royal ceremony had been fixed. He made it up to his cousin Peter by joining the drunken stag weekend on the Isle of Wight. The principal entertainment seemed to be a series of drinking games that left the groom legless and slumped in a doorway. He had apparently gone missing from the pub, prompting Prince Harry to shout out, 'We've lost the fucking stag!'

While the boys sobered up for the wedding, William flew to Kenya. He had been looking forward to it because it would be a Maasai-themed outdoor ceremony at Lewa Wilderness Lodge that would continue most of the weekend and include tribal elders pouring milk over Batian and Melissa and offering prayers for their long life and happiness. William may not have wanted it for his own wedding but he was always moved by the romance of this part of Africa.

The wedding in Windsor was less exotic but much more controversial because it was the first royal event of its kind to be sold to a glossy magazine. *Hello!* reportedly paid in excess of £500,000 for exclusive coverage. The magazine wasn't allowed to take photographs of the Queen or her immediate family on the day but they were able to take exclusive pictures of Kate and Chelsy, which basically swung the deal. The girls were smuggled in to St George's Chapel by a side door and when the wedding party gathered outside on the west steps after the ceremony, they were nowhere to be seen. Harry was there, exchanging a joke with his stepmother, Camilla, while the Queen, Prince Philip and Prince Charles were all beaming while the photographs were being taken. Peter Phillips is very popular within the Royal Family and had always kept well out of the limelight.

The gathering crowd outside missed the opportunity to see Kate in a black knee-length dress with sheer voile neckline and a pink jacket. She showed her thrifty side by basically wearing the same outfit but with a different coloured coat to the wedding of Harry Aubrey-Fletcher and Louise Stourton in January 2011. The readers of the magazine, however, were treated to the sight of Kate and Chelsy laughing heartily at a joke Harry was telling during the reception at Frogmore House in Windsor Home Park, about half a mile from the castle. Kate looked refreshingly natural.

The reception, which lasted well into the night and included fireworks and much dancing, was an extravagant display that wouldn't have been possible if Peter and Autumn hadn't followed a path already trodden by Cheryl Cole, Jordan, the Beckhams and the Rooneys and sold their big day for a fortune. Autumn's parents couldn't afford it and Peter's mother, Princess Anne, was reluctant to show off the Royal Family's wealth, although she did lend the bride a sparkling diamond tiara. *Hello!* sent three photographers and their resulting pictures covered sixty pages of the next issue. The magazine certainly got its money's worth. It was further proof that the Royal Family was a part of celebrity culture.

Some were unimpressed. Labour MP Ian Gibson thought the British public would be shocked by the pictures and observed, 'She is the Queen, not a footballer's wife.' The *Daily Mail* joined in the outrage, writer Geoffrey Wheatcroft calling the '*Hello!*-ification' of the Royal Family 'the gravest threat the Crown faces today'. He added that 'greed and vulgarity are simply fatal.' The furore quickly died down, although it is unlikely that a similar idea will be sanctioned in the future – certainly not for any wedding involving Prince William or his brother.

The wedding was of particular interest to Kate because

Autumn came from what the press would describe as a 'humble background'. Her father runs an electrical shop, her mother is a hairdresser and her two brothers are a chef and a builder respectively. The Queen, despite what royal commentators may have us believe, doesn't have any problem with people's backgrounds. She is, for instance, very fond of her daughter-in-law the Countess of Wessex, who, as Sophie Rhys-Jones, was a businessman's daughter working in PR when she married Prince Edward.

The Queen also likes Autumn. Just a few minutes before the service was due to begin, she sought out the bride and calmed her nerves by telling her how lovely she looked. Kate was able to observe for herself how the family behaved on such occasions and think ahead to the day when she might be the centre of attention. But first she had to speak to the Queen.

Kate was officially representing Prince William at the wedding, which, in the way protocol works on such occasions, was a considerable honour. Many assumed that she and the Queen had already been introduced. You would have thought they might have bumped into each other in the corridors of Clarence House if the Queen had been visiting, or at Highgrove if she came to tea. But it hadn't happened, even though Kate and William had been together for more than six years and in most ordinary relationships grandma would have been one of the first relatives to meet. At the wedding Kate couldn't just barrel over to the Queen and say, 'Hiya.' There were a lot of guests, all of whom would be hoping for a word with the monarch at some stage. Eventually, the Queen came over to where Kate stood patiently. Kate recalled at her engagement interview, 'She was very friendly and it was fine.' William added that his grandmother had wanted to meet Kate for a while: 'They had a nice little chat and got on really well.' The Queen, it should be noted, didn't meet Kate until she and William had come to a proper understanding about their future together.

While Kate felt entirely secure about her prospects, Chelsy was finding that university life in Leeds wasn't suiting her. She was seeing less of Harry than she had when she was living in Cape Town. Their relationship was still full of ups and downs and six months later they split yet again.

15

A Jigsaw Puzzle

By the time she met the Queen, Kate was no longer in full-time employment. Her working life had always been a bit vague, to say the least. Her original position at Jigsaw as assistant accessories buyer had been upgraded to assistant buyer but still didn't sound very glamorous. The job had started with the best of intentions on both sides. Belle Robinson, the fashion chain's joint owner, explained, 'She genuinely wanted a job but she needed an element of flexibility to continue the relationship with a very high-profile man and a life that she can't dictate.' Nobody was ever quite clear how many days a week Kate worked – it was either three or four – and exactly what she did when she got there. The impression was that Kate was able to drift in and out when it suited her.

The *Daily Mail* spoke to a former employee who said, 'Kate was never what you might call committed to the job. She never worked full time and appeared to take an inordinate amount of time off to go jetting around the world with her boyfriend. It certainly rubbed a few people up the wrong way. She was always treated as a special case.' The implication was that Kate was a nice enough girl but not really pulling her weight. Belle

Robinson said, 'She sat in the kitchen at lunchtime and chatted with everyone from the van drivers to the accounts girls. She wasn't precious.'

When she left in November 2007, nobody seemed to be falling over themselves to offer Kate a career in fashion. Belle Robinson told the *Daily Mail*, 'Signing up Kate Middleton wasn't really that lucrative. There was an initial buzz, but it quickly died down.'

Kate couldn't sit around and do nothing while William appeared to be doing so much. But she was sure of one thing – she didn't want to start another birthday battling through a scrum of paparazzi on the way to work. She wasn't unemployable, of course, but her CV was looking very thin. She would have been a terrific brand ambassador for fashion and beauty products but she knew she would be Queen one day and she couldn't endorse hair conditioner as if she were Cheryl Cole. One thing was absolutely clear: she couldn't make money from her royal connection. There was talk of her moving to New York for a while so she could live a more normal daily life but that was a non-starter because she was seeing too little of William as it was because of his military commitments.

Kate's lack of a proper job continued to be the biggest criticism of her. Every time it was mentioned, the nickname 'Waity Katie' was dusted off. Even the Queen was reported to have enquired, 'What is it exactly that Kate does?' Ironically, her social skills and charm were well suited to PR but she couldn't very well cultivate media contacts on the one hand and ask to be left alone on the other. Some news was positive – she made it onto *Vanity Fair*'s International Best Dressed List in 2008. She placed fourth behind Ivanka Trump, Michelle Obama and Carla Bruni-Sarkozy.

The solution to Kate's employment problem proved to be closer to home. She started working for the family firm, Party Pieces – the only course of action really open to her. A job there would take care of many problems: she wouldn't have photographers outside the door every minute; she was assured that nobody would speak about her; and she could fit her working schedule around seeing William and preparing herself for the royal role she expected to have in a few years' time. Part of that process was to improve her work for good causes.

Paddy Harverson and his team at Clarence House wanted to raise her profile in the right way and charitable work was one of the best means of doing that. William was already involved with many charities and Kate wanted to follow suit, albeit in a small way to start with. She set about organizing an exhibition by acclaimed celebrity portrait photographer Alistair Morrison, which raised money for UNICEF, the United Nations children's fund. Morrison had thought of a clever idea – installing a special photo booth at various hotels in New York and Los Angeles, as well as the Dorchester in London, and persuading celebrities to use it. Tom Cruise, Kate Winslet and Catherine Zeta-Jones were among those happy to oblige. Morrison's concept for the £60 book, called *Time to Reflect*, was that everyone, however distinguished or glamorous, was equal in the eyes of the passport camera.

Kate persuaded some of her friends to attend the opening, including Laura Parker Bowles and Guy Pelly. Her mother and father came up from Berkshire for the launch at The Shop at Bluebird on the King's Road, owned coincidently by the Robinsons. Everyone agreed that the exhibition, which ran for four weeks, was a big success. It was reported that Kate was planning a whole series at the venue but, in the end, this was the only one.

Being able to divide her time between Bucklebury and London meant Kate could stay at the former if she knew William was going to be at Highgrove and the latter if she was staying with him in Clarence House. Sometimes William came to stay at her family's house. He liked to do so because it was informal and he could relax; he even admitted once that he was happy to do his share of clearing the dishes and washing up.

Kate didn't fancy Lincolnshire much when William reported for duty at RAF Cranwell in January 2008. Traditionally, an heir to the throne was expected to do a certain amount of service in all branches of the military to prepare him for being head of the armed forces one day. William had passed his army training at Sandhurst, his tank course at Bovington and now it was the turn of the air force. He couldn't wait to learn how to fly. The boozy escapades of Bovington were a thing of the past and most weekends William would drive down to Clarence House in London, where Kate would be ready to cook his favourite bangers and mash supper. For the first time since St Andrews, they settled into a more contented domestic routine.

William proved a natural pilot. He qualified for his wings and was awarded the rank of Flying Officer. The ceremony at RAF Cranwell on a wet and windy April day was brightened by the appearance of Kate in an elegant tailored cream coat. She looked genuinely pleased and proud as Prince Charles, in his capacity as the RAF's Air Chief Marshal, pinned the badge onto his son's uniform. Kate was heard to say how gorgeous she thought William looked.

There was still time for the occasional good night out but, more frequently, this was linked to a charity event. They joined Harry, Chelsy and the gang at the annual Boodles Boxing Ball in aid of the Starlight Children's Foundation, which raises money for seriously ill children. All the usual suspects were there: Guy Pelly, Jamie Murray Wells and Thomas von Straubenzee, as well as Jecca Craig, who was seen laughing and joking with Kate throughout the evening – again demonstrating that Kate had no problem with Jecca whatever the papers wrote.

Kate looked a million dollars in a vivid pink dress by her current favourite fashion label, Issa. The Brazilian-born designer Daniella Issa Helayel was a friend of Pippa's. One of William's oldest friends, James Meade, the son of the Olympic horseman Richard Meade, was fighting in the event under the nickname

'The Badger'. Kate entered into the spirit of the evening, either wincing or cheering as his bout unfolded. At one point she put her head in her hands as if to hide when a particularly fearsome punch was thrown. Disappointingly, The Badger lost on points.

Chelsy, by contrast, was a little subdued. She spent much of the evening chatting with Richard Branson's daughter, Holly, and resting her arm affectionately on Harry's shoulder. She had apparently been worried about the semi-public event and the comparison with Kate that would inevitably follow. A friend recalled, 'She was very nervous about her choice of outfit as she always gets flack.' She settled for a rather demure blue dress to suit her mood.

A more flamboyant Kate, however, was determined to have a good time, dancing to DJ Rusty Egan at the subsequent party until 3a.m. When they weren't on the dance floor, William and Kate would slip back to their table to sink shots of Ivan the Terrible vodka. It was as if Kate and Chelsy had swopped personalities for the night. Kate was far more confident with William's commitment fresh in her mind. She no longer felt the need to be jealous of Chelsy's easygoing nature.

So far Kate's new working arrangements were going well. The principal drawback with her role at Party Pieces, however, was that nobody had any idea what she did and there was a sneaking suspicion it wasn't very much. Apparently she took photographs for the online catalogue and helped design the company's website but the only picture of her at work shows her carrying some cardboard boxes into the office.

She was troubled less by photographers when in Bucklebury, where the opportunity for 'citizen journalism' was also limited. Members of the public had realized they could make thousands of pounds if they snapped Kate on their mobile phone. The potential for people to make money out of the couple was always there, creating a new nuisance to deal with. In the summer of 2008 two men stole a memory stick from Pippa Middleton's car while it was parked in Kensington. It contained pictures of a previous Middleton family holiday to Mustique and included Kate practising yoga in a skimpy bikini and William larking about in a woman's hat. The thieves tried to negotiate a sale with the *Sun* newspaper, which reported them to the police. They were caught, prosecuted and sentenced to one hundred hours of community service.

The intention for William and Kate to keep below the radar at Bucklebury was somewhat ruined when William landed his Chinook helicopter in the field behind the house. William hadn't realized the implications of what the papers called a 'thoughtless act of bravado'. The public relations blunder happened while he was training at the Odiham base in Hampshire, just twelve miles from Oak Acre. There was a serious side in that he was practising his take-off and landing skills and was fully supervised by his instructors. A spokesman defended the escapade by claiming that helicopter crews routinely practised landing in fields and it was a vital part of his training – but presumably there were more suitable locations than his girlfriend's back garden.

It was an unexpected own goal by William. The bad publicity the 'vital training' brought was made even worse when it was revealed that he had also buzzed Highgrove on a trip that cost nearly £12,000, hovered over Sandringham, flew to a base in Northumbria so he could join Kate for the wedding of their friend Lady Iona Douglas-Home and used a helicopter to fly himself and Harry to Peter Phillips' stag weekend on the Isle of Wight. Apparently that flight was 'open water training'. The author Claudia Joseph calculated William's joyrides cost the taxpayer £82,434. It all gave the impression that the prince was just playing at being in the armed services.

Fortunately for William, some better publicity was around the corner and quickly led to his helicopter shenanigans being forgotten. He made a thirty-hour round trip to Afghanistan to learn about the role of the RAF in a war zone. On this occasion he wasn't expected to shake hands and boost morale but he did have a solemn duty – he was one of the official party bringing home the body of a fallen soldier, Trooper Robert Pearson, then the ninety-fourth serviceman killed in the conflict. Many observers thought the timing was opportune. His former protection officer, Ken Wharfe, said, 'I think the cynics amongst us will say it's an attempt to cover up the Chinook jollies.'

Kate knew that William wouldn't be in any danger on his mission but the mere mention of Afghanistan is enough to cause anxiety to anyone connected with the services and Kate was no exception. There was a world of difference between clapping and cheering as he landed his helicopter in the back garden and waving him off to the most dangerous of lands. Kate was relieved when he was home again. She also knew William would never be sent to serve in Afghanistan because of the risk of him being killed and the country losing the man who was destined to be king one day.

William was extremely frustrated by his situation. He told Matt Lauer that he wanted to go if he could, '. . . otherwise, what's the point of me doing all my training and being there for my guys when I can turn around to somebody and say, "Well, I'm far too important. I'm not going."'

William's brother Harry, who was serving in the army, had been allowed to go to the front line in December 2007. The mission had been top secret, with UK newspaper editors agreeing not to report it because of the added security risk it would pose, not just to Harry but also to his fellow soldiers. Annoyingly, an Australian magazine printed the scoop that he was there when he still had a month left of his tour of duty. To his fury, Harry was immediately put on a plane home, although he understood his commanders had no choice.

Even so, William was envious of Harry serving in a dangerous conflict and was overheard on a night out at the Whisky Mist club in Mayfair telling a friend, 'That's why we train, because we want to be there on the front line. I'm a bit jealous to be honest.'

Kate was becoming more integrated into the Royal Family week by week. Her most formal event to that point was attending the ceremony in which William was invested as a Royal Knight of the Garter in June 2008. She could see the funny side of the grand occasion, however, and giggled furtively with Harry when they caught sight of William's traditional costume – a blue velvet cloak and plumed cap with ostrich feathers sticking out the top.

William had undergone a lifetime of training for such events – they are his destiny. But Kate had to learn about them as she went along. She wasn't to the palace born but as part of the master plan, which they had both agreed to, she should learn to be a princess before she actually became one. Prince Charles wholeheartedly agreed with William's strategy, noting perhaps that it was a luxury not enjoyed by his first wife, Diana. It was a case of learn the ropes, keep your nose clean and you'll be fine. Kate was allowed out in public for charity events but was advised to cut back on Boujis nights, especially if William was away.

She helped to organize another charity evening – this time one where she wouldn't be able to rely on William's support. She joined Holly Branson in arranging a roller disco evening at the Renaissance Rooms in Vauxhall. The Day-Glo Midnight Roller Disco was in aid of Place2B, a youth counselling service, and Tom's Ward, the foundation set up by the Waley-Cohen family to honour the memory of Kate's school friend Tom. The money raised since his death in 2004 had funded a children's surgery ward at the John Radcliffe Memorial Hospital in Oxford.

Kate's claim that the split with William the previous year had made her stronger was again evident in the way she now seemed much more comfortable in her own skin. She was lightening up. She threw herself into the spirit of the occasion, helped by her old friend Sam Waley-Cohen, who lived quite near her in south-west London. Kate dressed up for the disco, looking like someone out of an eighties' dance troupe. She wore a green sequinned halterneck top, yellow hot pants that would have won the approval of Kylie and pink legwarmers. She was like a rocket ice lolly. For an expert skier and all-round sportswoman, Kate revealed herself to be useless on skates. She gingerly clung on to the rail and the arm of anybody passing she knew, before striking out on her own and promptly ending up flat on her back. Sam gallantly helped her up as she dissolved in a fit of giggles.

Rarely has Kate looked so happy in public. For some reason she received bad press after the event with some sniping comments suggesting that she had let the side down and been an embarrassment to the royals. Sam was annoyed on her behalf: 'The whole event was done in really good humour with everyone out to have a good time and raise money for charity. It just showed what a normal person Kate is. She was there to have fun and fell over. What's the problem here?'

While Kate was roller skating, William was at sea. He had moved on from the RAF to the Royal Navy where, after training in Dartmouth, he was posted for duty with HMS *Iron Duke,* a frigate on patrol in the Caribbean. He was able to fly the latest naval helicopters that he loved. The most exciting day in a rather low key few weeks was when he took part in a joint mission with the US coastguard: it captured a cocaine shipment worth £40 million in the lucrative drugs market. William was part of the Lynx helicopter team that located a 50-foot power-boat about a hundred miles off the coast of Barbados. When it was boarded, the coastguard discovered nearly a ton of coke stacked in forty-five neat bales. His captain, Commander Mark Newland, said, 'Sub Lieutenant Wales was my trained pair of eyes in the skies and a valuable member of the team.' He added that William had yet to be seasick.

One good thing about serving in the Caribbean was that William was handy for Mustique and was able to join Kate while she was holidaying on the island with her family. The highlight was a private party at Basil's Bar, their favourite place on the island. They were among a hundred guests celebrating the fortieth anniversary of the Mustique Company, which runs the island. Mick Jagger, who has a villa nearby, gave an impromptu concert for everyone. The rest of the time William spent sleeping on the beach, utterly exhausted after getting up at 4a.m. every day on board ship.

William's military service, which had been going on for more than sixteen months, was almost at an end. He just had time for some more training with the Special Boat Service (SBS), when he grew a typical naval beard, before coming to a decision that would shape the future for him and Kate.

William adored flying. He had been fascinated by planes as a child and never lost his enthusiasm for the freedom and the speed that went with flying. Both William and his brother thrived on the buzz of adrenalin it gave. Of all the training he had received since he'd been on parade at Sandhurst, it was the thrill of piloting the helicopters that stayed with him. After his stint with the SBS, he would be expected to move on to the next stage of his life as a full-time royal. But William wasn't ready to be a professional ribbon cutter. He had only just celebrated his twenty-sixth birthday.

He wanted to stay in an active military role and decided to become a full-time pilot with the RAF's Search and Rescue Force (SARF). It was an inspired choice. He had been frustrated when he wasn't allowed to use his skills and training and join the Household Cavalry when it was deployed to Afghanistan in 2007. Those operational limits would never change but in his new role he might well be posted abroad – to the less dangerous bases of Cyprus or the Falkland Islands. William had come a long way since he first sat down to a lecture on baroque art at St Andrews. The two weeks he'd spent with the Search and Rescue Team in Anglesey after he'd finished university had made a lasting impression on him.

William announced his decision in September 2008. It would

mean at least another eighteen months of training – this time in a Sea King helicopter – when he would learn the full extent of operations, from rescuing trawlermen in trouble to airlifting stranded hillwalkers and flood victims. He explained, 'The time I spent with the RAF earlier this year made me realize how much I love flying. Joining Search and Rescue is the perfect opportunity for me to serve in the Forces operationally, while contributing to a vital part of the country's Emergency Services.' It may not involve *Boy's Own* heroics but it is vital work. His father was said to be delighted that he had made such a worthwhile choice.

From Kate's point of view, it signalled the start of a more set-tled period in her life. If William was posted to a base in the UK, then they could enjoy some normality together before the mad-ness began.

16

Embarrassing Relations

Kate managed to survive more than seven years in a relation-ship with one of the most famous men in the world without a hint of scandal involving her or her family. She had to put up with a story alleging a pregnancy scare in 2008 but the rumour was quickly forgotten. Her family by and large had avoided the wrong sort of media attention: her father had never spoken out of turn; her mother had suffered petty snobbery about her upbringing and her lack of grace in chewing gum at William's Passing Out Parade; and her sister, Pippa, was sparky in a Calamity Jane sort of way, although she did once strip off her clothes, wrap herself in toilet paper and balance precariously at the top of a human pyramid.

James seemed disappointingly squeaky clean except for the evening of his twenty-second birthday in April 2009 when he was reported to be 'legless' after a family night out. He was photographed having a much needed pee up against a fence while his mother, Carole, did her best to chase away the photographers. Kate, apparently mortified, shielded her face as she walked by her urinating brother. The offending picture eventually showed up in an Australian magazine. According to

Women's Day, Carole acted 'like a cornered lioness protecting her cubs.' The magazine dramatically called the episode a scandal but none of the British media seemed interested.

But then, in July 2009, while Kate was watching yet another game of polo at the Beaufort Polo Club, the *News of the World* was putting the finishing touches to the first serious hit on her family. The newspaper was about to expose her Uncle Gary, who had been woefully indiscreet to the paper's investigation's expert, Mazher Mahmood, popularly known as the 'fake sheikh'. The banner headline said it all: 'Kate Middleton Uncle Drugs & Vice Shock' – a lurid tale of sex and drugs on the holiday island of Ibiza, where Gary lived.

Kate's uncle was described as a 'bald-headed 49-year-old braggart' in a story that combined outrage and salaciousness as the newspaper accused him of supplying illegal drugs and fixing up hookers. One can only imagine breakfast in the Middleton household as they digested all the ghastly details. To those looking on incredulously the story, which included his f-word greeting to William, was mostly a hoot. The most cringe-making detail was the revelation that William had been round for dinner at the family house in Bucklebury when the subject of Kate's figure had come up and, in particular, the size of her bust, which had been her obsession at school. Gary recalled, 'They were talking about boobs . . . William said that more than a handful is a waste.'

Unintentionally, someone had revealed for the first time that Kate and William talk about normal things at the dinner table like millions of other people and don't have a problem with the f-word. William is not a snob or a prude and wouldn't be the least perturbed by the over-the-top manner of Gary Goldsmith. The revelations did have a serious side, though, in that Gary seemed to be connected with drugs and prostitution. He offered the reporters the name of a pimp who could supply a Brazilian girl for the night as well as the number of a drug dealer called Sharon who would deliver to their door.

On another occasion, Gary greeted them dressed only in shorts with his belly hanging over the waistband and went into the kitchen, where he proceeded to prepare some lines of coke for sniffing through a 100 euro note. He also openly smoked marijuana joints, which he kept in a special box on the coffee table.

Gary Goldsmith grew up on the same disadvantaged streets of Southall as Kate's mother. And, like her, he has turned his life round to become hugely wealthy – amazingly, both the son and daughter of a jobbing builder have independently become millionaires. He had made his fortune and as a result never has to work again. His place in the sun is in Ibiza, where thousands of British teenagers go every year for 'sex, drugs and rock 'n' roll' away from the disapproving gaze of their parents. His girlfriend at the time was a shapely twenty-six-year-old former lap dancer called Antonia Bourke.

The fallout from the *News of the World* sting was a curious mixture of hand-wringing self-righteousness and snobbery. Nobody seemed quite sure what Gary's biggest crime was – the coke and other assorted substances, the sex, the tattoos and the perception that he was in some way naff, or perhaps just the fact that he was bald and his name was Gary? Everybody in the media seemed to agree he was the 'black sheep' of the family.

The story gave the press the opportunity to link Kate Middleton to the staple diet of sensationalism – cocaine, sex, lap dancing and misbehaving millionaires. The *Daily Mail* was in no doubt: 'The revelations have caused huge embarrassment to the Middletons and sent shockwaves around the palace, although William, who is close to Kate's family, is standing by them.'

The press declared open season on Gary's life. A woman called Julia Leake was revealed as having jilted Gary at the altar in 2007 because she could no longer cope with his drug-taking and mood swings. She told a friend, 'He is a lovely guy in his heart of hearts but I just can't help him anymore.'

They had married in a civil ceremony in London but she had ditched Kate's uncle before a £250,000 church blessing and reception in Ibiza. The most interesting part of Julia's story, according to her friend, was that William and Kate had been due to fly out to join the celebration. Kate's parents, as well as Pippa and James, had already travelled to La Maison de Bang Bang for the occasion. Gary was genuinely popular within his family circle and, as far as Carole Middleton was concerned, he would always be her kid brother. Apparently she rang Julia and said, 'I know what my brother's like and he needs a good woman to pull him through. Please come back.'

The reporting of the aftermath was classic journalism – say how worried and freaked out Kate was and then repeat all the salacious details just in case anybody had missed them the day before. The story gave the media the rather dubious permission to run headlines like 'Kate's Drug Shame' and 'Royal Outrage'. Even the US got in on the act with the *Globe* magazine, a supermarket tabloid, shouting on the front cover, 'William's Bride Caught in Cocaine Scandal'. The *Globe* also suggested that Camilla Parker Bowles demanded that Kate and William postpone any wedding plans.

Gary, meanwhile, appeared to be Billy No Mates. The lap dancer promptly left him after the story broke. He was, apparently, ashamed that he had embarrassed Kate and flew back to England to keep his head down in his £1 million mews house in West London.

The American media put the 'scandal' in perspective. Mary Jordan of the *Washington Post* observed that the whole discussion centred on class prejudice: 'Class in Britain is roughly equivalent to race in America – despite enormous strides towards equality, social standing simmers never far below the surface.' The renowned royal biographer, Robert Lacey, author of the ground-breaking book *Majesty*, agreed: 'I think class is the primary element in all of this.'

Perhaps Gary's biggest crime as far as the snobs were

The Sarah Burton wedding dress in all its glory. Above, a bride alone with her thoughts. Kate arrives outside the doors of Westminster Abbey. Below, her sister Pippa was a constant presence at the service, making sure the dress looked its best.

Celebrity watch. Sir Elton John and his partner, David Furnish, check their ties: 'Your Song' is one of Kate's favourites; the Beckhams: David checks that his pregnant wife, Victoria, is coping well; and the ever glamorous Zara Phillips with her fiancé, Mike Tindall: theirs will be the next royal wedding.

Chelsy Davy kept a low profile although her outfit was as vivacious as ever.

James Middleton, Kate's brother, looked poised throughout the day and gave a faultless reading of the lesson.

On the day, the Middletons mixed easily with William's family. Left, Michael Middleton with Prince Charles. Below, Both Carole Middleton and the Duchess of Cornwall looked a picture in their hats.

The service was the right blend of serious and cheerful. Left, kneeling to pray in front of the altar; below, gazing deep into each other's eyes as they hold open the order of service.

The watching audience gasped as William struggled to push the wedding band on to Kate's finger.

Westminster Abbey had never looked so atmospheric.

The Queen, waiting with Prince Philip for their carriage, called the day 'amazing'.

The open-topped landau is always a crowd pleaser and Kate and William waved happily as they were seen in public for the first time as man and wife. Below, finally there – Kate arrives at the Palace.

On the balcony... Kate makes sure her bridesmaids are included on her special day.

The best man and maid of honour: Harry and Pippa could relax after their formal duties of the day were finished.

The flypast. Kate joins the entire balcony to scan the skies as the magnificent war planes power overhead.

And finally they kiss. After so many years of hiding their love, they shared the moment in front of a billion people watching worldwide.

No wonder Kate exclaimed, 'Wow!' when she saw the size of the crowds who had come out to celebrate her wedding day.

Just like many other newlyweds, William and Kate drive away from their reception with L-plates on the front and 'JU5T WED' on the back. His dad's Aston Martin made a wonderful picture for the thousands who stayed in the Mall hoping to catch another glimpse of the couple.

The iconic Kate in the Sarah Burton dress she wore for her wedding party – elegant, statuesque and regal.

concerned was his taste in furniture – no tasteful antiques were on show at Bang Bang. Instead he had a jukebox, a games machine, a white grand piano and a pink Raleigh chopper bike from the eighties emblazoned with his GG motif.

More seriously, Kate and her family were genuinely shocked by the revelations – perhaps not by learning anything new about a well-liked and generous uncle's lifestyle but because this was the first time anything like this had ever happened to them. They were worried that the stories about Gary would give the world ammunition to declare Kate an unsuitable partner for Saint William of Highgrove.

Fortunately, not everyone took it so seriously. The humorist Craig Brown saw the funny side, pointing out that having a black sheep in the family virtually assured Kate's royal future. He noted the late lamented Major Ron Ferguson, father of the Duchess of York, who was a regular at a massage parlour; Princess Michael of Kent's dad was an SS officer in World War Two; and Diana herself was associated with a 'full farmyard of black sheep', including the authoress Barbara Cartland, Dodi Fayed and his father, Mohamed Al-Fayed.

Kate's family did the right thing under the circumstances. Michael Middleton told reporters camped outside the house in Bucklebury, 'You know we don't ever talk to the press and the situation remains the same.' Then they whisked Kate off for a break in the Caribbean – just as if she were a WAG having to deal with the tawdry sex life of her footballing partner. When fretting about something, Kate has a tendency to stop eating which, while very common, is not something to be taken lightly. The *Daily Mail* diarist Richard Kay, a friend of Diana's with impeccable royal connections, reported that the shock had 'almost affected Kate physically'.

None of the Middleton family has ever made any public comment about Uncle Gary and they almost certainly never will. That is their golden rule about family matters and they all stick together. The shock of the revelations about Gary only served to bring the family unit even closer. He learned a sobering lesson and, while he will never be allowed by the press to live down his indiscretions, he hasn't repeated them.

Fortunately, the Royal Family was nothing like as 'outraged' as the media would have liked. The public, fed a regular diet of this sort of thing, didn't take long to forget it. William was strongly advised not to accept any further invitations to La Maison de Bang Bang and couldn't offer any public support but privately he was overheard at polo reassuring Kate, 'I want to marry you, not your family.'

The evening before the *News of the World* exposé, Kate and William were having a quiet drink in The Potting Shed pub in the Wiltshire village of Crudwell. They undoubtedly would have been told to expect some revelations the next day. When they left, with their arms around each other, they walked towards William's car before stopping for a passionate embrace in the middle of the car park. Unsurprisingly, someone sneakily took a photograph but it was the first time they had been seen kissing in public for more than two years.

William's resolve to progress his relationship with Kate Middleton as quietly as possible was only strengthened by the headlines about her uncle. He had a hatred of such press, perhaps haunted by the stories about his mother. Prince Charles sent Kate a note telling her to 'try and put it out of your mind'. Her other uncles do not possess Gary's va va voom and are unlikely ever to hog the headlines. Mike Middleton's three brothers are Uncle Simon, a teacher from Berkshire; Uncle Nicholas, who works for the Ordnance Survey and lives in Oxfordshire; and Hampshire-based Uncle Richard, who is a computer systems and software consultant.

William's relatives are a different story, however, and make Gary seem like a novice. He isn't even the most embarrassing uncle – that title is held firmly in the grasp of Prince Andrew, who would cement his position as number one following the revelations in 2011 of his friendship with a notorious paedophile. Gary was also not the first to be duped by Mazher Mahmood. He had persuaded the Countess of Wessex to be indiscreet about, among others, Charles and Camilla, Tony and Cheri Blair and William Haig. She had been fooled into believing he was interested in putting business the way of her ailing PR company and allegedly was prepared to allow her royal connection to be used to sweeten the deal.

After the revelations over ten pages of the newspaper, Sophie resigned from her PR firm RJH and guidelines were established at Buckingham Palace to prevent future 'conflict of interest'. The vulnerability of a member of the Royal Family to an enterprising reporter has shaped the strategy over Kate's career or lack of it. It would be a disaster if she were caught using her position. For that reason any work she has done for Party Pieces was kept as secret as if she worked for MI5. The one occasion when she wrote on the company website that she used to love her mother's cakes as a child was hastily removed.

The fake sheikh had exposed Princess Michael of Kent in 2005, when he had posed as a potential buyer of her country house. She apparently called William's mother Diana a 'bitter' and 'nasty' woman and also thought the young prince was 'too young' to marry Kate at that time. He didn't stop at Uncle Gary either. He went on to expose the Duchess of York in yet another scandal. She was caught, in effect, selling a businessman access to her ex-husband Prince Andrew, who has an unpaid role as the UK's special representative for trade and investment. The financially strapped Duchess appeared on the *Oprah Winfrey Show* to say how sorry she was.

So many members of William's family have been touched by gaffes and scandals that you could forgive Kate's family if they were the ones wondering about the suitability of the potential in-laws and their relatives. The Royal Family receives so much intense scrutiny that such embarrassments are almost inevitable. Barely a week goes by without Prince Harry making the pages of the papers for the wrong reasons. Kate enjoys a good relationship with Harry but he does seem to attract trouble.

His bond with William is, in some ways, similar to that of Kate and her sister. They have always had a healthy rivalry but are very close, showing a united front against the world. Harry said of his brother, 'He is the one person on this earth I can actually talk to about anything. We understand each other.' But whereas Pippa always seemed a step ahead of Kate as they grew up, Harry was a step behind William. It hasn't been easy for him growing up in William's shadow and being compared to his charismatic older brother.

One of the best things Diana ever did for her younger son was to insist that Harry be sent to Eton too, even though she was advised that it might be too tough for him academically. He was never the brightest of boys and there were fears that he would find it all too much. He battled through, although his two A levels – a B in art and a D in geography – ruled him out of following William to university. The shy, almost tragic figure who shuffled behind his mother's coffin was transformed by the time he left the school into a confident young hell-raiser.

Kate had only just started dating William when she had a taste of what is was like for the brothers if either of them put their head above the parapet and were noticed. Harry was just seventeen when he was alleged to have been ejected from the Rattlebone pub in Sherstone, Wiltshire, for allegedly calling the French bar manager a 'fucking frog'.

Harry has had to apologize a few times over the years since that first occasion over his teenage 'drug shame'. He had to say sorry again when he was photographed wearing a German army uniform with a swastika armband to a fancy dress party. Harry was universally criticized for his spectacular lack of judgement. Nobody seemed to notice that William was also there: his costume was only offensive to the eye – a black leotard with leopard skin paws and matching tail. Guy Pelly went too, dressed as the

Queen. They must have been a rare sight as they arrived at Harry Meade's birthday party.

William always seems to escape censure even though, at the age of twenty-two, he should have realized the questionable taste of Harry's costume. Perhaps they thought they were safe among friends and wouldn't be found out. After the story appeared in the *Sun*, Harry apologized through Clarence House 'if I have caused any offence'. Andrew Pierce in *The Times* noted that Charles was away at the time and wrote, 'No authority figure was present to remonstrate with Harry about his disastrously ill-judged choice of costume.'

At the party, which Kate didn't attend, William gave a speech in which he remarked on the tightness of his costume, which apparently revealed every contour of the crown jewels. He reportedly told guests 'I really should go and rearrange all this, shouldn't I?'

Harry is perceived as a naughty boy and William isn't. Trouble seems to follow Harry around, whether scuffling with paparazzi outside Boujis, or calling a fellow soldier 'my little Paki'; being filmed calling another a 'raghead' or telling the comedian Stephen K. Amos that 'he didn't sound like a black guy'. Following the last incident he was reportedly sent on a course in equality and diversity. Yet again Clarence House issued a statement saying Harry was 'sorry for his remarks.'

Harry is an interesting mix of exuberance and sensitivity. He thrived in the army, 'passing out' eight months before William, which caused great amusement because it meant that William would have to salute Harry if he passed him in a formal situation. Like William, Harry has a great love of Africa. After a trip to Lesotho in 2006, he founded his charity Sentebale, which translates as 'Forget me not' in the local dialect. He was visiting the country when he was asked to write down what his ambitions were. He responded, 'Professional surfer, wildlife photographer, helicopter pilot and live in Africa.'

Both the brothers have embraced 'Boujis Nights', a nightclub and drinking culture, and Harry has been an enthusiastic smoker since his teens. William seemed to turn over a new leaf after he decided his long-term future lay with Kate.

Harry and Chelsy haven't been so settled. She ditched him by changing her status on Facebook in early 2009. She hadn't been happy in Leeds and was eager to go home to South Africa for a while before starting her legal career. She had also reacted badly to Harry's decision to follow William and train as a helicopter pilot.

While their split lasted a lot longer than Kate and William's, they were also back together long before anyone realized. Neither has ever been in love with anybody else. A friend in Cape Town revealed, 'She would definitely marry him if he proposed.'

17

The Return of Catherine

William and Kate's future was becoming clearer. His training would continue until the middle of 2010, when he would become a fully qualified search and rescue pilot. That would be a good time to think about a wedding. Then he would be expected to spend at least three years in the job. Kate, meanwhile, needed to continue her own preparations for a royal life.

Kate was becoming increasingly aware that she needed to set the right example and, taking a leaf out of William's book, she wanted an inner circle of people she could trust – her court after she and William eventually married. While her mother and father were obviously vital, it was her sister Pippa who was becoming the second most important person in her day-to-day life.

Pippa had become, in effect, her unpaid social secretary, sorting through invitations and booking restaurants, particularly when William was in town and they wanted a discreet meal out. When she first moved to London, it was Kate who would go into a restaurant first and have a quick look round, decide which table was the best and make sure there were no lurking paparazzi before going back out to get William. Now it was Pippa who did her best to ensure their privacy.

Kate may have given up trying to find meaningful employment in London, but her sister was thriving. Pippa found work with Table Talk, an upmarket catering company. They planned weddings and engagement parties, and provided canapés for drinks receptions. Things had moved on a bit from cocktail sausages and pineapple and cheese on sticks. Table Talk promised to serve mouth-watering canapés on themed canapé trays or perspex canapé boxes filled with seasonal flowers. Pippa was a planner you could phone up and tell what sort of event you were holding and she would do the rest.

Pippa's personal stock was rising. *Tatler* magazine named her 'the number one Society Singleton' in its annual list of two hundred of the 'coolest kids in town' in 2008. She featured in the magazine's Little Black Book of the most important young people in English society: 'Catherine's lil sis, this perma-tanned Chelsea girl confines herself to uber-beefy toff types. Low maintenance, you'll find her working out at the council gym on Chelsea Manor Street. Goes to a lot of parties, but mainly as the caterer.' The accolade was not quite as impressive as it sounded – Pixie Geldof was number four and James Blunt was number eight.

The 'uber-beefy' men she was linked to included her old flatmate, George Percy, a Scottish aristocrat called Billy More Nisbitt, whose family own a stately home in Edinburgh, and diamond heir Simon Youngman. A friend cattily told the papers, 'Pippa seems to have a clear idea of what her ideal man must have – a house in town, a country estate, a title or at least be in line for one and, of course, he must be good looking.' Another more complimentary source observed, 'She's very sexy, exuberant and cheerful.'

Besides her job, Pippa was often seen at fundraisers and society parties – and not just as the caterer. She had certainly been quicker than Kate to establish a life for herself in London. She persuaded her parents to stump up £11,000 for her membership to The Queen's Club, the exclusive tennis venue in West

Kensington. Kate would join her for tennis matches as often as possible. One day William dropped them off and caught sight of the crest, QC, on the gates and joked that it stood for Queen Catherine.

At weekends Pippa would attend shooting parties in the country. She told the royal correspondent Katie Nicholl that she had shot twenty-three birds during one shoot in Scotland. She had some way to go, however, to match the expertise of Chelsy Davy, who was a crack shot. Kate was not so enthusiastic but she and William were photographed carrying dead pheasants after a shoot at Windsor. She was wearing what appeared to be a real fur hat. She was also seen on a shoot at Sandringham, carrying a gun alongside William and Harry. The League Against Cruel Sports was not impressed. A spokesman said, 'This is the young generation of royals and they're not sending out a good message. I feel sorry for Miss Middleton. We got the impression that she didn't like blood sports. The royals appear to use shooting as some sort of induction ceremony.'

Kate's brother James was also doing well and made *Tatler*'s Little Black Book. The magazine said, 'Catherine's little bro and embryonic business tycoon is storming the baking world with his Cake Kit company. His ambition in life: "To make baking a cake hassle-free as well as idiot proof". Not ashamed to wear a pinny and hairnet.' James formed the Cake Kit company after leaving Edinburgh University just one year into a course in environmental resources. He had been on a plane back from Scotland when the idea suddenly came to him to set up a business selling themed birthday cakes. He looked to have inherited his parents' entrepreneurial skills. He perfected a disposable cake tin that he distributed through Party Pieces. At one point there were rumours that Kate would join him in a new cake venture but this came to nothing more than some nice coverage for James's company. He received some less welcome publicity when the *Daily Mail* published a photograph of him at a party wearing a wraparound dress in black with white spots that was said to have been borrowed from Kate. Mostly he manages to keep a low profile, which is exactly how Kate prefers it.

Subtly, Kate started to become Catherine again. She now knew she would be Queen one day and accepted advice from Palace officials that Queen Kate might not sound regal enough. Princess Kate also sounded like a Disney character so it was decided that Catherine was the way forward. Her parents had always called her Catherine and they were in favour of her using the name they had chosen. Kate began using her full first name in emails and on correspondence.

There was still a year to go before William graduated as a fully fledged search and rescue pilot so there was time for people to get used to the new name before any official announcement of an engagement. Her family and her oldest friends from Marlborough and St Andrew's prep called her Catherine automatically, so no change was necessary for them. But since leaving school she had always introduced herself as Kate, so newer friends called her Kate, including William. He did so without thinking and would have to get used to having a Catherine as his girlfriend. Not everyone thought it was a good idea. Chelsy Davy, for one, was unimpressed and continued to call her Kate. A friend said, 'She thinks this Catherine thing is ridiculous.'

Kate will be the sixth Queen Catherine in England. The first was Catherine of Valois, who married King Henry V in 1420. She was queen for just two years before he died, leaving their nine-month-old son, Henry VI, on the throne. Her principal claim to fame came after her death, when her coffin in Westminster Abbey was accidently opened and her remains became a grisly tourist attraction until she was reburied by the Victorians. The next three Catherines were all married to Henry VIII. Catherine of Aragon was divorced by the king after failing to produce a son in twenty-four years of marriage; Catherine Howard was beheaded after Henry discovered her adultery; and Catherine Parr had just four years as queen before he died. She remarried a few months later but died herself shortly afterwards, probably in childbirth, aged thirty-six. The final Queen Catherine was Catherine of Braganza, a Portuguese Catholic who wasn't popular with the British public. She failed to produce an heir for Charles II and, instead, suffered the humiliation of him fathering many illegitimate children. Catherine Elizabeth Middleton will hope to fare a great deal better than her predecessors.

The future King William, meanwhile, was enjoying his initial training at RAF Shawbury in Shropshire. As was the normal practice for recruits, he started small, learning the controls of a single engine Squirrel before graduating to the larger Griffin helicopters and finally moving on to the bright yellow Sea Kings he would be flying in his new job. William travelled south to see Kate as often as he could but the course was particularly demanding and he was given no special treatment because of who he was. The RAF had insisted that he pass all stages of his course on merit, which was sensible considering that the prince would have responsibility for people's lives.

William decided to rent a house in the countryside near the base so he could spend more time with Kate and unwind from his exhausting schedule. While there, Kate was still able to work online, helping Party Pieces and planning her charity ventures. The arrangements were similar to their house near St Andrews because they would again be sharing – this time with Prince Harry. He was learning to fly Apache helicopters and had begun training at Shawbury a few months after William. The arrangement made sense as it meant that security for both princes could be concentrated in one manageable location.

After a quiet summer Kate and William travelled to London for another charity event that Kate had helped to arrange. With no fuss in the press, she had joined the committee of the Maggie and Rose Art for Starlight project. Professional artists were enlisted to help children create paintings, which were then sold off to raise funds for the Starlight charity, a cause that had so moved Kate.

She was persuaded to join the committee for this event by her old friend Rose Astor, one half of Maggie and Rose, a members' club for mothers and children in Kensington. Kate immediately enlisted the support of her family. Party Pieces provided all the bunting and decorations for the big children's party in the afternoon, when the paintings were on display. Kate turned up to join in the fun and make sure it went smoothly.

Then, at the evening event for 800 guests, she hosted a table for ten, including her mother, sister and William. Her father hosted a second table with the help of her brother. Carole did her bit at the auction too, bidding £8,000 to secure a skiing holiday. William applauded warmly when a partially blind little girl fulfilled her wish to be a pop star for the day. The eleven year old was introduced to William, who kissed her on the cheek before she did a little twirl to show off the new dress that had been bought for her during her special day. Kate wore a grey halter-necked Issa gown that literally flowed to the floor and revealed her maturing fashion sense. William and Kate are a very charismatic young couple on such occasions, which bodes well for a lifetime of royal events.

William's presence made the evening for Kate. She was always there to support him at polo, his military ceremonies and his own fundraisers so it meant a lot to her for him to return the compliment for once and be at her side. The grand total raised by the end of the night was more than £120,000. Afterwards Kate's 'gang' went off to celebrate at Raffles in the King's Road, where more friends joined them, including Prince Harry.

Kate's old student friend, Jules Knight, who became a member of the classical singing group Blake after leaving university, was concerned that Kate was losing touch with her friends from St Andrews. He told the *Daily Mail* that he had spoken to Kate and said it was a shame she hadn't been in contact with them: 'She said, "I know I've been really bad, I should contact them but it's been difficult because I've been really busy."'

The Queen's lawyers wrote to the newspapers in October 2009, warning them not to publish any paparazzi photographs of Kate and William, which immediately lit the blue touch paper to speculation over the prospect of an engagement announcement. That wasn't the plan, however. It was more likely that they were trying to put a degree of privacy in place so they could enjoy their time together in the quiet surroundings of Anglesey.

Paddy Harverson, Prince Charles's Communications Secretary, 'Members of the Royal Family have a right to privacy when they are going about everyday, private activities. They recognize there is a public interest in them and what they do but they do not think this extends to photographing the private activities of them or their friends.'

Reading between the lines, William and Kate didn't want an enterprising photographer, or even just somebody with a mobile phone, taking pictures of them shopping in the supermarket or eating fish and chips on the promenade.

Five weeks later the couple went their separate ways for Christmas. As usual William was at Sandringham, while the Middletons hired a Duchy of Cornwall house. They spent the holiday at the 500-year-old Restormel Manor in Cornwall, a mile from the village of Lostwithiel. The nine-bedroom property, with its own indoor heated swimming pool and tennis court, cost £3,000 to rent from the Duchy – money effectively bound for the wallet of Kate's prospective father-in-law, Prince Charles. Kate had once stayed there with William and their friends and remembered it when her family was trying to decide where to go for their festivities.

On Christmas Eve, Kate and Pippa braved the bracing December air to play their daily game of tennis. They loved to play whatever the weather and it was a good way of working off the seasonal calories. A photographer, Niraj Tanna, took shots of them from a footpath that bordered the court. He later insisted it was a public footpath. Subsequently, his pictures of them enjoying their game were distributed by Rex Features, the London-based photographic agency, which syndicated them overseas, where some were published. Kate was apparently concerned that the photographer might also have taken pictures of her family enjoying their Christmas lunch the next day – something Niraj denied doing. She told William what had happened when they met up for New Year at Birkhall, their favourite venue for Hogmanay. He was immediately on the case, keen to ensure this sort of thing didn't become common practice in the future. Legal letters were sent by Prince Charles's lawyers, Harbottle & Lewis, who acted for Kate in the matter. Rex apologized and paid Kate an estimated £10,000 in damages as well as substantial legal costs.

The agency stated on its website: 'Although at the time Rex Features did not know that an infringement of privacy had occurred, we now accept that this was the case and that by distributing the photographs we were party to that invasion of privacy. Accordingly we have agreed to pay compensation to Ms Middleton and have undertaken not to syndicate any further private photographs of her. We apologize to Ms Middleton for what has taken place.'

It was an excellent result for Kate, who decided to donate the money to charity. The photographer told the *Guardian*'s Roy Greenslade, 'Under no circumstances did I harass her. She even wished me Merry Christmas on the day.'

The upshot was that the couple could feel more confident about being left alone after they moved to Anglesey in the spring of 2010. William had to complete the last six months of his training at RAF Valley, where he had been so inspired on his gap year. This time he wasn't just observing – it was the real deal.

Intriguingly, William was cramming the last eight months of his training into six, suggesting there might be plans in the offing that would be time consuming later in the year. Before they left, there was time for a week's holiday with Kate's family at Courcheval in France. William is clearly at ease with the Middletons and was heard sharing a running joke over dinner with Michael Middleton. 'Yes, Dad' he would say at every opportunity, much to everyone's amusement. Ski instructor Meret Visser, dining at a nearby table, observed, 'William was clearly very close to Kate's father. William and Kate looked like a honeymoon couple. He held her hand under the table, stroked her hair and kissed her cheek.'

Hello! carried pictures of the trip, which they trailed on the front cover of the magazine. In one of them, Kate is seen using her hand to hide her face from photographers – something she was doing with more frequency. She couldn't do that when she rode pillion on the back of a snowmobile: William was going so fast, she had to hang on for dear life.

Anglesey is a beautiful rugged island off the coast of North Wales. You can drive there by crossing one of the two bridges that span the Menai Strait. The locals like to think they have a separate identity to the rest of Wales. In wintertime Anglesey can be a bleak, god-forsaken place where the paradise islands of the Caribbean and the Indian Ocean must seem a million miles away. But in summer, when the traditionally awful British weather clears, it's a lovely spot and you can dream of owning one of the tiny islands scattered about it in the Irish Sea.

Kate loved it. She may have become more accustomed to topping up her tan on Mustique but she had never forgotten her childhood trips to Snowdonia, where she discovered a lifelong enjoyment of walking in Britain. William shared that enthusiasm and, on his days off, would seize the opportunity to explore the North Wales countryside, where nobody bothered them. Snowdonia itself was only twenty miles away. While there were undoubted similarities with their early days in St Andrews, William had at least upgraded his transport: Kate could hop on the back of his red and white 180 mph Ducati superbike to speed along the remote country lanes.

When the weather warmed up, they could swim in the sea or enjoy some waterskiing or sailing. William was overheard enthusiastically describing these attractions when he visited St Dunstan's, a charity for blind ex-servicemen in Llandudno. He was 'genuinely keen' according to an eyewitness.

Kate could see Snowdonia every morning, dominating the view from the house, which was very secluded and even had its own private beach for romantic evening strolls. The location of the house was kept a closely guarded secret for security reasons, which suited Kate. She much preferred the view of the mountains to that of a group of paparazzi outside her bedroom window. The one drawback was the level of protection they required. Some reports suggested that a special unit of fifteen local police officers was needed to keep the couple safe. This provoked some controversy when it was revealed the cost might be as much as £1.4 million a year.

It was a reminder of what Kate would face in the future. More immediately, though, she could enjoy what was, in effect, married life in all but name. The months in Anglesey were the closest she would ever to get to the normal married life the majority of couples enjoy. There wasn't actually much to do but she wasn't cut off from the outside world thanks to the Internet.

Shopping was a little trickier. The nearest major centre for upmarket boutiques and designer labels was Chester, a good hour and a half's drive away, so Kate preferred to wait for her next trip to London to browse in her favourite stores. For everyday things, however, 'Mrs Wales' was seen shopping at Morrison's and Argos in the town of Holyhead, the port for the ferry crossing to Dublin. Sometimes she would shop for groceries in the nearer Blaenau Ffestiniog. On one occasion when William was with her she had to queue up to pay. Someone managed to take a picture of her shopping basket, which revealed they would be eating pizza, chips and salad that night.

Janet Street-Porter wrote in the *Daily Mail*, 'Kate Middleton has discovered one of life's basic truths – go shopping for food with a bloke and you'll find he's "forgotten" his wallet.'

In the evenings when William was home they could pop in to the White Eagle at Rhoscolyn, where William would have a pint and Kate would choose a glass of white wine or sparkling water. If they were eating out that night, William favoured the pub's home-made burger and chips while Kate went for fish or a salad. One of the bar staff observed, 'They're just like any other young couple until you realize there are armed bodyguards at the next table.' Kate has become so used to their presence over the years that she barely notices they are there.

Kate travelled home to Bucklebury if William was going to be on duty for an extended period but mainly she was taking the chance to enjoy the peace and quiet of Anglesey. William finally qualified as a search and rescue pilot in September. This time there was no grand Passing Out Parade but a quiet ceremony at RAF Valley, where he joined six other trainees to receive his badge and certificate. His commanding officer, Wing Commander Peter Lloyd, told the men: 'You are exposed to your weaknesses and therefore have to adapt to them. There is nowhere to hide in a helicopter.'

William had completed seventy hours of live flying and a further fifty hours' simulator work during his twenty months. It was more than five years since he had left St Andrews and, at last, he could start the job for which he had been so well trained. He was joining 22 Squadron as a co-pilot on an RAF Sea King on a three-year posting. This would be dangerous work. He would be on call twenty-four hours a day to rescue people in the most hostile conditions.

But before he reported for duty, he had decided to take Kate away for a secret trip to Kenya. It would change her life forever.

18

A Royal Engagement

Before they left for their African holiday, William slipped an important small box into his rucksack; it contained his mother's engagement ring. If all went to plan, he would need it in a few days.

He was taking Kate back to Kenya, a place that had first touched his heart as a schoolboy and he had visited many times since. Kate now shared his love for the country he once described as a 'second home'. They stayed with the Craigs in their beautiful house at Lewa Downs, spending their days driving around the estate, watching the elephants and, of course, the rhinos. Some friends flew up from South Africa to join them and the party of four would go off on wildlife expeditions. They took a thirty-minute flight to a tented camp called Sarara, where they tracked a leopard unsuccessfully.

William asked Ian Craig if he could arrange an overnight trip as the next stage of his plan. William flew by helicopter to the remote Rutundu Log Cabins, where he had booked himself and Kate in for the night. Two cabins are available to rent 10,000 feet up the northern slopes of Mount Kenya with views over Lake Rutundu.

The cabin was pretty basic but perfectly formed. All the floors were polished wooden planks with some sheepskin rugs thrown over them. The days were spectacular, clear and sunny, with inspiring views over the rugged moorland slopes. It's a bit like an Alpine landscape in summer or even the Scottish Highlands that William knew so well. The nights, however, were cool with open fires burning to protect guests from the chill mountain air.

William had stayed at the cabin before but this was the first time for Kate. He knew they wouldn't see another person – and no paparazzi – in such a secluded spot. After they had unpacked the few things they needed for their overnight stay, they went fishing for rainbow trout on beautiful Lake Rutundu but by all accounts didn't catch their supper. In the early evening they returned to the cabin. William checked that the champagne he had brought was cooling nicely before they watched the sun setting. And there, gazing at the most wonderful of views, he proposed. Neither of them has revealed if he went down on one knee.

They had talked of marriage many times but that didn't make it any less of a surprise for Kate when the moment came. She admitted that the timing had been completely unexpected: 'It was a total shock when it came and I was very excited.' In their official engagement interview, William recalled that he had planned it to show his romantic side. Kate laughed, 'There's a true romantic in there.' He had been concerned at the horror stories of proposals going 'horribly wrong', so he was delighted it went so well.

William had remembered to take the ring from his rucksack. Kate thought it was 'beautiful'. It featured fourteen solitaire diamonds clustered around an impressive twelve-carat sapphire. The world would soon recognize it because Diana had flashed it modestly at her engagement announcement. William couldn't have revealed his true feelings about Diana more poignantly: 'My mother's not going to be around to share any of the fun – this was my way of keeping her close.' Kate realized the significance of the gesture as she admired the famous ring on the cabin's veranda.

Afterwards they toasted their future with the champagne. They lit candles as darkness fell, because the cabin had no electricity, and ate a dinner prepared by the cabin's staff, who then left the couple alone to enjoy their moment. They talked into the night before it was time to stumble off to the wooden four-poster bed.

They both wrote messages in the visitors' book the next morning, 21 October 2010. Kate put: 'Thank you for such a wonderful twenty-four hours! Sadly no fish to be found but we had great fun trying! I love the warm fires and candle lights – so romantic! Hope to be back again soon, Catherine Middleton.' William echoed that sentiment: 'Such fun to be back! Brought more warm clothes this time. Looked after so well, thank you guys! Look forward to next time soon, I hope.'

After nine years together, Kate finally had a ring on her finger, although she had to take it off for the journey home – it was too soon to let the world know her happiness. The first thing William had to do was tell Kate's father the news. He hadn't gone down the traditional route of seeking Michael's permission to ask Kate for her hand in marriage. He explained, 'I was torn between asking Kate's dad first and then the realization that he might actually say "No" dawned on me. So I thought if I ask Kate first then he can't really say no. So I did it that way round.' Carole Middleton, when she heard the news, was 'absolutely over the moon', said Kate.

Michael Middleton had some concerns about the pressure Kate would now be under but over the years he had seen for himself how protective William was of her. William was able to reassure him that he would do all he could to ensure the Middleton family would be able to live their lives normally. It was time to make plans for telling everyone. The Queen and Prince Charles were told first, of course, and were delighted for William.

Just when Kate was gearing herself up to tell the rest of the world, fate unhappily stepped in and her grandfather, Peter Middleton, died at his home in the village of Vernham Dean, Hampshire, on 2 November. He was ninety. Kate's other grandfather, Ron Goldsmith, had died in 2003, so Peter had been the last surviving grandparent. Sadly, none of them would experience the pride of seeing Kate walk up the aisle. The whole Middleton family, including Kate, was very upset and not in the mood to look cheerful for the cameras. Kate also didn't fancy agreeing to any wedding arrangements while she was helping her parents organize the funeral, which took place quietly at a church near his home. It was only after the funeral had taken place, on Friday, 12 November, that she thought it appropriate to reveal her own happier news.

The formal announcement was made on the British Monarchy Twitter page on Tuesday, 16 November 2010. It tweeted: 'The Prince of Wales is delighted to announce the engagement of Prince William to Miss Catherine Middleton.' Simultaneously Clarence House released a fuller statement confirming that the proposal had been in Kenya and the Queen had been told. It also revealed that the arrangements were up in the air: 'The wedding will take place in the spring or summer of 2011 in London. Further details about the wedding day will be announced in due course.'

Extraordinarily for such a big announcement, it seemed rather a botched job. Nobody explained why the 'further details', including when and where it would take place, had yet to be decided. It was five weeks since the proposal so one might have expected the church and the date to be sorted at the very least. A royal source observed, 'The wedding announcement was hasty and bungled. They didn't know on the day where it was going to be. Well, why not?'

The only people who did seem in control of the situation were the three well-dressed men who had gone into a Ladbrokes betting shop to forecast correctly that the wedding announcement would be in November. The bet had been placed in the betting office nearest to Sandringham in Norfolk, which added to the suspicion of a royal leak.

Several reasons may have contributed to what appeared to be a rushed announcement – all the more ironic considering how long William and Kate had been planning to get married. The first theory is that they weren't being allowed the wedding they wanted and had to make changes; secondly, they didn't want to lose control of the media on the day and were paranoid the news would get out and bedlam would ensue; and thirdly, that nobody was going to feel particularly joyful at the couple's news when the government cuts began to bite so they brought the date forward.

The wedding arrangements were put to the back of Kate's mind as she faced her first ordeal as Prince William's fiancée – a day in front of the cameras. Kate chose to wear the now famous deep blue Issa dress, which cost £399, and proudly paraded her engagement ring, sparkling on the third finger of her left hand.

The first task of the day was the engagement interview. The couple had chosen the ITN political editor Tom Bradby to conduct proceedings. He was one of the very few genuine friends that William and Kate had in the media. He met them socially from time to time and would occasionally have a drink and a chat but, as he admitted, 'I'm not over at their house all the time.' Kate was also friendly with Tom's wife Claudia, who has a jewellery design business, and the couple specifically asked for him to conduct the interview.

Tom, who comes from a military background and is also an acclaimed writer of historical thrillers, had shown himself to be entirely trustworthy over the years, which counted for a great deal with William. He had reportedly been the person who sparked the police investigation into phone hacking in early 2007, which eventually led to the jailing of *News of the World* royal correspondent Clive Goodman. Tom had apparently become suspicious after a story about him lending William some broad-casting equipment appeared in the paper containing information that only he, the prince and two other people had known about. It led to fears that William's phone voice mail messages had been intercepted. In some respects, the engagement was a reward for Tom's discretion about it all.

They settled into comfortable chairs in a private room in St James's Palace while the camera crew set up an interview that would be shown to millions around the world and would be the first time many people heard Kate speak. Tom was anxious to keep everything as calm as possible: 'I told them beforehand that I had to ask them some things and we had to go into particular areas, but I told them that my main aim was not to mess up their happy day.'

The principal concern was to avoid any chance of the notorious remark of Prince Charles during the interview marking his engagement to Diana. Anthony Carthew of ITN asked them how they felt, then asked, 'And, I suppose – in love?'. Diana enthused, 'Of course!' before Charles said, 'Whatever "in love" means.' Tom explained, 'I was very anxious not to have anything like that.' He admitted that Kate was a 'bit nervous' but pretty composed under the circumstances.

The interview, which was broadcast that night, confirmed that William had wanted to finish his flying training before pressing on with the engagement. He said, 'I couldn't have done this if I was still doing that.' Despite the rather stilted nature of the conversation, the couple were refreshingly open about their relationship and didn't mind chatting about their brief split and about the public criticism that Kate didn't have a job. She said she had worked very hard for her parents' company.

William, who referred to his fiancée as Kate throughout, was amusing when he spoke of the difficulties of keeping their engagement news a secret: 'We're like sort of ducks, very calm on the surface with little feet going under the water.' William does have a good sense of humour about things – it helps him get through what must sometimes seem an absurd life. Tom Bradby observes the many sides to his friend's personality: 'He has a potential career as a comedian. He loves to crack jokes all the time. He's also an extremely focused individual and is determined to live his life his way. He's got lots of sides to him'.

After the relative cosiness of her television interview, Kate had to face the press. By this time – late afternoon – the whole world knew that she was going to be a princess. After a quick check of her hair and make-up, she made her way through the corridors to the splendid and historic Entrée Room at the Palace for a cup of tea with the specially selected reporters and photographers assembled for the photocall. It was all very civilized. The huge room is opulently carpeted and wall papered in deep red with royal portraits on the wall. It couldn't have made a sharper contrast with the Kenyan log cabin, where William had proposed.

Then it was time for the cameras to start flashing. Kate was completely unaccustomed to something like this, although the constant use of flash lights was something she knew all about from her paparazzi pursuers. She also didn't have to worry about being asked any difficult questions – nobody was going to do that at such an upbeat occasion. Kate appeared poised, and revealed the remarkable self-control she has always had. She had obviously had some coaching from Clarence House staff in how to handle the occasion. The two important pieces of advice were: think before you speak and, if in doubt, look to William to jump in. Judy Wade of *Hello!* observed, 'She kept turning to William for guidance throughout. She hesitated occasionally as if to say the right thing but she handled it beautifully.'

Kate will not be enduring days like this too often in the future. She didn't give much away but did manage one revealing observation, 'Over the years William has looked after me. He's treated me very well, as the loving boyfriend he is, he is very supportive of me through the good times and the bad times.'

Meanwhile, other key players in the story were giving their reaction. Kate's father Michael Middleton spoke publicly for the first time since he had denied the relationship in 2003. Then he said he and his wife were very amused at the thought of being in-laws to Prince William. He may not have been laughing now but he looked pleased as punch next to his wife, Carole, who was positively beaming when they faced the cameras in the garden of their home in Bucklebury. Michael said, 'Catherine and Prince William have been going out for a number of years, which has been great for us because we have got to know William very well. We all think he is wonderful and we are extremely fond of him. They make a lovely couple, they are great fun to be with, and we've had a lot of laughs together.' Neither he nor his wife is likely to make any more statements about their daughter or son-in-law.

William's family was in high spirits – as if the news had lifted a cloud. The Queen said she was 'absolutely delighted', while Prince Charles was in jokey good humour when he visited the Poundbury model village in Dorset. He told one well-wisher, 'They've been practising long enough', before confiding to another, 'It makes me feel very old.' Prince Harry simply said, 'It means I get a sister, which I have always wanted.' The Prime Minister, David Cameron, described the announcement as 'a great day for our country', which was perhaps a little extravagant.

All that remained for Kate on this momentous day was to go back to Clarence House for a celebratory drink and watch herself on the telly. Then it would be a case of waiting to see what the morning papers had to say. They didn't disappoint and had clearly been prepared for the announcement for years. Page upon page covered the news from every possible angle. One aspect of the story dominated – the ring gave the press the opportunity to bring Diana's name to the front of the story.

'Sealed With Diana's Ring' said the *Daily Express* headline while the *Daily Mirror* proclaimed, 'With this ring, Di thee wed'. The *Sun* said, 'With Mummy's ring I thee wed'.

Presenting Kate with Diana's ring was a lovely tribute to his mother. As William explained, 'It's very special to me and Kate is very special to me – and it's only right the two are put together.' Prince Charles apparently knew that William wanted to give Kate the ring and had given his approval. He had originally bought it from the royal jeweller Garrard of Mayfair for £28,000 in February 1981. The cost today would probably be about £85,000. Unusually for a royal ring, it hadn't been custom made and anyone off the street could have chosen the same one if they could afford it. Now its history made it priceless. Willie Hamilton, the chief executive of the Company of Master Jewellers, observed, 'You can't put a price on Princess Diana's ring.' Willie had unwittingly gone to the heart of the matter – it was Diana's ring even though Kate was now wearing it. Quite simply, through William's fine and poignant intentions, Diana had hijacked the engagement announcement from beyond the grave.

Opinion was divided as to whether the ring weighed too heavily on Kate's finger or not. While Willie noted that the ring had 'meaning and continuity', Miranda Sawyer of the *Daily Mirror* thought the 'unlucky rock' was a 'symbol of Diana's rotten marriage'. She added, 'Over the past eight years, Kate has tried hard not to be like Diana – keeping out of the public eye, being discreet, unflirtatious, realistic. And then on the day of the engagement she was compared to no one else but her, Why? Because of that ring.'

The royal author Christopher Wilson commented, 'It is an incredibly heavy burden for Kate. The ring must weight ten tons on Kate's finger and it will continue. Kate is carrying the Diana legend around with her in the presence of that ring.'

Kate's only public comment on Diana had been during her television interview when she said, 'I would have loved to have met her, and she's obviously an inspirational woman to look up to.' William added, 'No one is trying to fill my mother's shoes.'

Having exhausted the ring story, the press could spend the next week speculating on the time and place of the wedding. Nobody really had a clue about the date, although they needed to find the best one to fit in the public holiday that had been announced. The venue was easier – a straight decision between St Paul's Cathedral and Westminster Abbey. Charles and Diana had married at St Paul's so the Abbey was an odds-on favourite, even though William's mother's funeral was held there. It was, in any case, slightly smaller, more manageable and nearer to Buckingham Palace, which would make a few savings on the day.

When Kate was seen the next evening having a private tour of the Abbey with her mother and father, it was considered a thumbs-up to the venue. She still had to speak to William about it because he had dashed back to Anglesey for his next shift at RAF Valley. They made their final decision at the weekend and discussed the various date options they had been given. In the end, Friday, 29 April was chosen as William and Kate's big day.

19

Dressed for Success

Within a week of Kate wearing her sapphire blue wraparound Issa dress for the engagement announcement, Tesco had launched their own version. It cost an affordable £16 – about £380 less than Kate had paid for hers. It sold out online within one hour. The supermarket wasn't alone in cashing in on the surge of interest in the royal bride-to-be. The High Street chain Peacocks managed to produce their variation for £14 and set up an online waiting list under the banner 'Waity Katie'. It wasn't just the dress that was being copied; cut-price 'Diana' engagement rings also flooded the marketplace. The jeweller H. Samuel was selling theirs for £179, and Debenhams had one for £6 – their fastest-selling piece of jewellery ever.

It was the start of the Kate effect: everything she wears, including her accessories and make-up, is now subject to intense scrutiny and can start a trend the moment the first photograph or TV clip is shown. Kate was canny in that for her first big day of public exposure she had chosen such a pretty and unfussy dress but to have it described as 'iconic' was overstating it. Quite honestly, as far as much of the media is concerned, Kate could wear a sack and still be praised to the skies for her fashion sense.

The engagement dress was never going to set the fashion world on fire. Alison Jane Reid, the former *Times* fashion writer who has studied Kate's changing style, observes, 'It was pretty but a safe option. I would like to have seen her being a little bit braver and adventurous. It was very elegant, sexy and restrained but I would have preferred her in a couture piece at that point to separate her old life from the life she is about to have. It would have been great to see her support a really hot British designer like Alice Temperley, Henrietta Ludgate or Emma Burton at Alexander McQueen.'

In the world of fashion the Issa dress looks quite chic but is self-evidently off the peg. Kate had bought it in Fenwick in Bond Street. The best thing about it was its simple design that many could imitate. Alison Jane explains, 'Many women could have a piece of Kate's style for a fraction of the cost of the original dress. I think that's empowering. It's fantastic that a woman who doesn't have £400, which is a lot of money for most of the population, can get a pretty good copy.'

If she didn't know it before, then Kate knew now that the first thing people would notice was her outfit no matter what she was doing. Everybody was falling over themselves to comment on Kate's style when she didn't really have one yet. Dame Vivienne Westwood, probably the most famous name in British fashion, summed it up, a little bluntly: 'I would have loved to have dressed Kate Middleton but I have to wait until she kind of catches up a bit somewhere with style.'

For a young woman not used to courting fame or self-serving publicity this must have been upsetting, especially as every single thing about her would be subject to such intense scrutiny. Joanna Lumley thought that Kate needed a 'fleet of stylists' to help her. That may have been interpreted as a barbed comment from the popular actress but she also more tactfully suggested that Kate needed to be vigilant or the 'fashion assassins' would start critiquing her every look.

Kate seemed to take this advice on board. She needed to

establish her fashion sense quickly and, sensibly, was reported to be seeking advice from the senior executives at *Vogue*, including the editor Alexandra Shulman and her deputy Emily Sheffield, who is the sister of Samantha Cameron and had also been a pupil at Marlborough College. Mario Testino, too, is one of *Vogue*'s principal photographers and had years of experience to pass on to Kate. She already had a fabulous glossy mane of hair, a slender frame and legs to die for but she lacked a proper fashion role model.

When she was younger, Kate loved the Kate Moss look and had the height to carry off some of the supermodel's frivolity, such as the sparkly shift mini dress she wore on a night out to Mahiki. But falling out of nightclubs in a short skirt isn't something she can continue to do as a princess. Nor will she be able to flash a bare midriff in the back of a cab any more. As Alison Jane Reid observes, 'She will have to save those outfits for private holidays.' Kate in her twenties also had an alarming knack of wearing outfits that made her look older than she was, most noticeably on her annual trips to Cheltenham Races, where she always seemed to favour deeply old-fashioned frumpy tweeds.

Her outfits were a bit hit-and-miss but certainly not all bad. The first wedding she went to with William, Rose Astor's in 2005, was a success. The giveaway that the cream jacket was off the peg was the way it pinched underneath the bust – a couture coat specially made for Kate wouldn't have done that. She looked beautiful in a cream coat and dress at Laura Parker Bowles's wedding in 2006, which *Hello!* fashion editor Francesca Fearon thought 'ticked all the boxes'.

Kate's early fashion problem was that she seemed in limbo, not wanting to make too much of a statement. She couldn't very easily move from Topshop to fashion icon without attracting a barrage of criticism that she was getting above herself. If she had bust the budget when she was merely William's jobless girlfriend, she would have been accused of cashing in and being a sort of upmarket WAG. Alison Jane Reid explains, 'She didn't have a role so she had to be careful not to be seen to be flaunting extremely rare couture pieces at that point. I think that would have been very tricky and disastrous.'

She had to play safe with outfits that suited her slender figure but that other young women could find in their favourite High Street stores. At the time, though, she wasn't being scrutinized so intensely. Shopping was something she enjoyed but overnight her fashion and her style had become a responsibility and she had to take it more seriously. Whether she likes it or not, she is going to be an unofficial ambassador for fashion, which is worth millions to the British economy. She has a duty of care to British designers.

Another woman in the spotlight having to deal with that kind of attention is the Prime Minister's wife, Samantha Cameron. She is a millionairess and can afford anything she likes but is careful to mix designer pieces with High Street. 'She doesn't want to be elitist,' explains Alison Jane.

Kate would do well to study the first ladies of other countries rather than follow the rather staid fashion of Princess Anne or Sophie Wessex. In the US, Michelle Obama has put vintage back on the map but perhaps the role model Kate could best follow is the President of France's wife, the former model Carla Bruni-Sarkozy. Like Kate, she is a willowy brunette and almost impossibly chic.

It's too soon to form a strong idea of how Kate's fashion will develop but her first outings after the engagement provided some pointers. She played it safe for the official engagement pictures. For the first photograph, Kate wore a cream chiffon blouse costing £95 from Whistles. In the second photograph, William was in a smart dark suit and Kate had chosen a simple £159 white dress from Reiss, one of the more expensive High Street chains. Unsurprisingly, Whistles and Reiss fell over themselves in rushing Kate's choices back on to the shelves of their stores. Apparently, the couple wanted to wear things that they already had hanging in their wardrobes and refused the offer of a stylist for the day, with Kate preferring to do her own make-up.

Again the spectre of Diana reached out to touch Kate. This time it wasn't just the ring that created associations with the late Princess of Wales but the choice of the photographer, Mario Testino. He had taken what was widely described as an 'iconic shoot' for *Vanity Fair* magazine, published just a month before Diana's death. The photographer had succeeded in catching Diana's natural beauty, so much so that both William and Harry said the photos were the 'most like her they had seen'.

As a result of that favourable impression, Testino had taken the twenty-first birthday portraits of both princes, as well as photographing Charles and Camilla on their first wedding anniversary. He was obviously a sound choice to capture Kate and William's happiness but, having said that, there are many photographers in the world and he was the one most closely identified with Princess Diana. At the photo shoot at St James's Palace, William joked in his usual self-deprecating way that he had chosen Testino because he was 'the only person who could make a moose look good.'

The two official pictures were stunning and revealed Kate and William to have the most perfect white teeth. They looked very much in love, which was the main thing. Testino observed, 'I have never felt so much joy as when I see them together.' He also praised Kate's 'natural grace' and 'open personality'.

In one photograph, William has a protective arm around Kate while she shows off her ring for the camera. The picture creates a great sense of love and happiness. Inevitably, comparisons were drawn with the engagement pose of Charles and Diana, which was taken by Lord Snowdon, William's great-uncle. In that famous picture, Diana is behind Charles with her arm around him. Charles has his arms folded and is generating zero warmth towards his future wife. Psychoanalysts could, with the benefit of hindsight, draw obvious conclusions from the imagery; the Testino photograph, however, would prompt them to comment on the togetherness of the couple. Even in the more formal photograph, William and Kate are clearly a partnership. It is not an act for the camera.

Kate continued her promising start when she stepped out in public for the first time as a royal fiancée at the Teenage Cancer Trust Gala evening, when she wore a cream and black silk Titan dress by Alice Temperley, the British designer much loved by the 'boho chic' set. The dress, with a trademark Temperley embellished neckline and worn with a simple black jacket, was just about the most elegant thing Kate had ever worn. It was the sort of dress one could imagine being worn by Sienna Miller, a fan of Temperley's creations. Alison Jane observes, 'Her clothes are beautifully finished and she could only be a British designer. She is renowned for her luxurious and quirky detailing.'

William was actually the guest of honour at the gala in the village of Thursford in Norfolk, which was raising funds for the first specialist cancer unit for young people at the renowned Addenbrooke's Hospital in Cambridge. After the show, Kate and William showed a genuine interest in the young cancer patients, who told them they were often put in wards alongside old people or babies when they were being treated.

The event, which raised £35,000, was a good, low-key start for Kate and an early indication that she could connect with the general public. Charities will be forming an orderly queue in the future to try to win her patronage. After events like this, William was lucky that he could disappear back to the wilds of Anglesey to continue his day job without worrying about his next outfit or how it might be judged by the press.

Now that he was fully qualified, his work was demanding. He had to contend with ferocious crosswinds while piloting his yellow Sea King helicopter to rescue a climber 3,000 feet up on Snowdon who had been stricken with a heart attack. When the victim found out he had been rescued by Prince William and his crew, he said simply, 'Tell him thank you. If it wasn't for him and his crew, I'd be dead.'

William was in noticeably good spirits after the engagement announcement. It was as if a weight had been lifted from his shoulders. He was spotted laughing and joking with his mates on a stag weekend to Blackpool. They hired a private box at Blackpool football club and watched the team beat Premiership rivals Wolves. The one small cloud on his horizon was that he would have to work over Christmas.

Traditionally the single officers volunteered to work so their colleagues with children could enjoy time with their families. It meant William and Kate would be apart yet again on Christmas Day, although it gave her the chance to have one last traditional celebration with her family in Bucklebury before a lifetime of royal festivities began. William had Christmas lunch in the canteen at RAF Valley, where he drank orange juice and wore his flight suit in case his crew was scrambled for an emergency.

Kate was in front of the fire in the sitting room at home as her family toasted her future. Like millions of families, they could slob around on the day, watching television and opening presents while the turkey roasted, and perhaps venture out for a walk to work up an appetite. It would be the last time she would be able to enjoy such informality.

When she finally spends Christmas at Sandringham, Kate will be issued with a timetable and room plan when she arrives. This will have been worked out by the Master of the Household, just one of the numerous royal staff who will loom large in Kate's life in the coming years. Everything that happens is done in exactly the same way each year and is based entirely on protocol.

William and Kate, for instance, will be expected to arrive second to last, as protocol dictates that you arrive in reverse order of seniority – the further down the line of royal succession you are, the earliest you roll up. Princess Anne, who has slipped down from third at birth to tenth now, is usually the first to arrive. Charles, first in line, arrives last and gets the best room.

Gifts are always exchanged on Christmas Eve, a German tradition. They must not cost too much and should be jokey. Princess Anne one year chose the star gift when she gave Charles a leather toilet seat, which apparently remains a prized possession.

On Christmas morning the family all brave the elements to attend a morning service at the local church, St Mary Magdalene. They then return to Sandringham for Christmas lunch before, rather sweetly, everything stops so that family and staff can watch the Queen's Christmas broadcast.

Christmas night with the royals is a formal affair, with the men in black tie and the women in evening dresses. The Queen likes to play games – charades is the most popular. Nobody is allowed to leave until the Queen herself decides to call it a night even if they had overindulged and just wanted to go to sleep. The Queen is very set in her ways and Kate will have to conform: there is no choice in the matter. Only once William becomes king, and not before, will she have the chance to do things her way.

Kate's last wedding before her own was on her twenty-ninth birthday, 9 January 2011. It may not have been her big day but at least she could spend it in William's company. He was an usher at the wedding of his old friend from Eton, Harry Aubrey-Fletcher, who was marrying Louise Stourton in a village near Harrogate in Yorkshire.

Some of the VIP guests, including Kate, arrived at the church in a black Routemaster bus with 'Wedding Party' on the front. Kate could be seen laughing merrily with Holly Branson as the bus pulled up. It would have been a brilliant choice for her own wedding – boosting London as a unique tourist destination. William, meanwhile, had nipped across the road for a swift pint and some cottage pie with Prince Harry and the other ushers and scuttled hastily back to the church when he saw the bus pull up so that he could help show everyone to their seats.

Kate wore black. Her outfit was pored over in forensic detail by the media. She had chosen a tailored velvet dress coat by the designer Libélula held together by a pretty silver clasp. The plunging neckline of the coat revealed an adventurous amount of cleavage courtesy of a favourite black silk Issa dress underneath, but the most eye-catching element was the elaborate felt beret from established British milliners Whiteley Fischer perched jauntily on her head.

Hats are particularly fashionable at the moment. Peter Whiteley, director of the family firm, said, 'Once someone like Kate starts wearing them, I'm sure more people will follow.' For perhaps the first time Kate was showing how her own fashion taste and personality could come to the fore in the future. She loves hats and fascinators. Alison Jane Reid observes, 'Kate has a perfectly symmetrical face so she looks wonderful in hats. She can really carry them off and that will give her confidence.'

The one slight shadow cast over the outfit was that Kate was starting to look decidedly thinner. The commentators called it 'wedding slim', merely a good, healthy result of a couple of months spent getting in shape for her own wedding. Nobody at this stage was suggesting that Kate was 'wedding thin' or 'wedding skin and bones'.

All the Middleton women were said to be dieting frantically, with Carole favouring the popular Dukan regime. It's a protein-based diet and bans most carbohydrates. Carole apparently lost four pounds surviving on cottage cheese and prawns. It sounded distinctly faddy and according to the *Daily Mail* had been condemned as a 'health hazard'. Hopefully Kate has not been persuaded to follow suit.

Just when the fashion portents looked promising for Kate, she completely mucked it up when she went for an 'engagement lunch' with her future stepmother-in-law on 24 February. She wore a short tan jacket over a stripy patterned dress, black tights and a pair of black boots. Her outfit seemed to be in two parts. Alison Jane Reid observes, 'I didn't like it at all. It was a uniform – the sort of thing you would wear if you were a New York lady who lunches – that didn't say anything about her personality. And she was wearing far too much black eyeliner, which actually makes her look ill.'

Camilla hosted the small get-together, which included her daughter Laura and Kate's sister Pippa, at Koffmann's in the Berkeley Hotel, Knightsbridge, one of the best restaurants in London. Lunch lasted three hours and much was made of Camilla giving Kate some advice about married life as a royal. In fact, it was just four women enjoying a good gossip over a long lunch with wine. Being within full view of other diners meant it wasn't the place for a few well-chosen quiet words.

Instead the women chatted and laughed together as if they were all the best of friends and did this sort of thing every week. In case there were any doubts about how Kate and Camilla got on, this was just the occasion to banish them. If it had been suggested by the master strategists of Clarence House, then it was another example of how astutely Paddy Harverson and his sidekick Miguel Head were conducting the Kate publicity campaign in the run-up to the wedding.

Amusingly, and quite realistically, a fellow diner commented that all four women seemed to be talking at once and the poor waiters couldn't get a word in. One diner apparently heard Kate ask, 'What happens if William doesn't turn up?', which resulted in giggles all round. They also had a laugh discussing the wedding 'buffet', with Kate, tongue in cheek, suggesting mini pizzas and Camilla adding that sausages on sticks were always acceptable. One of the things not generally known about the publicity shy Duchess of Cornwall is that by all accounts she has a great sense of humour and is genuinely very witty.

Camilla was never an aristocrat although she was brought up as a society girl. She enjoys smoking – although always trying to give up – and a nice glass of red and she knows how to keep a notoriously touchy royal happy. She makes no pretensions about working out but dresses smartly for a 63-year-old woman.

Kate's ease in Camilla's company begs the question of how the new princess would have got on with Diana if the latter were still alive. Diana would have put William's happiness first and foremost. His love for Kate would have been enough for his mother. But, privately, according to one royal source, Diana would probably have been jealous of Kate: 'Diana would have upstaged her. Upstaging is what she did. She upstaged the Queen at the State Opening of Parliament and she would have upstaged Kate.'

Fellow diners at Koffmann's couldn't get too close to Kate and Camilla's table, as two armed protection officers were enjoying lunch at the adjoining table. Kate had become used to it over the years she had been with William, but since the engagement she'd had her own round-the-clock detail. Her 'shadows' were with her all the time. When she drove herself, one would sit in the passenger seat while two more would be following in another car.

Their constant presence did come in useful sometimes. Never again would she face the embarrassment of being photographed removing a parking ticket from her windscreen. When she popped into the Peter Jones store in Sloane Square, she had no need to pay and display. Instead, one of the protection squad was able to persuade the traffic wardens not to give her a ticket.

A couple of weeks after her lunch with Camilla, Kate was again the centre of attention when she joined William for her next royal engagement, naming a new inflatable lifeboat, the *Hereford Endeavour*, on their home patch in Anglesey. If Camilla had given Kate any tips about public events like this one, they must have included the words 'Be Yourself' because the novice seemed to have fun from start to finish, waving happily behind her fiancé's back.

One little girl presented Kate with flowers, her first official posy, and said, 'You're very pretty.' Kate smiled broadly and replied, 'Thank you. You are too.' She joked with another shivering youngster, 'You look nice and warm,' prompting laughter all round. She seemed completely at ease at the low-key event, chatting amiably with young and old, even allowing one pensioner to kiss her hand gallantly. She was word-perfect singing 'Land of My Fathers' and let slip that she had been taking Welsh lessons in preparation for the day when she would become Princess of Wales.

Kate looked elegant in a beige herringbone coat cut just above the knee. Keen Kate watchers spotted that she had first worn the £700 Katherine Hooker design to Cheltenham in 2006. Then it reached several inches below the knee and was part of a rather frumpy ensemble that included a Russian-style fur hat. The remodelled coat was much more successful, topped off by a silk and velvet fascinator with a spray of pheasant feathers and a tunic button bearing the insignia of the Royal Welch Fusiliers. The design, by Wiltshire milliner Vivien Sheriff, was an indication of Kate's growing confidence in her style, although she was worried that the keen Welsh wind was making her hair look messy.

William entered into the cheerful spirit of the occasion, staging a mock bow as he applauded Kate performing the naming ceremony and pouring the champagne over the £160,000 boat. It was hardly the *QE2* but Kate found it all exciting. William is a master of these occasions, able to put people at their ease with a joke or a witty aside. On one memorable occasion he was meeting some young people as part of his role as a patron of Centrepoint, the homeless charity. One young woman became totally tongue-tied when it came to her turn to speak to the prince. William bent down and whispered in her ear, 'Imagine me naked,' which gave her a fit of giggles. Kate may not want to use this particular line but putting people at their ease is a skill William has had from an early age.

Kate faces a lifetime of spending hour upon hour just saying hello to people but for the moment that duty was new and great fun. The next day the couple were in Scotland, returning to St Andrews, where William made a speech to undergraduates launching the university's 600th anniversary charity appeal. It was a welcome return, especially as the ceremony was held in the quad outside Sallies, where Kate had so enjoyed her first year foam fight and William had fallen drunk into the bushes. They were seen happily pointing out places and things they remembered. Kate chatted to one of her old tutors, Professor Brendan Cassidy, and told him she had kept all her essays. When he told her he had kept his as well to show his children, she replied, 'I will probably do the same.'

Kate wore a vivid red suit created by Luisa Spagnoli, an Italian ready-to-wear label famously worn by film star Sophia Loren. Kate had bought the matching skirt and jacket for £495 from the Hollie de Keyser boutique in Knightsbridge. She finished the outfit with a pair of black suede knee-high Aquatalia boots that she bought in Russell & Bromley. Afterwards, Kate and William flew by helicopter to London to sign a book of condolence at the New Zealand High Commission for victims of that country's earthquake.

It had been a hectic couple of days but Kate appeared to be well rehearsed, ready with a dazzling smile at all times. The newspapers and magazines couldn't resist taking every opportunity to compare Kate and Diana, digging out pictures of the Princess of Wales interacting with the crowds and wearing a similarly coloured red suit. The pensioner whom she allowed to kiss her hand had done the same to Diana in 1995. Poor Kate must have been secretly gnashing her teeth as Diana continually rained on her parade. One friend commented, 'She is not another Diana. She is completely her own person.'

After England, Wales and Scotland, Kate just had Northern Ireland to go to so none of the home nations would feel left out. She flew to Belfast with William and joined in some traditional Shrove Tuesday pancake tossing outside the City Hall. She confided to an eleven-year-old girl her tender feelings for William: 'He's a very nice man and I'm looking forward to spending the rest of my life with him.'

This was probably the first occasion when Kate had shown how her future style might develop. She wore a beige trench coat from the legendary British design house Burberry. Claire Brayford of the *Daily Express* was impressed: 'Following a series of surprising style choices, Kate has invested in arguably the most versatile, iconic and just plain stylish item a woman can own.' Fortunately she decided to wear an elegant pair of black high heels, for once avoiding boots, which would have ruined the effect. Alison Jane Reid thought the Burberry coat revealed Kate's growing confidence in her clothes: 'She really shone. The outfit gave her *joie de vivre* and for the first time she really looked her age.'

All four of Kate's public outfits since the formal announcement of her engagement showed just how far her fashion sense had come in a short time. The only slight jar came in Belfast when one of the cheering crowd told her not to lose any more weight. Kate apparently laughed and said it was all part of the wedding plans. That seemed a good response at the time but many people were shocked six weeks later to see how much more weight she appeared to have lost. Surely it was not part of the plan to look *so* thin just ten days before the wedding.

Kate's problem is one many women face: when she loses a few pounds, she doesn't just drop a dress size, she also loses weight from her face, leaving her looking gaunt and older than her years. Pictures can be misleading but those of her crossing the King's Road on a shopping trip for honeymoon clothes appeared to reveal a 'skin and bones' figure, according to concerned newspapers. Kate seems to have gone from a size ten to a size eight. She has always been prone to losing weight, even as a young schoolgirl, when she was described as a '100-miles-an-hour kind of girl'. There will only be concern on her big day if the wedding dress falls off her. The *Daily Star* had the answer: 'Kate, You Need Cake'.

20

The Big Day

Prince William could hear the gathering crowd through the open window of his private apartment at Clarence House. It was the evening before his wedding but already hundreds of people were in high spirits as they faced a long and chilly night in the open air. He turned to his brother Harry and suggested they go out to say hello.

At 8.30p.m. the royal brothers strolled through the gates of Clarence House on to the Mall to be greeted by a sea of sleeping bags, makeshift tents and Union Jacks of all shapes and sizes – some of them showed his smiling face next to his bride's. Well-wishers started up a chant of 'For he's a jolly good fellow'.

William, in a dark jumper and open-necked white shirt, happily let those with cameras or mobile phones take his picture. He high-fived, shook hands and chatted amiably to people. He asked one woman if she was going to sleep in the small tent she had put up, joking, 'Have you got a Jacuzzi in there?' and told another, 'All I've got to do tomorrow is get my lines right.'

He said he was a bit nervous but he didn't seem so. Harry cracked jokes about the prospects of rain for the next day and cheekily invited himself into one woman's tent. One fourteen-year-old girl, who shook William's hand, said it was 'the best moment of my life'.

The walkabout, though brief, was a PR master stroke – another indication of William's skill when it came to letting the public into his life. He seems instinctively to know how to communicate with people and is able to be natural and not as aloof as previous generations of his family.

The brothers went back indoors to a quiet family dinner with their father. Kate, meanwhile, was coping with her nerves five minutes away in the Goring Hotel. She had spent part of the day at Westminster Abbey for one last rehearsal that William had somehow managed to avoid.

When she arrived at the hotel where she would spend her last night as a single woman, she smiled and waved to a cheering crowd as her sister and mother looked on happily. They had been to lunch with Camilla at Clarence House and then Kate had had a one-hour manicure to ensure her nails would look in tip-top condition for any close-ups of the wedding ring. Camilla had recommended her own manicurist, Marina Sandoval from the Jo Hansford salon in Mayfair.

The Goring had given their top floor suite a makeover for a reported £150,000 so Kate could wake up on her wedding day in complete luxury in a four-poster bed. Kate was keen to have her family around her in the £5,000-a-night suite, as it would be the last time they would be together before all of their lives changed forever.

Kate's wake-up call was for 6.30a.m., when a tray containing tea and fruit juice was delivered to the suite. She was too excited to have much of an appetite. All the important business of the day seemed to be about to happen before she barely had time to get out of bed. One of the first visitors was her hairdresser, James Pryce, her regular stylist from the Richard Ward salon. Richard himself was looking after Pippa's and Carole's hair but James had the job of styling the bride. He later confessed that he had had quite a few practice runs and 'hadn't slept for weeks'.

Kate had been adamant that she didn't want to change her trademark look of long flowing hair, although she realized that traditionally a royal bride wore her hair up with a tiara holding everything in place. In the end she compromised a little, with James creating a style that was up enough to accommodate a tiara but down enough to be recognizably Kate.

The tiara was Kate's something borrowed. The Queen lent her the 1936 diamond halo tiara by Cartier for the occasion. It was a personal favourite of the Queen's because it had been a present from her mother on her eighteenth birthday. Kate chose to look after her own make-up, believing she knew what suited her best. She had taken lessons from a make-up artist and was using products from Bobbi Brown, a leading American brand.

And then it was time to put on the dress. The name of the designer had been kept under wraps as if it were an MI5 secret. A woman had been smuggled into the Goring the day before, wearing an elaborate fur hat to hide her identity. To give the dress maximum impact, a canopy had been erected at the front of the hotel to prevent anyone from getting a sneaky peak and spoiling the big surprise of the day. It would also serve to protect the dress from the predicted rain, which thankfully failed to appear.

Finally, after all the preparations, it was time to leave the hotel. The police had blocked off the street so the crowd could only peer hopefully in Kate's direction as she was helped into the waiting Rolls Royce with her father Michael, as supportive as ever, by her side.

By the time they set off for Westminster Abbey at 10.51a.m., Prince William had been there for forty minutes and some of the guests for more than two hours, but they had the consolation of listening to the London Chamber Orchestra and one of the Abbey's organists.

Sir Elton John was already in his seat next to his partner, David Furnish. The Beckhams were there as predicted. Victoria Beckham, six months pregnant, seemed a little self-conscious and unsure of herself but looked immaculate in an elegant navy blue day dress with a slash boat neck from her own collection. She had specially commissioned her pillbox hat from the milliner Philip Treacy, as well as having her Louboutin shoes with six-inch heels customized to take the strain of her pregnancy.

It's always fun on these occasions to recognize people in the congregation but, in reality, there weren't that many well-known faces. Chelsy Davy slipped in without attracting much attention. She and Kate are getting on better these days and Chelsy had been one of the first to text congratulations after the engagement was announced. It's a relief to William that the two women are on friendlier terms because he has always liked Chelsy and she is such an important figure in his brother's life.

She had chosen a turquoise mini dress and matching jacket by Alberta Ferretti, accessorized with a veiled pillbox hat. Not everybody liked the outfit: Alison Jane Reid thought it 'rather tight and trashy' but she was clearly a young woman out to enjoy herself at a friend's wedding. Chelsy didn't get to speak to Harry during the ceremony but was able to spend time with him at the reception and evening party.

David Cameron's wife Samantha raised some eyebrows by not wearing a hat to the Abbey. She can be a bit of a rebel when it comes to etiquette but she did fly the flag for British fashion by wearing a Burberry dress and a jewelled hairpiece by Erdem. It may not be the sort of fashion statement that Kate will want to make in the future.

The singer Joss Stone was there. She had become friendly with William after performing at the Concert for Diana in 2007. Kate's distant cousin Guy Ritchie had been invited, along with Prince Charles's friend Rowan Atkinson and some figures from the world of sport, including Sir Trevor Brooking, Sir Clive Woodward and England rugby captain Mike Tindall with his fiancée Zara Phillips. He will be the next commoner to marry into the Royal Family later this year.

Kate is not really a celebrity person. She and William invited Tom Bradby and his wife Claudia, as well as Ben Fogle, who had made a documentary with William about the prince's love for Africa, but this was a day more for ordinary people than for those we knew from the television. William had, for instance, invited a young stroke victim he'd met in his role as patron of the homeless charity Centrepoint. Shozna had been left homeless and with little confidence but the charity had helped her rebuild her life. She had intended to be one of the crowd watching the wedding in the Mall until she received her invitation. Shozna was nervous about the grand royal occasion and said, 'I felt I was in a dream.' William had himself slept rough in freezing temperatures in 2009 to highlight the problem of homelessness in Britain.

In some ways it seemed a pity that so many diplomats and dignitaries the couple had never met were invited but it is the nature of these occasions to blend royal duty and private life together. It will also be the balance that Kate will have to find in her own life as a member of the Royal Family.

Carole Middleton had taken her place at the front of the bride's family's side of the Abbey before the royals trooped in. The diet had worked because she looked slim and elegant in a sky blue wool crêpe dress with satin piping by Catherine Walker & Co. The designer, who died in September 2010, had been credited with transforming Princess Diana into a global style icon. Kate's brother James, looking tanned and handsome, was at his mother's side, helping to keep her calm as the excitement began to build. The Middleton family would prove to be the stars of the wedding day.

The Royal Family trickled in. Camilla wore a champagne silk dress with a matching duck egg blue and champagne coat with pleat detail and hand embroideries by Anna Valentine. The Queen wore a primrose crêpe wool dress by Angela Kelly that reflected her immaculate taste at the age of eighty-five.

And then Kate arrived. It was 11a.m. At last the world could devour the dress. It turned out that she had chosen the Manchester-born designer Sarah Burton at Alexander McQueen, one of the most famous of modern British fashion houses. Lee McQueen, as he was widely known, had sadly taken his own life in February 2010.

Sarah was a popular choice within the world of fashion. Now thirty-six, she had worked alongside McQueen for fourteen years. She had begun on a student placement and he had been impressed enough to offer her a job when she graduated from Central Saint Martins College of Art and Design. After his death she was appointed creative director and had to assume the mantle of one of the fashion greats. Alison Jane Reid observes, 'No one understands his love of theatre, obsession with historical detail or his love of embellishment better than Sarah.'

The designer found her new role intimidating but she impressed with her designs for Madonna, Gwyneth Paltrow and Lady Gaga. She also designed the wedding dress for Sarah Buys, who married Camilla's son Tom Parker Bowles, which gave Kate an indication of what could be created for her. Fashion critics thought Sarah Burton brought a new 'romantic sensibility' to the fashion house. She explained that she couldn't forget the influence of McQueen but wanted to move forward: 'I'm not going to wipe the slate clean but you can never stay still and you have to stay true to yourself.'

The world gasped with delight at the dress she had made for Kate. The creation had the priceless attribute of informality, making Kate seem natural and unmistakably the girl we had come to know over the past ten years. Kate's hairdresser, James Pryce, had explained that her number one priority on her wedding day had been to please her husband, ensuring that he recognized his bride when she stood next to him at the altar. Her hair was Kate and so was her dress. She may have been about to style herself Princess Catherine but the dress was Princess Kate.

It came as no surprise to learn that the bride had been closely involved with Sarah Burton in formulating the design. It was neither too fussy nor as overblown as Princess Diana's creased meringue of 1981. The effect was very regal, with a flowing, 2.7-metre train that Kate's sister Pippa did a masterful job of negotiating around the steps of the Abbey. The gown, which would have cost upwards of £50,000 to make, featured a delicate, ethereal, sculpted bodice in English and French lace, a tiny waist and an intricately constructed skirt of ivory and white satin gazar arches and pleats that moved and fluttered like a dream.

One little girl interviewed for television said that the dress looked like it was floating. Alison Jane Reid observed, 'It gave Kate a stunning silhouette and extraordinary confidence. It showed off her slender frame to its best advantage, creating an overall effect that was romantic and sexy. The dress was beautifully constructed and displayed a timeless artistry.'

Sarah Burton had been keen to show off the skills of British workmanship, paying tribute to the Arts and Crafts movement. The lace design, for instance, used a technique from Ireland of the 1820s. Individual flowers were hand-cut from lace and engineered by hand on to ivory silk tulle to create a unique design incorporating the four national flowers of the United Kingdom – the rose, thistle, shamrock and daffodil.

The sheer veil allowed us to see Kate's delighted expression throughout her journey down the aisle. The tiara finished the overall effect beautifully, as did the earrings, a wedding day gift from her proud parents. Designed by Robinson Pelham, they featured diamond-set stylized oak leaves with a pear-shaped diamond-set drop and a pavé-set diamond acorn suspended in the centre. The inspiration came from the new Middleton coat of arms. She carried a simple bouquet that included sweet William (signifying gallantry), lily-of-the-valley (the return of happiness), hyacinth (constancy of love) and ivy (fidelity).

The Queen may have been one of those present in the church who recognized the influence of one of the most beautiful and revered wedding dresses of the twentieth century: that worn by the film star Grace Kelly when she married Prince Rainier of

Monaco in 1956 – another beautiful and wealthy commoner to marry a prince and invigorate a monarchy.

Everyone had the chance to have a proper look as she made her way slowly down between the tree-lined avenue that had been specially created in the Abbey for the wedding. The seven-metre-high trees will all be replanted, probably at Highgrove, when the Abbey is returned to normal. The couple might have preferred a quiet country affair but this would be the nearest they could get to a wedding in the local church at Bucklebury.

William clearly appreciated Kate's efforts and when she arrived by his side at the altar he turned to greet her with the words, 'You look beautiful.' No bride could wish for more. He had been alerted by Harry that she was on her way down the aisle but had managed to restrain himself from turning round to look. He was obviously moved because he added, 'It looks fantastic,' just to make sure Kate understood how he felt.

He also joked lightly to Michael Middleton, 'We're supposed to have just a small family affair.' William need not have been concerned about either his new father-in-law or his bride. They were both utterly composed. At one point Kate appeared to be breathing quite shallowly but that may have been due more to a tight corset than nerves.

William did not fluff his lines and neither did Kate. She managed to say his full name, William Arthur Philip Louis, with precision and clarity. William's mouth twitched a little after she'd successfully negotiated his name – perhaps they'd practised together. She did not promise to obey her new husband but instead confirmed her intention to 'love him, comfort him, honour and keep him.' Most noticeably, when Kate and William exchanged their vows, they gazed deeply into one another's eyes.

The crowds outside applauded and clapped as the ceremony unfolded, many of them singing along to 'Jerusalem', the most rousing of all British hymns. Even more joined in for a chorus of 'God Save The Queen', which everyone in the Abbey sang with gusto except, of course, the Queen herself. The choice of the hymn 'Guide Me, O Thou Great Redeemer' was interpreted as a tribute to Diana because it was the last hymn sung at her funeral. James Middleton read the lesson perfectly; it was a passage from Romans 12 that stated: 'Live in harmony with one another; do not be haughty, but associate with the lowly.'

One potential problem had everyone holding their breath. For a split second the wedding ring didn't slip easily on to Kate's finger and William had to get serious about shoving it past the knuckle. It was worth it, however, because it was a beautiful and simple band of Welsh gold. The late Queen Mother had started the tradition of wearing Welsh gold when she married the future George VI in 1923. Both Diana and Camilla and now Kate had used gold from an ingot presented to the Queen by the Royal British Legion in 1986. William, for some reason, had chosen not to wear a ring.

A little surprisingly, considering his job as a pilot, William was married in the mounted dress uniform of the Irish Guards. He is honorary colonel of the regiment. The bright red tunic was extremely dashing and photogenic but the only sign of his career in the RAF was his helicopter wings badge.

Pippa, a star throughout the service, was attentive again at the end as the couple prepared to leave, once more making sure her sister's train was looking its best when Kate greeted the crowds. Her own dress, also by Sarah Burton, was for many the equal of Kate's wedding dress and had the critics raving about its elegance and 'stunning simplicity'. Bridesmaids' dresses can often be a nightmare of frills and bows but this satin-based crêpe in ivory would have made a superb dress for the bride at a less traditional wedding.

Outside the Abbey, William put on a smart black forage cap, which carried the badge of the Blues and Royals regiment, and a pair of white gloves, before helping his new wife into the open state carriage. The weather had been kind and Kate was able to show the world her beautiful dress from her seat in the 1902 landau that had been built for the coronation of Edward VII.

The carriage had also been used by Diana and Charles on the journey back to Buckingham Palace after their wedding. Diana was missed by many on the day but she didn't overshadow it. Much of the crowd was, in any case, too young to remember her wedding thirty years before. This was Kate's day and it was her dress, her smile and her happiness that occupied people's thoughts.

While everything went like clockwork inside the Abbey, vast crowds, which some estimates put at one million people, were braving all sorts of difficulties to catch a glimpse of the royal newlyweds. I was one of those twenty deep in the Mall as the cars made their serene progress to the Abbey. It was impossible to see anything, as the view was obscured either by periscope contraptions that had been sold at stalls in the park or by children hoisted onto the shoulders of their parents.

Nobody seemed to mind much though. It was like being at a rock festival, except that instead of Coldplay and Kings of Leon the odd military band would march past jauntily. Every so often a cheer would ring out but nobody had a clue who had gone by. The elderly lady standing next to me, when I told her I thought it was the Queen's car, replied, 'The Queen! She's a legend.' Another woman told me that she was sick of souvenirs: 'I've got my Wills and Kate mug from the Co-op and that will do for me.'

When everyone was in the Abbey I retired to a pub near St James's Park station to watch it on TV with a Buck's Fizz. A Japanese tourist next to me spent the whole service taking pictures of the television screen. Everybody seemed to think a drink was a good idea because soon quite a crowd had gathered and we all clapped and cheered when William succeeded in getting the ring on her finger.

The sun came out when they began the prayers, as if in response to the Bishop of London when he described it as a 'joyful' day. As soon as William and Kate were in the landau, I walked back towards the Palace to try to catch a glimpse of the balcony scene. I didn't hold out much hope – even less so when I was trapped with hundreds of people in a street where we could go neither forward nor back. Time moved on until it was past one o'clock and everyone was resigned to missing the main event. Suddenly we started to move forward, slowly at first and then in a half run as we realized that they were opening up the top of the Mall by the Victoria Memorial and the people on our street were among the first to be allowed in.

When I came to a stop, I was right by the Palace gates in as good a position as I could possibly have hoped for. The excitement was almost tangible. Next to me a man from New York and another from Philadelphia couldn't believe their luck. Behind me was a sea of thousands and thousands of people. And then Kate and William were there on the balcony, smiling at us. They didn't look like movie stars – they looked better than that. 'Wow,' said Kate as she realized just how many people had turned out for her big day.

And they kissed – simply and naturally with perhaps a hint of embarrassment. After so many years spent hiding their love from prying eyes here they were, providing the ultimate proof of that affection in front of a billion people. The Queen led the rest of the family onto the balcony. She was clearly enjoying herself and had been heard to say, 'It's amazing' when her carriage arrived back at the Palace.

William and Kate looked up when a magnificent Lancaster bomber led a small flypast. It was nothing too fancy. Kate bent down to offer words of reassurance to her young bridesmaids, including Grace van Cutsem, who had covered her ears at the great wall of noise from the crowds below. The crowd started chanting, 'Kiss, Kiss, Kiss!', imploring them to have a second embrace. And they listened. William turned to Kate and said, 'Let's give them another one. I love you', so they kissed again before following the Queen back inside for the reception. It had only been a minute or two but it was enough – we were happy.

Kate and William had made a connection with the people on their big day. They were happy to share the occasion although they did manage one tender and private moment as their landau travelled through the archway into the Palace: Kate simply put her hand on top of William's.

Throughout, they looked the part and had managed to appear completely natural in the most rarefied of circumstances. They continued to add touches to their day that everyone could relate to. When it was time to leave the reception to return to Clarence House, William drove them in a vintage Aston Martin, his father's pride and joy, given to him by the Queen on his twenty-first birthday. On the front was an L-plate and on the back some balloons and a number plate that read 'JU5T WED'. It was a simple touch but the right one.

Kate has a huge reservoir of public affection to draw on as a result of her big day. Inevitably she will soon face questions about when they are going to start a family. The chances are that it won't be long. She has always been very family oriented and, from an early age, friends recall that her one wish was to be a mother.

In the short term she and William want to return to Anglesey, where he will continue to work as a pilot. It's up to her how high profile a life she wants to lead. She is unlikely to be in the papers every day but she now has the prestige to make a difference to the country and the people in it.

But that is something for the future. First it was time for a party at the Palace. She had woken up on 29 April 2011 as Kate Middleton, a beautiful unassuming girl from Berkshire; she ended the day as Princess Catherine, the new Duchess of Cambridge and the woman destined to be queen. But to the millions of people watching on the streets of London and on their televisions around the world, she will always be Kate.

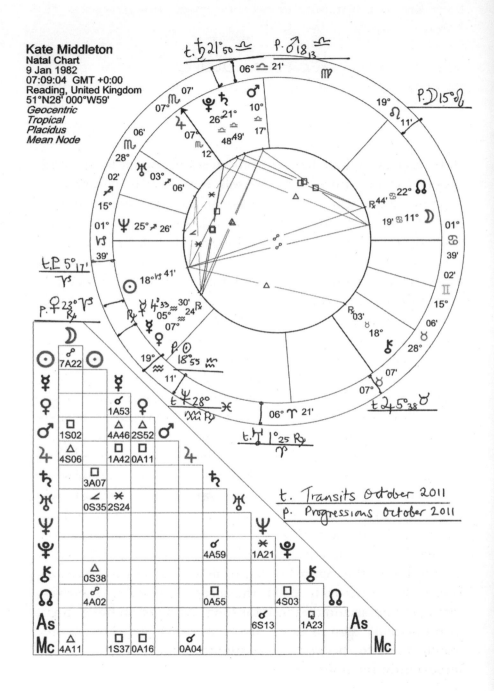

Kate Middleton
Natal Chart
9 Jan 1982
07:09:04 GMT +0:00
Reading, United Kingdom
51°N28' 000°W59'
Geocentric
Tropical
Placidus
Mean Node

t. Transits October 2011
p. Progressions October 2011

Kate's Stars

Kate has charm, Kate has taste but most fortunately for all, and indeed for our future queen herself, Kate has backbone. Born in chilly January, her Sun is in steely, capable Capricorn, the first of many indications that here is a character who can set aside short-term gratification for long-term goals. Her Sun sign is ruled by Saturn, Lord of Reality and Restrictions, Lord of the Slow and Steady Ascent. It is fitting that her rise to prominence comes during a period of recession, a time when most have been forced, often uncomfortably, to acknowledge limitations and the damage that excess can incur. Kate is, in effect, the dignified face of a more responsible and considerate Britain.

The Sun is associated with an individual's identity and self-esteem. Not only is Kate's Sun in Saturn's sign, but it also forms a hard link to the planet of authority and boundaries. This provides a double dose of disciplining energy, shaping her view of who she is and what she deserves. Kate would have grown up with an innate sense of responsibility and an ambitious urge to make the most of circumstances. Regardless of a comfortable, privileged upbringing, she would be unable ever to think well of herself unless she worked hard. Easy lessons are forgotten. It is the hard lessons that are remembered and force growth. Kate already knows this. Saturn brings trials and tests early; it creates insecurities and fears that only the acceptance of duty and striving seem to ease and then not for long. With taskmaster Saturn in the sociable sign of Libra, likely arenas for any life lessons would relate to the world of aesthetics, diplomacy and, most importantly, relationships.

Kate

Kate would have perceived her parents playing very different roles within her home. Despite her mother's career, it is likely her parents followed traditional gender patterns in terms of domestic responsibilities. The Moon placed in Cancer suggests a mother who is sensitive and fiercely protective, to whom nurturing is instinctive and who would know, not least through her own experience, the great importance of emotional security. Links between the Moon and Mars suggest someone who might be too ready to jump in and fight battles on Kate's behalf, but also a mother who can be enterprising and courageous. Kate's mother, Carole, taught her about emotional closeness and she, in turn, will replicate the same caretaking strengths to others who are important to her. Carole may well have had a restless streak, an explorative nature and a desire for freedom that would need to be integrated, perhaps not always easily, with the demands of a family. One would expect a genuine concern for the well-being of others and someone appreciative of traditional splendours, customs and grand buildings. This, together with an ability to find solutions to tricky problems, would make her a very useful person for Kate to have at her side.

Kate's Sun forms a tight link to Uranus, planet of individuality and all that is unique – an indication that her father Michael was a charismatic and dynamic figure in the home. Further links between her Sun and the weighty planets Saturn and Pluto suggest his dominant role in her upbringing. The importance of fair partnership and presenting a united front to the children would have been part of the family ethos. The planetary picture suggests a man who would have found it difficult to express his deep emotions easily. Doubtless he was a busy person, aware of the value of time, and there would have been occasions, particularly in childhood, when Kate felt overlooked, forcing her to develop her own means of validating her worth. This strong-willed, thorough man, with his patience and precision with details and his rationality, would have provided Kate with a role model and, most importantly, lessons about responsibility and sharing power. Inevitably he would have instilled in her the positive virtues of self-restraint, decorum and maintaining the boundaries that protect privacy. It is an obvious observation, but valid nonetheless, that Kate will be drawn to powerful men with a strong sense of their own entitlement.

Relationships with her siblings would have been warmly affectionate, thriving on competition and argument – Kate knows her own mind. She has been grounded within a stable family background with close bonds between parents and offspring, where the need to love and be loved has been clearly modelled, supporting her strong instinct to establish a family of her own.

Growing up, the usual scuffles with parents and peers will have given Kate some very useful training for the inevitable future power struggles with authority figures and, with suitable reflection, will enable her to spot the weaknesses in her defences. Kate has Venus, the planet that signals what we value, and Mercury, planet of the mind, in the sign of rebellious Aquarius – a strong indication that she will work out her own ethical code and will not easily join the pack unless there is good reason to. She values independence and those who can think for themselves and can be stubbornly resistant to peer pressure.

There are many traits of character that fit Kate for her forthcoming public role. Mercury, Lord of Communication and Ruler of Mentality, makes many positive links to the planets Mars, Venus and Uranus and a tight link to Jupiter. Kate has a sharp mind with plenty of mental energy and can understand ideas that aren't always obvious to others. She can go beyond narrow logical thinking, embrace big ideas and be enthusiastic and inspirational about pet projects. She can be forthright when she needs to be: others will know where they are with her. Her chart has a 'cardinal' emphasis – an indication that she is someone who puts her ideas into action. She is a 'doer'. These qualities will be coupled with charm, tact and amiability, allowing her to talk to people in a manner that can win them over.

Kate

Almost inevitably given such skills, her position and beauty, there will be comparisons made to Prince William's mother, Diana. Kate has the Moon in the sign of Cancer, within a few degrees of the position of Diana's Sun, suggestive of the enormous importance of the mother role in the public's perception of both women. However, Diana's Moon, the planet that rules one's ability to empathize, was in democratic Aquarius, where traditionally it is less at ease. This does, however, confer the ability to understand instinctively and value the levelling effect of emotions – someone living in a shoebox can feel just as intensely as someone in a mansion. Diana's connection was to the emotion rather than the circumstances and, of course, she provided extraordinary support to many individuals.

Kate's Moon suggests enormous sensitivity and an urge to protect but can be clannish – that is, her family and, by extension, her country are where her heart lies. She will be proactive in many good causes but there will be a very different feel to the manner in which she connects to her public – she is her own person and those strengths that are unique to her will be evident. The position of her Moon does suggest a natural appreciation of the nation's heritage and changing place in the world. It seems clear that she will very successfully use her intelligence and intuitive talents to support William in reshaping the image of the country, very much enhancing its status as we move through the twenty-first century. Her approach in seeing everyone as part of a family, albeit one with an acknowledged hierarchy, will enhance social cohesion. The value she places on standards of behaviour and ambition supported by hard work will cast her, in later years, in the role of firm but loved parent.

Kate will become part of a powerful family and have inside knowledge of complex political scenarios. There are those who wonder how well she will survive, implying her background has not readied her for hothouse scheming. They need not worry. The link between her Sun and Pluto, Lord of Manipulation and what lies hidden, gifts her with exceptional sensitivity to under-currents of power. Kate has an instinct for what is unexpressed, a perceptive nose for what lies beneath the surface of seeming calm. She will become able to handle with innate skill those with agendas. All that she needs, she already has. However, the tense nature of the Pluto/Saturn/Sun links suggest this will not be before she has developed greater assertiveness in wresting control when challenged and passed further tests to her self-esteem.

Kate will shortly experience her Saturn Return, a time when Saturn completes its 29-year cycle around the zodiac and returns to the same position it occupied at the moment of birth. This turning point will prompt an assessment of her life's progress and will reveal that she has served a very productive apprenticeship in the art of strategy, although she is not yet a master.

Within the royal household there are those who will form a particular affinity with her and help her progress. The rela-tionship between Kate and her mother-in-law, Camilla, Duchess of Cornwall, will be one of sympathetic understanding. Both women have their Moons in Cancer, suggestive of emotional rapport. The friendship will develop cautiously on both sides but is therefore likely to last. It will have a sporadic nature – not confined to routine, but essentially very supportive and cheer-ing. In effect, they could be seen as rivals – there are those who doubt the ascension of Prince Charles to the throne. This undercurrent is shown clearly in the charts through the posi-tions of their Suns, which lie in the heavens opposite each other. Both women, though, have been nurturing consorts to their starry partners; both women know how to discipline their drive and play the waiting game (Camilla has a lovely link between Mars, Lord of Direction, and Saturn, Lord of Delay). Both have a natural reticence and fear intrusive exposure. There is an intellectual spark between them and they will find each other stimulating and positive company.

Kate

The Queen will be a hard act to follow but she will be of profound importance in the development of Kate's future role. A link between Jupiter, Lord of Fortune and Success, and Pluto, Lord of Power, in the combined charts of Queen Elizabeth and her grandson's bride is enormously encouraging. It suggests that together – if only in the manner in which they help and support William – they can instigate creative and far-sighted changes. Their relationship will be marked by great deference on Kate's part but also deep and sincere mutual feelings. They share a realistic approach to challenges and tasks and a pragmatism that can help build something real in any joint undertakings. Should they unite behind a specific project, they would make a formidable, unbeatable team, primarily because of a similar instinct to make personal sacrifices for the success of the goal. In the combined chart, Pluto sits opposite the Sun, suggesting their friendship may attract the antagonism of others or indeed that ultimately, many years down the line, Kate will succeed, albeit only in the consort role, to the near ultimate position of power within the family.

There is a similar planetary signature in the combined charts of Charles and Kate – a link between Pluto and the Sun, which always suggests power struggles at some level. This will be an intense and transformative relationship born of the fact that the direction of each life conflicts in some way. Again this could simply suggest the inevitable decline of one star and the rise of another. What is important is that Kate has already experienced within her family and in her early years – evidenced by the Sun/Pluto link in her chart – exactly the same sort of dynamics before. As the intern, she will feel pressure to fit the type of unspoken role Charles feels is appropriate, with little room for any moderately independent spirit of her own. But this type of energy can reverse. With maturity, Kate will have the resources and skills she needs to use influence and be the person she wants to be. This is an important part of their relationship but not the only thing worth mentioning. A dynamic and positive link between Mars, Lord of Clear Goals, and Uranus, Lord of Unexpected Change, suggests unusual success at finding solutions to any problem they turn their minds to. They will find common ground in their interests in heritage projects and aesthetics: investing active time in this field will consolidate mutual respect and affection.

As for William and Kate, we have here a meeting of minds, bodies and souls. A delightful link between William's Moon, the planet that rules his Sun, and Kate's Jupiter suggests that when it comes to appreciating her original and adventurous ideas and plans, her husband will never cease to be a comrade in arms. He will value her generosity of spirit and optimism, confident that they share mutual far-sighted visions. William will feel safe and supported when leading the Royal Family and transforming this figurehead institution into something that establishes a benchmark of power wielded in a positive, fair and inspiring way. This planetary link suggests they are in for the long haul – whatever form that might take – and that the union is indeed a meeting of higher minds. Children are an essential part of the deal but a component that Kate will embrace with enthusiasm, revealing an ability to widen their horizons in the most beneficial way.

Kate will find her marriage liberating; William, in contributing his understanding, will find a greater sense of purpose and wisdom in his own life. Their combined chart reveals that as a team they are natural leaders, keen to initiate and act but needing the freedom to do things their own way, tear up the rule book and negotiate their own modus operandi. They have a brilliant ability to talk things through and make light of arguments and it is this willingness to be honest with each other that will act as the balm to all injuries and rescue the partnership time and again from potential conflict.

Beyond the personal fit between William and Kate, it is clear that this newcomer to the royal firm will bring vital assets. The position of Chiron in Kate's chart, a planet viewed as a maverick and alien, which doesn't belong and doesn't follow the same patterns as other planets in the solar system, signals the role she will play, forcing reflection on aspects of malfunction within the institution. William has joined forces with someone of mettle, who will bring out his desire to lead with courage and humanitarian vision and make healing changes for the future.

Looking ahead for Kate, October 2011 will be a significant month. There is a link between Uranus in her horoscope chart and the transiting planet in the sky. It will be a period when she becomes aware that certain allegiances are meant to be left behind so she can form new friendships that better fit her emerging identity. Her intuitive instincts will be strong and those close to her will recognize her fresh and original approach.

During her Saturn Return, Kate will learn key lessons in how to grow into her own power and authority, resist any unfair pressure from those with their own agenda and cultivate relationships embracing equality and fair play. All of these things will be facilitated by motherhood – an event that would be a classic example of the planetary pattern – and it is quite possible that Kate will enjoy a family of her own and the responsibilities that will bring at this time. Saturn moves from its position to join the mighty planet of regeneration, Pluto, in the later summer months of 2012, so either period could see that obvious transition to adulthood, forcing Kate to leave the world of the child irrevocably behind.

Madeleine Moore
April 2011

Life and Times

9 Jan 1982 Catherine Elizabeth Middleton is born in the maternity unit of the Royal Berkshire Hospital, Reading. Her parents, Carole and Michael Middleton, had recently moved into a semi-detached house called West View in the village of Bradfield Southend to ensure their children were brought up in the country.

21 June 1982 Prince William is born at St Mary's Hospital, London.

June 1983 Catherine is christened at St Andrew's, her local church on the banks of the River Pang.

6 Sept 1983 Philippa Charlotte Middleton is born.

May 1984 The Middleton family move to a one-storey house in the Jordanian capital of Amman, where Michael has secured a temporary posting as a manager for British Airways. Kate learns to sing 'Happy Birthday' in Arabic.

Sept 1986 The family return home from Jordan. Kate begins at St Andrew's preparatory school in Pangbourne, an imposing Victorian manor house set in fifty-four acres. Her mother dreams up the idea of a mail order company called Party Pieces.

15 April 1987 Kate's younger brother, James William Middleton, is born.

Sept 1991 Arrives for the first day of the winter term only to discover everybody else had started the day before – her mother had got the date wrong.

June 1995 Named best all-round sportswoman at the school; she excelled at hockey, netball and swimming. Takes part in sixth form review in which she is told that she will marry 'a handsome man, a rich gentleman.'

Kate

July 1995 Her parents move into their dream house in the wealthy hamlet of Chapel Row on the outskirts of Bucklebury, two miles from their old home.

Sept 1995 Begins at the prestigious Downe House school for girls but is not happy there and her parents withdraw her after two terms.

April 1996 Starts at Marlborough College and settles in well, telling the headmaster 'I am so happy' when he asks her how she is getting on. She plays hockey and tennis for the school.

Sept 1997 Watches the funeral of Princess Diana on television in the common room of Elmhurst, her house at Marlborough.

July 1998 After passing eleven GCSEs, spends a month on a school hockey trip to South America, travelling in Argentina and Brazil, where she visits the breathtaking Iguazu Falls. She is snogging an Argentine boy when her mother phones.

Sept 2000 Begins her gap year by travelling to Florence for a twelve-week course in Italian and history of art at the British Institute.

Jan 2001 Follows in the footsteps of Prince William by joining a Raleigh International expedition to Chile, where she helps build an adventure playground for children in a remote mountain village. Another member of the team said Kate 'was always in control of herself'.

June 2001 Becomes a corporate crew member on board a BT Global Challenge yacht moored in Southampton. Kate sails every day but is also responsible for serving food and drinks to guests and keeping the boat clean.

Sept 2001 Begins a four-year degree course in art history at St Andrews University in Fife. She shares a room in St Salvator's Hall, two floors below Prince William, who starts the same course a week later.

Nov 2001 Becomes part of William's set in 'Sallies' after they chat properly on the touchline of a rugby match. They are often seen talking on the stairs outside her room.

Dec 2001 Helps to persuade William to continue at St Andrews when he has a 'wobble' about university life. He agrees to go back but changes to a geography degree.

Feb 2002 Sashays down the runway at a charity fashion show in a see-through dress. William, in the front row, whispers, 'She's hot!' The £30 dress is sold in 2011 for close to £80,000.

May 2002 Celebrates the end of first year exams with William and has to be carried drunk up to her room by a fellow student. William stumbles into the bushes outside Sallies and has to be pulled out by his bodyguard.

June 2002 Attends Valedictory Dinner in Sallies' dining room. Is voted 'prettiest girl' while William wins the 'King of Sallies' award.

July 2002 Works as a waitress for the Snatch Bar at Henley rowing regatta. Her boss says she is 'Berkshire's most beautiful woman'.

Sept 2002 Moves into a maisonette in Hope Street, St Andrews, with William and two friends, Fergus Boyd and Olivia Bleasdale. William likes to take his turn cooking but Kate usually has to rescue his attempts.

Nov 2002 Her parents buy a flat in Chelsea that Kate can use as a London home. Attends her first shooting party at Sandringham.

May 2003 Kate's parents deny she is William's girlfriend. Michael Middleton says, 'We are very amused at the thought of being in-laws to Prince William.'

June 2003 William slips quietly into Kate's twenty-first birthday party in a marquee at her parents' home. She attends his celebration at Windsor Castle but the media thought he was interested in another girl, Jecca Craig, a friend from Kenya.

Sept 2003 The couple move in to a farmhouse on the outskirts of St Andrews, where they share with two old school friends of William's. It is very private, with two acres of land.

April 2004 Joins William on his annual skiing holiday to Klosters with his father. Pictures of them together on the slopes appear in the *Sun*, confirming that they were a couple.

July 2004 The couple enjoy their first summer holiday together on Rodrigues, an island in the Indian Ocean, where they stay in a £25-a-night guest house.

March 2005 Takes a break from revising for finals to join William again on the annual trip to Klosters. William tells a reporter that he won't marry until he is twenty-eight or thirty.

Kate

June 2005 Attends her first society wedding with William when his friend Hugh van Cutsem marries Rose Astor. They graduate from St Andrews with 2:1 degrees. The Queen attends the ceremony but Kate doesn't meet her.

Jan 2006 At Klosters, Kate and William are pictured sharing a tender kiss on the slopes. She throws a champagne party for him at Clarence House before he begins his training at Sandhurst.

March 2006 Attends the Cheltenham Gold Cup without William but is invited into the royal box to have lunch with Charles and Camilla.

July 2006 Her formidable grandmother, Dorothy Goldsmith, dies from cancer, aged seventy-one. Kate reads a poem at her funeral.

Nov 2006 Gets her first permanent job when she is hired as a junior accessories buyer by Jigsaw, the High Street chain. She and William had stayed at the store owners' villa in Mustique for their summer holiday.

Dec 2006 Watches William's Passing Out Parade at Sandhurst and is seen telling her mother, 'I love the uniform. It's so sexy.'

Jan 2007 On her twenty-fifth birthday she is surrounded by paparazzi as she leaves her Chelsea flat to go to work. Clarence House issues a statement that William is very unhappy about the harassment of his girlfriend.

April 2007 William is pictured grabbing the boob of a Brazilian student in a Bournemouth nightclub. He and Kate split. Although the separation lasts little more than a week, they don't tell the media they are back together.

July 2007 Joins The Sisterhood, a female crew planning to row the Channel for charity but pulls out because of the publicity. Goes to the Diana memorial concert at Wembley but is not seated next to William. At the after show party they dance together.

August 2007 Spends an idyllic holiday on the tiny island of Desroches in the Indian Ocean, where she and William reach an understanding over their future together.

Nov 2007 Gives up her job at Jigsaw and starts working for the family firm's website.

April 2008 William lands his Chinook helicopter in the back garden of Kate's family home in Bucklebury.

May 2008 Meets the Queen for the first time at the wedding of Peter Phillips and Autumn Kelly. William is away in Kenya and Kate is officially there to represent him.

June 2008 Wears a vivid pink satin Issa dress to the annual Boodles Boxing Ball and is seen next to William cheering the fighters.

July 2008 Places fourth in *Vanity Fair*'s International Best Dressed List.

Sept 2008 Wears luminous yellow hot pants, a green top and pink leg warmers to a charity roller disco. William announces he will become a Search and Rescue pilot.

July 2009 Kate's Uncle Gary is exposed by the *News of the World* in a story alleging involvement in sex and drugs. It is the first time her family hit the headlines in this way.

Dec 2009 Pictures appear in foreign magazines of Kate and Pippa playing tennis on Christmas Eve. She takes legal action and the picture agency apologizes and makes an out-of-court settlement.

Sept 2010 William qualifies as a pilot at a low-key ceremony on Anglesey, where the couple have been living for six months.

Oct 2010 William takes Kate on holiday to Kenya, where he proposes at a remote log cabin. He places his mother's sapphire engagement ring on her finger.

Nov 2010 Kate's grandfather Peter dies at the age of ninety. His granddaughter's engagement is announced on Twitter on 16 November and she wears a blue Issa dress for the official engagement interview.

Feb 2011 Names her first boat, the *Hereford Endeavour*, on a blustery day in Anglesey. Everyone agrees that Kate is a natural. The day after, they return to St Andrews to launch the university's 600th anniversary appeal.

March 2011 Tosses pancakes outside Belfast City Hall wearing an elegant Burberry trenchcoat. Tells a little girl she is looking forward to spending the rest of her life with William.

29 April 2011 Kate's wedding day.

Acknowledgements

I was surprised when Mike Jones, the commissioning editor at Simon & Schuster, asked me to write a book about Kate Middleton. I'm more used to writing about world famous pop stars but he convinced me that Kate was the biggest celebrity around and was a perfect subject. Thanks for the vision, Mike, because I really enjoyed finding out more about the woman who will one day be our queen.

The team at the publishers have been excellent as usual. Thanks to editor Rory Scarfe for his enthusiasm and keeping me on schedule; editorial assistant Emily Husain for dealing with author problems; Liane Payne for her eye-catching jacket design; Julia Marshall for overseeing production; Emma Harrow for publicity; and Grainne Reidy and Richard Clarke for looking after sales so expertly.

My agent Gordon Wise continues to guide my career with great skill and his assistant at Curtis Brown, John Parton, is a welcome addition to the team. I am grateful to Alison Sims for her research and to Jen Westaway for transcribing my interviews. Arianne Burnette has been fantastic, copy-editing the manuscript under huge time pressure. There would be no book without her help. Ella Rotherstein is responsible for Sean Smith online and, together with Dorchester Web Design, has set up a brilliant new website for me at www.seansmithceleb.com.

My old friends Christopher Wilson, Garth Gibbs, Richard Mineards and David Newman have given me the benefit of their experience and excellent advice. Alison Jane Reid is one of the UK's leading fashion writers and her insight and knowledge have been invaluable. When not interviewing the most famous people of our time, she is promoting green and organic style for publications including the *Independent* and *The Lady* magazine.

I wanted to say a special thank you to Jessica Hay, who has received some unkind and undeserving press. She has only warm and positive things to say about her old school friend from Marlborough College.

Generally speaking, the nation still worries about being sent to the Tower if they talk about the Royal Family. Time and time again I was asked not to mention a name by people worried about speaking of Kate. That's a pity because their stories made Kate more real for me and, I hope, for the readers of this book too. I have respected their wishes, however, and thanks to everyone who helped.

Finally, thank you to Jo Westaway for her patience and support and for standing in the Mall with me to watch Kate and William share a wedding day kiss with a cheering world.

Select Bibliography

Christopher Andersen, *William and Kate: A Royal Love Story* (Simon & Schuster, 2011)

James Clench/the *Sun, William & Kate: A Royal Love Story* (HarperCollins, 2010)

P. D. Jephson, *Shadows of a Princess* (HarperCollins, 2000)

Robert Jobson, *William's Princess* (John Blake, 2006)

Claudia Joseph, *Kate: The Making of a Princess* (Mainstream, 2010)

Andrew Morton, *Diana: Her True Story* (Michael O'Mara, 1992)

Katie Nicholl, *The Making of a Royal Romance* (Arrow, 2011)

Ingrid Seward, *William & Harry: The People's Princes* (Carlton, 2008)

Inspector Ken Wharfe with Robert Jobson, *Diana: Closely Guarded Secret* (Michael O'Mara, 2002)

Christopher Wilson, *The Windsor Knot: Charles, Camilla and the Legacy of Diana* (Citadel, 2003)

Picture Credits

Solo Syndication: 1, 2, 3, 4, 5, 6, 7, 8

Getty Images: 9, 10, 12, 19, 32, 33, 35, 36, 39, 40, 41-65

Rex Features: 11, 14, 15, 16, 17, 18, 20, 22, 23, 24, 28, 30, 31

Egotastic: 13

Spirit Pix: 21

Mark Stewart, Camera Press London: 34

Mirrorpix: 25, 26, 27, 29, 37, 38

Index

Sean Smith is the UK's leading celebrity biographer and the author of the number one bestseller *Cheryl*, the definitive biography of Cheryl Cole, as well as a bestselling biography of Robbie Williams. His books about the most famous people of our times have been translated throughout the world. His subjects include Kylie Minogue, Justin Timberlake, Britney Spears, Victoria Beckham, Jennifer Aniston and J.K. Rowling. Described by the *Independent* as a 'fearless chronicler', he specialises in meticulous research going 'on the road' to find the real person behind the star image.